Greek Capitalism in Crisis

Despite the depth of the Greek crisis, the exorbitant burdens placed upon the working people and the massive popular resistance movement to capitalist policies, there is a definite lack of consistently Marxist analyses of the Greek problem. International debates regarding the Greek crisis have been dominated by orthodox (Neoclassical and neo-Keynesian) approaches.

The heterodox side of these debates has been occupied by Radical Political Economy approaches (usually radical post-Keynesian or Marxo-Keynesian perspectives). Moreover, they are dominated by the financialisation thesis which is quite alien to Marxism, neglects the sphere of production and professes that the global crisis is simply a financial crisis that has nothing to do with 'real' accumulation and the profit rate.

This book argues that by emphasising the sphere of production and profitability, classical Marxist analysis better explains the Greek crisis than its orthodox and heterodox competitors. The contributors present critiques of the prevalent approaches and offer studies of the Greek crisis that use the methodology and the analytical and empirical tools of classical Marxist Political Economy. In particular, it is shown that the Greek crisis was caused by falling profitability and the ensuing overaccumulation crisis. The 'broad unequal exchange' existing between the euro-centre and the euro-periphery contributed to Greek capital's falling profitability. This book enriches the debate about the Greek economic crisis by demonstrating the insights that can be drawn by considering the Marxist alternative to the dominant mainstream and heterodox approaches.

Stavros Mavroudeas is Professor of Political Economy at the University of Macedonia, Greece.

Routledge frontiers of political economy

1 **Equilibrium versus Understanding**
Towards the rehumanization of economics within social theory
Mark Addleson

2 **Evolution, Order and Complexity**
Edited by Elias L. Khalil and Kenneth E. Boulding

3 **Interactions in Political Economy**
Malvern after ten years
Edited by Steven Pressman

4 **The End of Economics**
Michael Perelman

5 **Probability in Economics**
Omar F. Hamouda and Robin Rowley

6 **Capital Controversy, Post Keynesian Economics and the History of Economics**
Essays in honour of Geoff Harcourt, volume one
Edited by Philip Arestis, Gabriel Palma and Malcolm Sawyer

7 **Markets, Unemployment and Economic Policy**
Essays in honour of Geoff Harcourt, volume two
Edited by Philip Arestis, Gabriel Palma and Malcolm Sawyer

8 **Social Economy**
The logic of capitalist development
Clark Everling

9 **New Keynesian Economics/Post Keynesian Alternatives**
Edited by Roy J. Rotheim

10 **The Representative Agent in Macroeconomics**
James E. Hartley

11 **Borderlands of Economics**
Essays in honour of Daniel R. Fusfeld
Edited by Nahid Aslanbeigui and Young Back Choi

12 **Value, Distribution and Capital**
Essays in honour of Pierangelo Garegnani
Edited by Gary Mongiovi and Fabio Petri

13 **The Economics of Science**
Methodology and epistemology as if economics really mattered
James R. Wible

14 **Competitiveness, Localised Learning and Regional Development**
Specialisation and prosperity in small open economies
Peter Maskell, Heikki Eskelinen, Ingjaldur Hannibalsson, Anders Malmberg and Eirik Vatne

15 **Labour Market Theory**
A constructive reassessment
Ben J. Fine

16 **Women and European Employment**
Jill Rubery, Mark Smith, Colette Fagan and Damian Grimshaw

17 **Explorations in Economic Methodology**
From Lakatos to empirical philosophy of science
Roger Backhouse

18 **Subjectivity in Political Economy**
Essays on wanting and choosing
David P. Levine

19 **The Political Economy of Middle East Peace**
The impact of competing trade agendas
Edited by J.W. Wright, Jnr

20 **The Active Consumer**
Novelty and surprise in consumer choice
Edited by Marina Bianchi

21 **Subjectivism and Economic Analysis**
Essays in memory of Ludwig Lachmann
Edited by Roger Koppl and Gary Mongiovi

22 **Themes in Post-Keynesian Economics**
Essays in honour of Geoff Harcourt, volume three
Edited by Claudio Sardoni and Peter Kriesler

23 **The Dynamics of Technological Knowledge**
Cristiano Antonelli

24 **The Political Economy of Diet, Health and Food Policy**
Ben J. Fine

25 **The End of Finance**
Capital market inflation, financial derivatives and pension fund capitalism
Jan Toporowski

26 **Political Economy and the New Capitalism**
Edited by Jan Toporowski

27 **Growth Theory**
A philosophical perspective
Patricia Northover

28 **The Political Economy of the Small Firm**
Charles Dannreuther and Lew Perren

29 **Hahn and Economic Methodology**
Edited by Thomas Boylan and Paschal F. O'Gorman

30 **Gender, Growth and Trade**
The miracle economies of the postwar years
David Kucera

31 **Normative Political Economy**
Subjective freedom, the market and the state
David Levine

32 **Economist with a Public Purpose**
Essays in honour of John Kenneth Galbraith
Edited by Michael Keaney

33 **Involuntary Unemployment**
The elusive quest for a theory
Michel De Vroey

34 **The Fundamental Institutions of Capitalism**
Ernesto Screpanti

35 **Transcending Transaction**
The search for self-generating markets
Alan Shipman

36 **Power in Business and the State**
An historical analysis of its concentration
Frank Bealey

37 **Editing Economics**
Essays in honour of Mark Perlman
Hank Lim, Ungsuh K. Park and Geoff Harcourt

38 **Money, Macroeconomics and Keynes**
Essays in honour of Victoria Chick, volume I
Philip Arestis, Meghnad Desai and Sheila Dow

39 **Methodology, Microeconomics and Keynes**
Essays in honour of Victoria Chick, volume II
Philip Arestis, Meghnad Desai and Sheila Dow

40 **Market Drive and Governance**
Reexamining the rules for economic and commercial contest
Ralf Boscheck

41 **The Value of Marx**
Political economy for contemporary capitalism
Alfredo Saad-Filho

42 **Issues in Positive Political Economy**
S. Mansoob Murshed

43 **The Enigma of Globalisation**
A journey to a new stage of capitalism
Robert Went

44 **The Market**
Equilibrium, stability, mythology
S.N. Afriat

45 **The Political Economy of Rule Evasion and Policy Reform**
Jim Leitzel

46 **Unpaid Work and the Economy**
Edited by Antonella Picchio

47 **Distributional Justice**
Theory and measurement
Hilde Bojer

48 **Cognitive Developments in Economics**
Edited by Salvatore Rizzello

49 Social Foundations of Markets, Money and Credit
Costas Lapavitsas

50 Rethinking Capitalist Development
Essays on the economics of Josef Steindl
Edited by Tracy Mott and Nina Shapiro

51 An Evolutionary Approach to Social Welfare
Christian Sartorius

52 Kalecki's Economics Today
Edited by Zdzislaw L. Sadowski and Adam Szeworski

53 Fiscal Policy from Reagan to Blair
The left veers right
Ravi K. Roy and Arthur T. Denzau

54 The Cognitive Mechanics of Economic Development and Institutional Change
Bertin Martens

55 Individualism and the Social Order
The social element in liberal thought
Charles R. McCann Jnr.

56 Affirmative Action in the United States and India
A comparative perspective
Thomas E. Weisskopf

57 Global Political Economy and the Wealth of Nations
Performance, institutions, problems and policies
Edited by Phillip Anthony O'Hara

58 Structural Economics
Thijs ten Raa

59 Macroeconomic Theory and Economic Policy
Essays in honour of Jean-Paul Fitoussi
Edited by K. Vela Velupillai

60 The Struggle over Work
The "end of work" and employment alternatives in post-industrial societies
Shaun Wilson

61 The Political Economy of Global Sporting Organisations
John Forster and Nigel Pope

62 The Flawed Foundations of General Equilibrium Theory
Critical essays on economic theory
Frank Ackerman and Alejandro Nadal

63 Uncertainty in Economic Theory
Essays in honour of David Schmeidler's 65th birthday
Edited by Itzhak Gilboa

64 The New Institutional Economics of Corruption
Edited by Johann Graf Lambsdorff, Markus Taube and Matthias Schramm

65 The Price Index and its Extension
A chapter in economic measurement
S.N. Afriat

66 Reduction, Rationality and Game Theory in Marxian Economics
Bruce Philp

67 **Culture and Politics in Economic Development**
Volker Bornschier

68 **Modern Applications of Austrian Thought**
Edited by Jürgen G. Backhaus

69 **Ordinary Choices**
Individuals, incommensurability, and democracy
Robert Urquhart

70 **Labour Theory of Value**
Peter C. Dooley

71 **Capitalism**
Victor D. Lippit

72 **Macroeconomic Foundations of Macroeconomics**
Alvaro Cencini

73 **Marx for the 21st Century**
Edited by Hiroshi Uchida

74 **Growth and Development in the Global Political Economy**
Social structures of accumulation and modes of regulation
Phillip Anthony O'Hara

75 **The New Economy and Macroeconomic Stability**
A neo-modern perspective drawing on the complexity approach and Keynesian economics
Teodoro Dario Togati

76 **The Future of Social Security Policy**
Women, work and a citizen's basic income
Ailsa McKay

77 **Clinton and Blair**
The political economy of the third way
Flavio Romano

78 **Marxian Reproduction Schema**
Money and aggregate demand in a capitalist economy
A.B. Trigg

79 **The Core Theory in Economics**
Problems and solutions
Lester G. Telser

80 **Economics, Ethics and the Market**
Introduction and applications
Johan J. Graafland

81 **Social Costs and Public Action in Modern Capitalism**
Essays inspired by Karl William Kapp's theory of social costs
Edited by Wolfram Elsner, Pietro Frigato and Paolo Ramazzotti

82 **Globalization and the Myths of Free Trade**
History, theory and empirical evidence
Edited by Anwar Shaikh

83 **Equilibrium in Economics**
Scope and limits
Edited by Valeria Mosini

84 **Globalization**
State of the art and perspectives
Edited by Stefan A. Schirm

85 **Neoliberalism**
National and regional experiments with global ideas
Edited by Ravi K. Roy, Arthur T. Denzau and Thomas D. Willett

86 **Post-Keynesian Macroeconomics Economics**
Essays in honour of Ingrid Rima
Edited by Mathew Forstater, Gary Mongiovi and Steven Pressman

87 **Consumer Capitalism**
Anastasios S. Korkotsides

88 **Remapping Gender in the New Global Order**
Edited Marjorie Griffin Cohen and Janine Brodie

89 **Hayek and Natural Law**
Erik Angner

90 **Race and Economic Opportunity in the Twenty-First Century**
Edited by Marlene Kim

91 **Renaissance in Behavioural Economics**
Harvey Leibenstein's impact on contemporary economic analysis
Edited by Roger Frantz

92 **Human Ecology Economics**
A new framework for global sustainability
Edited by Roy E. Allen

93 **Imagining Economics Otherwise**
Encounters with identity/difference
Nitasha Kaul

94 **Reigniting the Labor Movement**
Restoring means to ends in a democratic labor movement
Gerald Friedman

95 **The Spatial Model of Politics**
Norman Schofield

96 **The Economics of American Judaism**
Carmel Ullman Chiswick

97 **Critical Political Economy**
Christian Arnsperger

98 **Culture and Economic Explanation**
Economics in the US and Japan
Donald W. Katzner

99 **Feminism, Economics and Utopia**
Time travelling through paradigms
Karin Schönpflug

100 **Risk in International Finance**
Vikash Yadav

101 **Economic Policy and Performance in Industrial Democracies**
Party governments, central banks and the fiscal-monetary policy mix
Takayuki Sakamoto

102 **Advances on Income Inequality and Concentration Measures**
Edited by Gianni Betti and Achille Lemmi

103 **Economic Representations**
Academic and everyday
Edited by David F. Ruccio

104 **Mathematical Economics and the Dynamics of Capitalism**
Goodwin's legacy continued
Edited by Peter Flaschel and Michael Landesmann

105 **The Keynesian Multiplier**
Edited by Claude Gnos and Louis-Philippe Rochon

106 **Money, Enterprise and Income Distribution**
Towards a macroeconomic theory of capitalism
John Smithin

107 **Fiscal Decentralization and Local Public Finance in Japan**
Nobuki Mochida

108 **The 'Uncertain' Foundations of Post-Keynesian Economics**
Essays in exploration
Stephen P. Dunn

109 **Karl Marx's Grundrisse**
Foundations of the critique of political economy 150 years later
Edited by Marcello Musto

110 **Economics and the Price Index**
S.N. Afriat and Carlo Milana

111 **Sublime Economy**
On the intersection of art and economics
Edited by Jack Amariglio, Joseph W. Childers and Stephen E. Cullenberg

112 **Popper, Hayek and the Open Society**
Calvin Hayes

113 **The Political Economy of Work**
David Spencer

114 **Institutional Economics**
Bernard Chavance

115 **Religion, Economics and Demography**
The effects of religion on education, work, and the family
Evelyn L. Lehrer

116 **Economics, Rational Choice and Normative Philosophy**
Edited by Thomas A. Boylan and Ruvin Gekker

117 **Economics versus Human Rights**
Manuel Couret Branco

118 **Hayek versus Marx and Today's Challenges**
Eric Aarons

119 **Work Time Regulation as Sustainable Full Employment Policy**
Robert LaJeunesse

120 **Equilibrium, Welfare and Uncertainty**
Mukul Majumdar

121 **Capitalism, Institutions and Economic Development**
Michael Heller

122 **Economic Pluralism**
Robert Garnett, Erik Olsen and Martha Starr

123 **Dialectics of Class Struggle in the Global Economy**
Clark Everling

124 **Political Economy and Globalization**
Richard Westra

125 **Full-Spectrum Economics**
Toward an inclusive and emancipatory social science
Christian Arnsperger

126 **Computable, Constructive and Behavioural Economic Dynamics**
Essays in honour of Kumaraswamy (Vela) Velupillai
Stefano Zambelli

127 **Monetary Macrodynamics**
Toichiro Asada, Carl Chiarella, Peter Flaschel and Reiner Franke

128 **Rationality and Explanation in Economics**
Maurice Lagueux

129 **The Market, Happiness, and Solidarity**
A Christian perspective
Johan J. Graafland

130 **Economic Complexity and Equilibrium Illusion**
Essays on market instability and macro vitality
Ping Chen

131 **Economic Theory and Social Change**
Problems and revisions
Hasse Ekstedt and Angelo Fusari

132 **The Practices of Happiness**
Political economy, religion and wellbeing
Edited by John Atherton, Elaine Graham and Ian Steedman

133 **The Measurement of Individual Well-Being and Group Inequalities**
Essays in memory of Z.M. Berrebi
Edited by Joseph Deutsch and Jacques Silber

134 **Wage Policy, Income Distribution, and Democratic Theory**
Oren M. Levin-Waldman

135 **The Political Economy of Bureaucracy**
Steven O. Richardson

136 **The Moral Rhetoric of Political Economy**
Justice and modern economic thought
Paul Turpin

137 **Macroeconomic Regimes in Western Industrial Countries**
Hansjörg Herr and Milka Kazandziska

138 **Business Ethics and the Austrian Tradition in Economics**
Hardy Bouillon

139 **Inequality and Power**
The economics of class
Eric A. Schutz

140 **Capital as a Social Kind**
Definitions and transformations in the critique of political economy
Howard Engelskirchen

141 **Happiness, Ethics and Economics**
Johannes Hirata

142 **Capital, Exploitation and Economic Crisis**
John Weeks

143 **The Global Economic Crisis**
New perspectives on the critique of economic theory and policy
Edited by Emiliano Brancaccio and Giuseppe Fontana

144 Economics and Diversity
Carlo D'Ippoliti

145 Political Economy of Human Rights
Rights, realities and realization
Bas de Gaay Fortman

146 Robinson Crusoe's Economic Man
A construction and deconstruction
Edited by Ulla Grapard and Gillian Hewitson

147 Freedom and Happiness in Economic Thought and Philosophy
From clash to reconciliation
Edited by Ragip Ege and Herrade Igersheim

148 Political Economy after Economics
David Laibman

149 Reconstructing Keynesian Macroeconomics, Volume 1
Partial perspectives
Carl Chiarella, Peter Flaschel and Willi Semmler

150 Institutional Economics and National Competitiveness
Edited by Young Back Choi

151 Capitalist Diversity and Diversity within Capitalism
Edited by Geoffrey T. Wood and Christel Lane

152 The Consumer, Credit and Neoliberalism
Governing the modern economy
Christopher Payne

153 Order and Control in American Socio-Economic Thought
U.S. social scientists and progressive-era reform
Charles McCann

154 The Irreconcilable Inconsistencies of Neoclassical Macroeconomics
A false paradigm
John Weeks

155 The Political Economy of Putin's Russia
Pekka Sutela

156 Facts, Values and Objectivity in Economics
José Castro Caldas and Vítor Neves

157 Economic Growth and the High Wage Economy
Choices, constraints and opportunities in the market economy
Morris Altman

158 Social Costs Today
Institutional analyses of the present crises
Edited by Wolfram Elsner, Pietro Frigato and Paolo Ramazzotti

159 Economics, Sustainability and Democracy
Economics in the era of climate change
Christopher Nobbs

160 Organizations, Individualism and Economic Theory
Maria Brouwer

161 Economic Models for Policy Making
Principles and designs revisited
S.I. Cohen

162 Reconstructing Keynesian Macroeconomics, Volume 2
Integrated approaches
Carl Chiarella, Peter Flaschel and Willi Semmler

163 Architectures of Economic Subjectivity
The philosophical foundations of the subject in the history of economic thought
Sonya Marie Scott

164 Support-Bargaining, Economics and Society
A social species
Patrick Spread

165 Inherited Wealth, Justice and Equality
Edited by Guido Erreygers and John Cunliffe

166 The Charismatic Principle in Social Life
Edited by Luigino Bruni and Barbara Sena

167 Ownership Economics
On the foundations of interest, money, markets, business cycles and economic development
Gunnar Heinsohn and Otto Steiger; translated and edited with comments and additions by Frank Decker

168 Urban and Regional Development Trajectories in Contemporary Capitalism
Edited by Flavia Martinelli, Frank Moulaert and Andreas Novy

169 Social Fairness and Economics
Economic essays in the spirit of Duncan Foley
Edited by Lance Taylor, Armon Rezai and Thomas Michl

170 Financial Crisis, Labour Markets and Institutions
Edited by Sebastiano Fadda and Pasquale Tridico

171 Marx and Living Labour
Laurent Baronian

172 A Political Economy of Contemporary Capitalism and its Crisis
Demystifying finance
Dimitris P. Sotiropoulos, John G. Milios and Spyros Lapatsioras

173 Against Utility-Based Economics
On a life-based approach
Anastasios Korkotsides

174 Economic Indeterminacy
The dance of the meta-axioms
Yanis Varoufakis

175 Freedom, Responsibility and Economics of the Person
Jérôme Ballet, Damien Bazin, Jean-Luc Dubois and François-Régis Mahieu

176 Reality and Accounting
Ontological explorations in the economic and social sciences
Richard Mattessich

177 Profitability and the Great Recession
The role of accumulation trends in the financial crisis
Ascension Mejorado and Manuel Roman

178 Institutions and Development after the Financial Crisis
Edited by Sebastiano Fadda and Pasquale Tridico

179 The Political Economy of Gunnar Myrdal
A reassessment in the post-2008 world
Örjan Appelqvist

180 Gender Perspectives and Gender Impacts of the Global Economic Crisis
Edited by Rania Antonopoulos

181 Hegel, Institutions, and Economics
Performing the social
Carsten Herrmann-Pillath and Ivan A. Boldyrev

182 Producer Cooperatives as a New Mode of Production
Bruno Jossa

183 Economic Policy and the Financial Crisis
Edited by Łukasz Mamica and Pasquale Tridico

184 Information Technology and Socialist Construction
The end of capital and the transition to socialism
Daniel E. Saros

185 Beyond Mainstream Explanations of the Financial Crisis
Parasitic finance capital
Ismael Hossein-zadeh

186 Greek Capitalism in Crisis
Marxist analyses
Edited by Stavros Mavroudeas

Greek Capitalism in Crisis

Marxist analyses

Edited by Stavros Mavroudeas

Routledge
Taylor & Francis Group
LONDON AND NEW YORK

First published 2015
by Routledge
2 Park Square, Milton Park, Abingdon, Oxfordshire OX14 4RN

and by Routledge
711 Third Avenue, New York, NY 10017

First issued in paperback 2016

Routledge is an imprint of the Taylor & Francis Group, an informa business

British Library Cataloguing in Publication Data
A catalogue record for this book is available from the British Library

Library of Congress Cataloging in Publication Data
Greek capitalism in crisis: Marxist analysis / edited by Stavros Mavroudeas.
pages cm
1. Marxian economics–Greece. 2. Greece–Economic policy–21st century. 3. Financial crises–Greece. I. Mavroudeas, Stavros, editor of compilation.
HB97.5.G6964 2014
330.9495–dc23 2014000972

ISBN 13: 978-1-138-22685-2 (pbk)
ISBN 13: 978-0-415-74492-8 (hbk)

Typeset in Times New Roman
by Wearset Ltd, Boldon, Tyne and Wear

Contents

Figures

Tables

Contributors

George Androulakis is Assistant Professor of Business Administration, University of Patras. His scientific field is quantitative methods. He studied mathematics at undergraduate and postgraduate level in the department of Mathematics, University of Patras and his PhD thesis was on specialised optimisation functions with or without restrictions. His research interests focus on developing new methods of optimising functions using computational intelligence optimisation methods in applications to practical or theoretical problems, such as neural networks in education, in portfolio management, finding the best Runge-Kutta methods, finding the best point time series, etc., in applications of quantitative methods for modeling related to issues concerning the science of management, such as models on the factors affecting e-commerce, IT Outsourcing process, in quantitative indicators and features on automated tests of knowledge and/or skills to use computers. He is a member of the Greek Association of Marxist Studies.

George Economakis studied at the Economics Department of the University of Athens (BA in Economics 1984), Panteion University (MSc in Regional Development 1988), Panteion University (PhD in Political Economy 1998). He is working as Assistant Professor in Political Economy at the Department of Business Administration of the University of Patras. He is a member of the Greek Association of Political Economy and the Greek Association of Marxist Studies. He has published in many academic journals and co-authored several books.

Stelios Gialis studied Rural and Surveying Engineering at the Aristotle University of Thessaloniki and graduated in 1996. He received his PhD in Economic Geography and Regional Development from the Polytechnic School, Aristotle University of Thessaloniki, in 2004. He is Assistant Professor in the Department of Geography, University of the Aegean. He has several years of research and teaching experience in economic and labour geography, regional development, water management (water privatisation issues) and GIS. He is currently affiliated to the University of Georgia, US and the Hellenic Open University. He is doing post-doctoral research which is jointly funded by the Greek General Secretariat of Research and Technology and the EU. He has published in many academic journals including *International Journal of Urban and Regional Research*, *Human Geography: A New Radical Journal of Geography*, *Migration Letters* and *Capitalism–Nature–Socialism*. He is a member of the Greek Association of Political Economy and the Greek Association of Marxist Studies.

Alexis Ioannides is Assistant Professor of Labour Economics at the Department of Social Administration of the Democritus University of Thrace. He took his PhD in Economic Science, from the Economic Department of University of Macedonia and MSc in Economics from the same department. He also has a BSc in Physics, Department of Physics, Aristotle University of Thessaloniki. His research interests focus on the areas of labour economics and social policy, including the fields of working time determination, wage differentials, flexibility and mobility in the labour market. Other fields of research interest are those of political economy, labour theory of value, as well as econometric and statistical methods. He is also the author of a book in labour economics and of several articles published in scientific journals, and collective books. He is a member of the Greek Association of Political Economy and the Greek Association of Marxist Studies.

Thanasis Maniatis is Associate Professor at the Department of Economics, University of Athens, Greece, where he teaches Marxist Political Economy at the undergraduate and graduate program. He has published articles on topics including the labour theory of value, productive and unproductive labour, theories of crisis, Marxian categories in the US and the Greek economy, measurement of absolute poverty, the welfare state and the social wage in journals such as the *Review of Radical Political Economics*, *Capital and Class*, *Cambridge Journal of Economics* and *Review of Political Economy*. He is a member of the Greek Association of Political Economy and the Greek Association of Marxist Studies. His research interests include the empirical investigation of the current crisis from a Marxist perspective, the estimation of absolute poverty in advanced capitalist economies and the role of the welfare state.

Maria Markaki studied at the School of Mechanical Engineering of the National Technical University of Athens (BA in Mechanical Engineering 2002) and took her PhD in Economics from the School of Applied Mathematical and Physical Science of the National Technical University of Athens. She is working as a Researcher at the Laboratory of Theoretical and Applied Economics of the National Technical University of Athens. She has published in several academic journals. She is a member of the Greek Association of Political Economy (board member 2012–13) and the Greek Association of Marxist Studies.

Stavros Mavroudeas is Professor of Political Economy at the University of Macedonia. He studied at the Economics Department of the National Kapodistriakon University of Athens, from where he received his BA Economics

(1985, First Class Honours). He subsequently studied at the School of Oriental and African Studies, University of London, from where he received his MSc Economics (1986). He received his PhD from Birkbeck College, University of London (1990). He has worked as Lecturer (1992–96), Assistant Professor (1996), Associate Professor (2002–13) and Professor (2013 to today) in Political Economy at the Department of Economics of the University of Macedonia. His teaching and research fields include: political economy, history of economic thought, labour economics, economic growth and development economics. He has published in several academic journals such as the *Review of Political Economy*, *Review of Radical Political Economics*, *Science and Society*, *International Critical Thought*, *Economie Appliquee*, *Capitalism Nature Socialism* and *International Journal of Pluralism and Economics Education*. He has authored several books in English and in Greek (such as *The Limits of Regulation* – Edward Elgar) and also many chapters in collective volumes. He is a founding member of the Greek Association of Political Economy and serves in its board as Secretary (2009–13). He is also a member of the Greek Association of Marxist Studies.

Dimitris Paitaridis studied at the Public Administration Department of the Panteion University (BA in Public Economics, 2003) and at the Economics Department of the University of Macedonia (MSc Economics, 2005 and PhD Economics, 2012). He is an adjunct faculty member of the Public Administration Department of the Panteion University, teaching macroeconomics for the BA and MA courses. He has published articles in various academic journals such as *Research in Political Economy*, *Review of Radical Political Economics* and *International Journal of Social Economics*. His research interests include theoretical and empirical issues on political economy and history of economic thought. He is a member of the Greek Association of Political Economy.

Demophanes Papadatos teaches economics as Adjunct Faculty in the Department of Public Administration, Panteion University, Greece. He studied Economics at Panteion University (BA in Economic and Regional Development, Department of Economic and Regional Development) and the New School for Social Research (MA in Economics, Department of Economics, USA). He received his PhD in Economics from the School of Oriental and African Studies (SOAS) of the University of London, UK. He has published articles in international academic journals and collective volumes. He also works in the Greek banking sector. His research interests include finance, monetary theory as well as economic development and macroeconomics. He is a member of the Greek Association of Political Economy and the Greek Association of Marxist Studies.

Christos Papatheodorou is Professor of Social Policy at the Democritus University of Thrace, Department of Social Administration. Since 2010 he has been head of the Research Unit 'Social Policy, Poverty and Inequalities'

(Labour Institute, Greek General Confederation of Labour). He is a graduate in Economics (First Class Honours) from the Department of Economic Sciences, University of Athens and holds an MSc in Social Policy Analysis from the University of Bath, and a PhD from the London School of Economics and Political Science. He was also a postdoctoral fellow at LSE-STICERD and a Researcher at the Institute of Social Policy, National Centre for Social Research (Athens). He was Senior Research Associate for the Greek Observatory on Poverty, Inequalities, Income and Social Exclusion, UADPhilEcon, University of Athens (2007–9). He is a founder member of the Hellenic Social Policy Association and was chairman 2010–11 and a board member 2002–8. He is also a member of the Greek Association of Political Economy. His research interests and publications are in the fields of political economy of social policy, economic inequality, income distribution and redistribution, poverty, social protection and distributional impact of government policies. His work has been published in books, academic journals, book chapters and research reports, and has been presented in many conferences.

Costas Passas studied at the Maritime Studies Department of the University of Piraeus (BA in Maritime Economics, 2003) and the Economics Department of the University of Athens (MPhil in Economics, 2006). He is currently a PhD student at the Economics Department of the University of Athens and a research associate at the Labour Institute of the Greek General Confederation of Greece (INE/GSEE-ADEDY). He has published articles in academic journals such as the *Review of Political Economy*, and various reports in publications of the INE. His research interests include theoretical and empirical issues in political economy and history of economic thought. He is a member of the Greek Association of Political Economy.

Abbreviations

ADF	Augmented Dickey–Fuller Test
BD	Budget Deficit
CAD	Current Account Deficit
CDO	Collateralised Debt Obligations
CPI	Consumer Price Index
EAP	Economic Adjustment Programme
EC	European Commission
ECB	European Central Bank
ECU	European Currency Unit
EEC	European Economic Community
EFSF	European Financial Stability Facility
EMU	European Monetary Union
EU	European Union
EUROSTAT	European Statistical Agency
FD	Fiscal Deficit
FDI	Foreign Direct Investment
GATT	General Agreement on Tariffs and Trade
GDP	Gross Domestic Product
GVA	Gross Value Added
HELSTAT	Hellenic Statistical Agency
HICP	Harmonised Index of Consumer Prices
IEA	Institute for Economic Affairs
IMF	International Monetary Fund
LFS	Labour Force Survey
LIO	Labour Inspectorates Organisation
LTV	Labour Theory of Value
MOU	Memoranda of Understanding
MVA	Marxian Value Added
NATO	North Atlantic Treaty Organisation
NSRF	National Strategic Reference Framework
NUTS	Nomenclature of Territorial Units for Statistics
OCA	Optimal Currency Area
OCC	Organic Composition of Capital

OECD	Organisation for Economic Co-operation and Development
PIBS	Perceived Inflation Balance Statistic
PIGS	Portugal, Ireland, Greece, Spain
PIIGS	Portugal, Italy, Ireland, Greece, Spain
PIP	Public Investments Programme
REH	Ricardian Equivalence Hypothesis
RULC	Real Unit Labour Cost
SAP	Structural Adjustment Programme
TCC	Technical Composition of Capital
TDH	Twin Deficits Hypothesis
ToT	Terms of Trade
TRPF	Tendency of the Rate of Profit to Fall
ULC	Unit Labour Cost
UNCTAD	United Nations Conference on Trade and Development
VCC	Value Composition of Capital
WTO	World Trade Organization

Introduction

Stavros Mavroudeas

Nowadays the Greek economy is under the spotlight of international attention as one of the major epicentres of the Eurozone crisis. As such it is considered to have a disproportionate to its size impact on the world economy also.

The whole affair began in 2009 when official circles and Mainstream commentators, rather abruptly, 'discovered' that the Greek economy was suffering from alarming levels of its twin deficits (fiscal (FD) and current account (CAD) deficits). Previously, Greece had for quite lengthy periods high FD and public debt but was able to finance them via either internal or/and external borrowing without serious problems. Greece's accession to the European Monetary Union's (EMU) placed FD and public debt under the constraints of the Maastricht Treaty. However, these were violated not only by Greece but by almost every other EMU country since these constraints proved to be rather unsustainable. The Greek crisis erupted when the newly elected government revised upwardly the estimates of the Greek fiscal deficit amid internal and external talks for 'Greek statistics' (i.e. manipulation of statistics by successive Greek governments). This ignited a crisis of confidence in international markets concerning Greece's ability to meet its debt obligations which resulted in the widening of bond yield spreads (particularly the one related to the German bund) and the increase of the cost of risk insurance on credit default swaps. This led, in April 2010, to the downgrading of the Greek government debt to junk bond status by the international credit rating agencies which signified that international private capital markets practically ceased to fund Greece's sovereign debt. The Greek government requested EU assistance which took the form of two assistance programmes (Economic Adjustment Programmes (EAP)) encapsulated in respective Memoranda of Understanding (MOU) signed between the Greek government and the so-called troika (i.e. EU, ECB and IMF since the latter, after much deliberation, took part in the programmes). The second programme was required because of the obvious failure of the first, despite its numerous revisions. However, the second EAP is also performing badly and failing to meet its milestones and projections.

The EAP austerity and capitalist restructuring policies, agreed between the troika and Greek capital, had a catastrophic impact on the Greek economy. The economy contracted by more than 25 per cent and the real per capita GDP declined annually by 5.96 per cent for the 2010–13 period. The burden of this adjustment fell on the working class and the middle strata. Wages were reduced by approximately 35–40 per cent, the labour market was deregulated, dismissals' restrictions were relaxed, casual and unpaid work increased and the official unemployment rate jumped from 12.6 per cent (2010) to 28 per cent (2013).

Once the crisis of Greek capitalism erupted there was a plethora of works from all economic perspectives debating its nature and causes and the economic policies for surpassing it. Mainstream analyses (coming from Orthodox economics) offered explanations and policy proposals aiming to support the capitalist system. Their main preoccupation was to absolve the capitalist system of any inherent systemic instability and to whitewash their previous optimistic accounts of Greek capitalism and their failure to forecast its crisis. The majority of them proposed explanations positing labour as the main culprit of the crisis and supported troika's capitalist restructuring strategy. A minority voiced dissenting views – mainly regarding the EMU's deficiencies – but also suggested modified capitalist restructuring strategies. Moreover, Mainstream perspectives fail to appreciate the fundamental structural dimensions of Greek capitalism's crisis and instead relegate it either to policy errors and/or to weak structural deficiencies. On top of that, they consider the Greek crisis as independent from the 2007–8 crisis which they understand as simply a financial crisis.

On the other side of the fence, there was a proliferation of Radical Political Economy analyses (stemming from post-Keynesian and Marxo-Keynesian perspectives). These Radical approaches recognised the crisis-prone nature of capitalism and placed the blame for the crisis on Greek and European capitals. They also criticised the EMU's neoliberal architecture and argue either for its dissolution or for its radical overhaul. However, they refrained from proposing a strategy leading to socialist transition and focused on overturning neoliberalism. Furthermore, most of the Radical analyses ascribe to the financialisation thesis which focuses on the monetary sphere and neglects inordinately the sphere of production. Thus, while they relate the Greek crisis to the 2007–8 global crisis, they consider the latter as merely a financial crisis (similarly with Mainstream analyses). In addition, they disregard completely crucial elements of capitalism's modus operandi; which plays no role whatsoever in their analyses. Hence, their explanations of the Greek crisis recognise only weak structural causes and their policy proposals are equally short-sighted.

The chapters included in this collective volume follow a different perspective. They argue that the classical Marxist Political Economy approach grasps more realistically the reality of Greek capitalism and its crisis. Its emphasis on the primacy of the sphere of production within the total circuit of capital (production – exchange – distribution) can recognise the deep structural problems that permeated Greek capitalism – even during its superficially successful periods – and led to its current crisis. The problem of profitability rightfully lies at the centre of this analysis; in contrast to both Mainstream and Radical approaches. Consequently, the 2007–8 global crisis is related to Greek capitalism's crisis and both of them to the problem of profitability. Hence, they offer a strong structural explanation by attributing the fundamental causes of the Greek crisis to problems grounded in the sphere of production. More specifically, they discern two main structural components. First, it is argued that 2007–8 economic crisis is a crisis à-la-Marx (i.e. stemming from the tendency of the profit rate to fall – TRPF) and not a primarily financial crisis and this represents the 'internal' cause of the Greek crisis. Second, it is shown that – apart from the 'internal' dimension of the Greek problem – there is also an 'external' dimension. This is expressed by the existence of relations of imperialist exploitation (i.e. broad unequal exchange) that exist within the EU and which divide it between North (euro-core) and South (euro-periphery) economies. Greece obviously belongs to the second group and suffers its consequences. Finally, the analyses included in this volume broadly agree that the exit from the crisis, in order to benefit the labouring majority of Greece, must follow a transitory programme leading to a socialist economy.

The volume consists of three parts. The first part ('Critiques of mainstream and heterodox analyses of the Greek problem') consists of chapters criticising the Mainstream but also the Radical views and explanations regarding the Greek problem. The second part ('Marxist explanations of the Greek crisis') gathers studies of the Greek crisis that use the methodology and the analytical and empirical tools of classical Marxist Political Economy as distinguished from Neoclassicism, Keynesianism and Radical Political Economy. More specifically, emphasis is placed upon the sphere of production and the profitability. The third part of the volume consists of chapters studying particular aspects of the Greek economy such as poverty and deprivation, the labour market, and atypical employment and regional issues.

The first part contains five chapters. In the first one ('Mainstream accounts of the Greek crisis: more heat than light?') Stavros Mavroudeas and Dimitris Paitaridis present a critique of the Mainstream explanations of the Greek crisis. They distinguish three main streams. The first one argues that it is a Greek 'disease' of profligacy leading to twin deficits. The second one maintains that the Greek sins were exacerbated by EMU's structural deficiencies (i.e. being a non-optimal currency area) that cannot be rectified. The third stream argues that EMU's flaws can be rectified. It is shown that all versions adhere to the Twin Deficit Hypothesis (TDH) and maintain that exorbitant wage increases are the culprit for both the FD and the CAD. Then it is analysed how Mainstream explanations fail analytically because they do not account properly for the 2007–8 global crisis and the deep structural causes of the Greek crisis. Additionally, TDH's validity and the causal role of wage increases are being disputed.

In Chapter 2 ('Fiscal crisis in Greece: whose fault?') Thanasis Maniatis examines empirically whether it is the working class responsible for the public deficits and the accumulated public debt in Greece. By subtracting labour taxes from labour benefits derived from public spending, the net social wage obtained by the working class for the period 1995–2011 is estimated. The net social wage ratio expresses the net social wage as a percentage of the GDP and reveals the significance of workers' positive or negative net fiscal position for the system as a whole. The results suggest that the net social wage is almost always negative in the years examined indicating that the subsidisation of the income of labour is not the cause of the Greek fiscal crisis.

The third chapter ('Explaining the rising wage–productivity gap in the Greek economy'), by Thanasis Maniatis and Costas Passas, adds another critique to the Mainstream mantra that exorbitant wage increases caused the crisis. They show that during the neoliberal period that followed the stagflation crisis of the 1970s distribution of newly produced value shifted towards the side of capital. They examine econometrically the factors behind this shift in the distribution of income in the Greek economy during the neoliberal period of 1986–2008 as expressed in the rising wage–productivity gap and the resulting increase in the rate of surplus-value. As expected, variables such as the capitalisation of production, increased trade openness, consumer inflation and especially the decline in the unionisation rate explain the rise in the wage–productivity gap.

Chapter 4 ('The Greek EU–IMF Memoranda: a problematic strategy for Greek capitalism') by Demophanes Papadatos analyses the strategy of the troika EAPs. More specifically, it argues that they are a special modification of the IMF's structural adjustment programmes. Whereas the originals were procyclical and austerity programmes, the Greek EAPs are even more because they are front-loaded strenuous and they lack the debt restructuring (in their initial versions) and devaluation pillars. This explains both the deeper than expected recession they caused and also their persistent failure to meet their projections and milestones. Papadatos shows that Greek capital, in collaboration with international capital, is trying to implement a rigorous strategy in order to solve the sustainability problem of its huge debt and at the same time to transform itself from a state-driven capitalism into a private sector-led system even amid a global economic crisis. Nevertheless, this restructuring strategy goes far beyond its historical and social boundaries creating the objective conditions of a revolutionary process in Greek society.

In the fifth chapter ('Financialisation and the Greek case') Stavros Mavroudeas criticises the financialisation analyses that dominate the Radical explanations of the Greek crisis. First, the financialisation thesis is disputed for exaggerating finance's significance in modern capitalism and for erroneously discovering a new phase or stage of 'finance-led' capitalism. Then the three main financialisation explanations of the Greek crisis are criticised for failing to grasp the significance of the real economy and for making erroneous and/or unsubstantiated claims about the Greek economy. Finally, it is shown that the supposed channels of financialisation are too weak and short-lived in the Greek economy and, thus, financialisation explanations introduce it only exogenously (as the impact of the 2007–8 crisis). It is argued that this is an unrealistic explanation of the Greek crisis.

The second part of the volume contains three chapters. The first one ('The law of the falling rate of profit in the post-war Greek economy) by Thanasis Maniatis and Costas Passas discusses the law of the falling rate of profit in the context of the post-war Greek economy. The main Marxian variables are estimated for the 1958–2009 period and the different phases of capital accumulation and growth are outlined and discussed. Then, the existence of a negative trend in the Marxian and the net profit rates over the whole period are examined econometrically. It is proved that the organic composition of capital determined the movement of the profit rate. Then the existence of a statistically significant negative trend for both measures of profitability (the Marxian and the net profit rate) provides empirical support for the operation of the law of the falling rate of profit in the post-war Greek economy.

Chapter 7 ('Profitability and crisis in the Greek economy (1960–2012): an investigation') by George Economakis, George Androulakis and Maria Markaki also studies empirically the Greek economy and its crisis. From this study three main conclusions are drawn. First, that the Greek debt crisis is essentially a competitiveness crisis. Second, it rejects the hypothesis that the pressure of international competition was crucial for the profitability of the Greek economy, on the grounds that the latter was mainly on productive sectors not exposed to the international competition (non-tradable goods and services). Third, it finds that the deep depression that followed the troika austerity policies has led to a sharp decline of profitability, mainly due to the activation of the underconsumptionist factor of the crisis.

The third chapter of this part ('The Greek crisis: a dual crisis of overaccumulation and imperialist exploitation') by Stavros Mavroudeas and Dimitris Paitaridis also studies empirically the post-war development of the Greek economy. It finds that the TRPF operates for both the 1973 and the 2007–8 crises in the Greek economy. Moreover, it argues that the Greek crisis has two interlinked structural causes. The internal cause is the overaccumulation crisis of Greek capitalism that erupted in 2007–8. It stemmed from the tendential fall of the profit rate that began after the 1974 crisis, was aggravated by the simultaneous fall of the military dictatorship and was not resolved decisively by the subsequent neo-conservative restructuring policies. The external cause is the failure of Greek capital's contemporary 'Big Idea' of participating in the European imperialist integration project. Greek capitalism instead of being elevated from a middle-range second-generation capitalism to a first-class imperialism is actually being downgraded within the international division of labour. The combined result is the current crisis of Greek capitalism.

The last part of the volume consists of three chapters. The first ('Economic crisis, poverty and deprivation in Greece: the impact of neoliberal remedies), by Christos Papatheodorou, examines the impact of the current economic crisis and of the austerity programmes on social inequality and poverty in Greece. The analysis reveals that the dominant perspectives on crisis and poverty in public discourse, which serve to legitimise the neoliberal remedies and maintain that they offer the correct solution to the problems of the Greek economy, are not empirically sound. It is shown that the economic crisis has broader devastating effects on poverty and deprivation that surpass the increase of unemployment and the shrinkage of GDP. These effects are amplified instead of being rectified by the troika policies remedies that promote fiscal discipline, reduction of public spending, particularly on social protection and labour market deregulation.

Chapter 10 ('A comparative study of aspects of employment and unemployment in Greece before and after the crisis'), by Alexis Ioannides, examines the condition of the labour market. It is shown that the crisis and the neoconservative policies push forward a major restructuring of it at the expense of the workers. First, it is demonstrated that unemployment is much larger than the official statistics admit. The additional hidden unemployment is estimated by using Labour Force Survey micro-data. The exceptionally high unemployment rate worsens the workers' position in all areas. Thus, it is proved that workers are forced to work more unpaid overtime than before and in the same time they work fewer (paid) hours than they wish to. These facts weaken the Neoclassical explanation for the labour market functioning and vindicate the Marxist one.

The third chapter ('Recession and atypical employment: a focus on contemporary Greek metropolitan regions'), by Stelios Gialis, studies the changes in atypical employment in the context of austerity measures in contemporary, crisis-hit Greek regions. Contrary to mainstream mantras, it argues that Greek regions' problem was not that they were insufficiently incorporated into the global capitalist economy but, rather, whether they were too well incorporated. This is substantiated by exploring atypical employment across Greek regions through the use of recent data on part-time, temporary, self-employment and family work and relating them to changes in permanent employment and unemployment. The findings are discussed within the context of the historical peculiarities of the Greek economy and the restructuring of its labour markets and welfare structures during past decades.

Part I

Critiques of Mainstream and Heterodox analyses of the Greek problem

1 Mainstream accounts of the Greek crisis

More heat than light?

Stavros Mavroudeas and Dimitris Paitaridis

I Introduction

Since the eruption of the Greek crisis, official circles (both academic and governmental) rushed forward a series of explanations. There were several reasons behind this rush. First, the blatant contradiction between their triumphant till 2007 evaluations of the Greek economy as a fast-growing one with good prospects within the EU and the abrupt threat of a sovereign bankruptcy had to be covered. Second, and more important, the vicious capitalist restructuring required in order to save Greek capitalism had to be justified. These reasons do not preclude explanatory and policy differences. On the contrary, these exist and reflect – to a great extent – different international, national and even sectoral interests and capitalist fractions.

The official or Mainstream explanations of the Greek crisis are based on Orthodox economics. The latter derive from Neoclassical economics (and especially its hardcore neoliberal versions) but also – to a great extent, particularly regarding policy issues – from New Keynesianism (that is the contemporary conservative Keynesian perspective). In fact, as it will be shown, in policy matters New Keynesian theses (e.g. the Twin Deficit Hypothesis (TDH), the role of fiscal multipliers) play a significant role. Consequently, Mainstream explanations of the Greek crisis derive from both the Neoclassical and the New Keynesian perspectives and particularly from their convergence in the so-called New Consensus Macroeconomics (Arestis (2009)).

Mainstream explanations emphasise policy errors and do not recognise 'deep' structural problems (i.e. those pertaining to the fundamental mechanisms of the capitalist system) as causes of the Greek crisis. This is typical of Orthodox economics as they consider capitalism free of internal destabilising elements. Hence, crises can occur only because of policy errors and/or of 'weak' structural causes (i.e. processes and mechanisms that are policy constructs and not fundamental elements of capitalism). Moreover, Mainstream explanations consider only superficially and through deforming analytical lenses the sphere of production. Thus, in their analyses the profit rate does not play any role whatsoever. Again this is a derivative of the fundamental nature of Orthodox economics (in both its Neoclassical and Keynesian versions) as economics of the sphere of circulation (as opposed to the Classical and Marxist Political Economy traditions that are economics of the sphere of production). Thus, Mainstream explanations are pre-occupied with fiscal, trade and current account balances but pay insignificant attention to the productive structure of the Greek economy.

Finally, Mainstream explanations agree on two important conjunctural issues. First, they consider the 2007–8 global economic crisis as simply a financial one. This means that it was the outcome of the unregulated financial liberalisation of the world economy that created unsustainable financial bubbles and had no roots in the production sphere. Only in retrospect it affected the real economy. Again, this view is a corollary of the fundamental tenets of Orthodox economics that see everything solely in terms of exchange relations (and especially financial ones). Moreover, this view facilitates putting the blame for the crisis to some 'irresponsible' agent (like financial speculators) and not to the fundamental elements of the capitalist system. Second, Mainstream explanations divorce the Greek crisis from the 2007–8 global crisis. By the time that the former was erupting the official discourse was arguing that the global crisis was over; apart from the subsequently justified fears of a 'double dip' (i.e. a return of the crisis). Thus, national official circles systematically argued that the global crisis did not affected Greece as its economy was less financially leveraged than other economies. International circles, on the other hand, wanted to put the blame to whatever problematic spots appeared in the world economy to 'national perpetrators'.

This chapter reviews the mainstream explanations of the Greek crisis and offers an analytical and empirical critique of them. It classifies them in three main categories:

a. The first category considers the Greek crisis as a 'Greek disease' (i.e. caused by special national policy errors and structural deficiencies). Therefore, it emphasises mainly *policy errors* and recognises structural deficiencies only as a consequence of these nationally specific policy errors. This perspective is usually conferred by pundits coming from the dominant EU circles.
b. The second category, usually stemming from Anglo-Saxon commentators, argues that whatever national 'disease' was aggravated by EMU's structural deficiencies (i.e. being a non-Optimal Currency Area (OCA) which is prone to asymmetric shocks that exacerbate national 'diseases'). Thus, this second perspective emphasises the European *structural dimension.* It argues that EMU's fundamental flaws cannot be rectified and its collapse is on the table.
c. The third category is a 'middle-of-the-road' blend: *policy-driven (national disease) cum EMU's rectifiable structural flaws*. It is argued that while the Greek crisis has national origins it abated existing flaws of the EMU. However, these flaws can be rectified.

All these versions are criticised for failing to comprehend the 'deep' structural characteristics of the Greek crisis. Instead, they either attribute it to policy errors or recognise only 'weak' structural causes. The first perspective, faithful to the typical Neoclassical approach to economic crises, considers the Greek case as a national specificity created by bad policies. The second perspective recognises a rather 'weak' structural cause. It concerns mainly the sphere of circulation (i.e. how the common currency is related to diverse national economies) and has not much to do with the sphere of production per se. Concomitantly, the Greek and the Eurozone crises have to do mainly with EMU's architecture. The third perspective also attributes the structural problems to the sphere of circulation (with the additional argument that, contrary to the second perspective, these problems can be surpassed) and neglects the sphere of production. Thus, all three mainstream perspectives *fail to appreciate the fundamental structural dimensions* of the problem at hand. According to them the Greek crisis, the Eurozone sovereign debt crisis and moreover the 2007–8 global crisis have nothing to do with the sphere of production. The 2007–8 global crisis is considered solely a financial one, having nothing to do with real accumulation. A more robust account should refer to the deeper structural problems that arise from the sphere of production.

Over time mainstream explanations of the Greek crisis evolved from monistic explanations to a more eclectic mix. The more articulate of them usually attribute its origins at two sets of causes: (a) *internal causes* (e.g. exorbitant public expenditure, weak tax collecting mechanism, corruption) and (b) *external causes* (e.g. EMU's deficiencies, the repercussions of the 2007–8 crisis). Notwithstanding, behind these eclecticist mixes lay versions (or combinations) of the three previously delineated explanations.

Moreover, the great majority of Mainstream explanations, irrespective of their differences, ultimately understand the internal causes of the Greek crisis through the lenses of the TDH. This is their hardcore analytical device since all of them identify the Greek crisis as simply a (fiscal) debt crisis which evolved in an external debt crisis (i.e. *in toto* as simply a *debt crisis*). Then wages are posited as the factor triggering both the fiscal and the current account deficits. The typical argument is that Greek nominal unit labour costs (ULC) increased faster than those of the other European countries. Thus they worsened both the FD and the CAD. Even those emphasising the deterioration of competitiveness over the worsening of fiscal deficits put the blame on the wages.

There are a number of well-known problems with this argument. First, there is an extensive literature disputing whether nominal ULCs are a convincing measure of competitiveness. Second, as the Kaldor paradox argues, competitiveness is not an exclusive virtue of low wages. On the contrary it depends not only on costs (costs competitiveness) but also on qualitative factors (structural competitiveness). Third, Greek wage increases were not exorbitant as labour productivity increased faster than in other more developed European economies and, also, wages lagged constantly behind productivity increases. Thus, the Greek real ULCs (i.e. the wage share in the product) have been falling continuously for several decades.

But the mainstream explanations of the Greek crisis have also wider problems. First, they totally underestimate the role of the 2007–8 capitalist crisis. This, as said before, is unanimously considered as a mere financial crisis without origins and causes in the sphere of real accumulation. Second, they consider the Greek crisis as independent of the 2007–8 crisis. The latter has only an exogenous impact on the Greek economy by worsening the international economic environment and setting off grey expectations about sovereign debts.

The chapter is structured as follows. The following three sections analyse the three main categories of Mainstream explanations. The fifth section offers a critique of the analytical and empirical arguments of the Mainstream explanations. Finally, the last section concludes.

II A Greek 'disease'

The first Mainstream explanation variant argues that the Greek crisis is the outcome of special national policy errors and structural deficiencies. Thus, it can be branded a 'Greek disease'. However, it has nowadays become a bit arcane as developments surpassed it. It was expressed vociferously at the beginning of the Greek crisis and before the eruption of the Eurozone crisis. In its initial version it centred mainly upon the public sector as this basically came under attack with the first Economic Adjustment Programme (EAP). Subsequently, after the first EAP's reviews and as the private sector came also under attack, it was expanded to the whole Greek economy. In a nutshell, it identified the Greek 'disease' with two major deficiencies of the Greek economy: (a) large and persistent fiscal deficits financed through borrowing (which created large external debts) and (b) a falling competitivess. It argued that these deficiencies were caused by particular Greek national characteristics (special policy errors and structural deficiencies), i.e. it is a Greek 'disease'. Therefore, it emphasises mainly *policy errors* and recognises structural deficiencies only as a consequence of those nationally specific policy errors. Again, unsurprisingly, this version was expressed predominantly by the EU, the ECB, commentators and think-tanks of the euro-core countries but also by the Greek governments that signed and support the troika EAPs. Of course it was echoed and popularised by Greek and international media in order to justify and legitimise the first EAP.

The gist of this version is that Greece is a special type of economy (and country) which is prone to fiscal profligacy. It is argued that it is characterised by large and persistent fiscal deficits and a falling competitiveness, characteristic of the 'lazy' European South as opposed to the 'prudent' European North. More specifically, the Mainstream mantra maintains that the Greek economy is characterised by low productivity, high wages and a big public sector. High wages are the product of the big public sector which is clientelist (thus voters are bought through provision of employment and wages). In addition, the public sector has low productivity and a falling ability to collect taxes (due to clientelism fomenting tax evasion). Consequently, fiscal deficits are accumulated. These are financed through loans resulting in a widening external debt (expressed in a deteriorating current account). Cheap borrowing was possible because since the entrance to EMU Greece benefited from low interest rates. In addition, Greece exploited EU's benevolence by forfeiting statistical data and thus violated the provisions of the Maastricht Treaty (that founded the euro). With the advent of the 2007–8 crisis international financial markets started scrutinising fiscal deficits and external debts. Consequently, the unsustainability of the Greek debt was discovered and the Greek crisis erupted. Thus, the deep fiscal cuts of the first EAP were justified. This was a political choice since the Greek and EU establishment aimed to pass piecemeal the EAP strategy. Therefore, it focused initially on the public sector and public employees by staging a truly defamation campaign aiming at creating a rift between public and private sector employees. The slant of the 'lazy and corrupt public employees' is the trademark of this first version.

However, as soon as the first EAP started failing and lagging dismally behind its own projections and timetables, austerity policies had to be expanded to the private sector. In order to justify this expansion the problem of competitiveness was surfaced. It was argued that not only the public but also the private sector is characterised by low productivity, high wages and rigid labour market regulation culminating in a falling competitiveness. Consequently, the current account worsened not only because of public borrowing but also because of diminishing exports and increasing imports. High wages fuelled consumption which was directed towards imports, since domestically produced goods were uncompetitive. The trademark of this new propagandistic campaign was that Greek workers collectively (private and public sector) are overpaid and inefficiently working.

Typical examples of this perspective are offered by papers from the governing EU and ECB bodies and from the Bank of Greece. For example, in the beginning of the first Greek EAP (EC (2010): 6) the origins of the Greek crisis are defined as:

- a persistent fiscal and external imbalances that led to a significant increase in government and external debt;
- b rigid product and labour markets.

These Greek vulnerabilities were exposed by the 2008–9 global crisis. Subsequently – and while not at the origin of the problem – the banking sector was affected by the economic and confidence crisis (p. 7). The same verdict is professed, in more damning terms, in the introduction to the second Greek EAP (EC (2012): 9). The origins of the Greek crisis are again attributed to:

- a unsustainable fiscal policies, partly hidden by unreliable statistics and temporarily high revenues;
- b rigid labour and product markets;
- c loss of competitiveness and rising external debt.

It is again reiterated that 'while not at the origin, the banking sector was affected by the economic and confidence crisis'. In a similar vein, Gibson *et al.* (2012: 500–1) find the origins of the Greek crisis in the large fiscal deficits and the falling competitiveness of the Greek economy:

> Although entry into the euro area contributed to a period of prolonged and robust growth, and low (by Greece's historical standards) inflation, two deep-seated problems remained unaddressed; the country continued to run large fiscal imbalances and the country's competitiveness – already a problem upon euro area entry – continued to deteriorate.

It should be noted that in its 2010 version this explanation emphasised fiscal and external imbalances with the emphasis on the former. The problem of competitiveness was mentioned but in a somehow subdued manner. Moving to the second EAP competitiveness is brought forward and emphasised.[1]

Finally, the same arguments are reiterated, in rather pedantic terms, by the neoconservative Greek economists grouped in the greekeconomistsforreform.com (e.g. Azariadis (2010), Dellas (2011), Ioannides (2012), Meghir *et al.* (2010)). Their arguments have nothing exceptional apart from some minor differences between them (for example some prioritise the fall in competitiveness over the fiscal deficits, e.g. Ioannides (2012)).

The Greek 'disease' explanation suffered a hit when other country members (Ireland at the end of 2010, Portugal at the beginning of 2011) of the EMU faced problems and entered also in bail-out programmes through EAPs with the troika. What was previously characterised as a special Greek 'disease' was now discovered to be a far wider problem. The initial reaction was to attribute the expansion of the problem to *contagion from Greece*.[2] This, which is indeed a rather weak argument,[3] was supplemented by collectively branding these countries (in fact all the PIGS – Portugal, Ireland, Greece and Spain) as EMU's outcasts: economies prone to fiscal and banking profligacy. Consequently, instead of a Greek, a South 'disease' was discovered. Thus, beginning with non-other but the ECB (ECB (2012)), several economists (e.g. Kosters (2009), Panetta (2011), Weidman (2012)) identified fiscal profligacy as the root of EMU's sovereign debt crisis. However, as the EU's crisis expanded beyond the PIGS and started touching Italy and even euro-core countries (e.g. Belgium, Netherlands and France) the popularity of the South 'disease' explanation started receding.

In analytical terms, the Greek (or South) 'disease' explanation hinges upon the TDH which contends that there is a strong link between the current account balance and the government budget balance. A twin deficit occurs when an economy has a current account deficit plus a fiscal deficit with the causality running from the latter to the former. In the Greek case this argument is expressed as follows. The increasing FD was caused by the profligate and clientelist state (mainly because of exorbitant wage increases but also because of widespread tax evasion). In order to finance this FD the country borrowed heavily. This has increased public debt. Since, after the accession to the EMU, external borrowing was cheap and indeed favoured by the EMU's rules then the public debt became external debt; thus deteriorating the already existing CAD. At this point a supplementary argument is brought forward: the current account worsened not only because of the FD but also because of the falling competitiveness of the whole economy. Therefore, it is argued that the TDH is verified. However, this elegant theoretical construction has rather shaky empirical foundations. The applicability of the TDH for Greece is far from unambiguous (see Section V).

III EMU is not (and cannot, at least easily, become) an OCA

The second Mainstream perspective argues that, whatever national Greek 'disease' exists, it is aggravated by EMU's structural deficiencies. That is, EMU is characterised as a non-OCA which is prone to asymmetric shocks that exacerbate national 'diseases'. Thus, this second perspective emphasises the European *structural dimension.* It argues that EMU's fundamental flaws cannot be rectified (i.e. EU cannot become something similar to the US) and its collapse is on the table. This view centres only passingly on the Greek case per se. It takes it, as well as those of the other PIGS, as a springboard to spearhead its main criticism: EMU is inherently faulty. This perspective is expressed mainly by Anglo-Saxon commentators either neoliberal (e.g. Feldstein (2010a)) or neo-Keynesian (e.g. Krugman (2012a)).

Characteristically, Feldstein (2010a) argues:

> The European economic and monetary union is doubly flawed. First, it forces diverse countries to live with a single interest rate and exchange rate that cannot be appropriate for all members. Second, combining a single currency with independent national budget policies encourages fiscal profligacy. The Greek situation is a manifestation of these flaws.

And elsewhere, Feldstein (2010b) maintains that 'The crisis in Greece and the debt problems in Spain and Portugal have exposed the euro's inherent flaws.' Feldstein's position is reiterated by the Thatcherite Institute for Economic Affairs (IEA). In a 216-page study, edited by P. Booth (2013) it gives a characteristically damning account of the EMU from a neoliberal perspective. The central conclusion is that the EMU is inherently flawed – by not being an OCA – and that it should be either broken up in an orderly way or radically reorganised along even more neoliberal lines.

The same line is towed by *The Economist* (2010):

> The Greek crisis only confirms the folly of binding a group of disparate countries together in a currency zone with no mechanism, such as a central fiscal authority, to address its internal imbalances. The north–south divide in the euro area looks more marked than ever. The north, exemplified by Germany, relies on exports to power its growth, saves hard and runs trade surpluses. The southern economies, such as Greece, have leant too heavily on consumer spending, have weak public finances and rely on foreign capital to supplement their low savings.

But also, from the neo-Keynesian side of the fence, Krugman echoes the same argument. In a series of works he forcefully supports the OCA theory (e.g.

Krugman (2012b)) and he argues that the existing crisis is nothing but the consequence of the Eurozone's difficulties dealing with asymmetric shocks (Krugman (2012a)).

To be more accurate, these predominantly Anglo-Saxon accounts do not absolve Greece from being responsible for the problem. On the contrary, they usually – particularly the neoliberal accounts – press forcefully the Greek profligacy argument. But, as said before, the crux of their argument is against the EMU. This emphasis has a twofold explanation.

The first explanation is geopolitical or has to do, in Marxist terminology, with the intra-imperialist contradictions. The euro is one of the main instruments through which European capitals (and the EU as their expression) strive for world supremacy against the US. As such it attracted US antipathy from its very beginning. Even in academic analyses this reason cannot be fully disguised. Again Feldstein (1997), commenting about the upcoming EMU, expressed it in almost explicit terms: 'the adverse economic effects of a single currency on unemployment and inflation would outweigh any gains from facilitating trade and capital flows' and that, while 'conceived of as a way of reducing the risk of another intra-European war', it was 'more likely to have the opposite effect' and 'lead to increased conflicts within Europe and between Europe and the United States'.

The second explanation is academic and has to do with the OCA theory (McKinnon (1963), Mundell (1961)). According to this theory in order for a currency union (that unites several diverse in character and structure economies) to be such an area it has to fulfil several crucial requirements. These are the following:

a It must have high productive factors mobility. This implies not only high capital but also high labour mobility.
b It must generate a viable process of structural economic convergence. This particularly implies similar business cycles and trade patterns.
c It must have a fiscal mechanism (i.e. some degree of fiscal integration) so that transfers could be made from well-doing economies to those underperforming and/or hit by 'asymmetric economic shocks'.

The majority of the US views opined that EMU is far from being such a currency area. The first feature regarding the labour factor is notoriously missing.[4] The second feature is also very erratic in the sense that periods of economic convergence are succeeded by periods of divergence. Finally, the last feature is simply negligible.[5] The absence of these features was supposed to be covered by the Stability and Growth Pact rules (that supplemented the Maastricht Treaty) regarding public deficit and debt. These were systematically violated by all EMU economies (except one); beginning with Germany and France. But also these rules are hopelessly inadequate to fill the gaps in a currency union comprising unevenly developed economies facing 'asymmetric shock' because of a major global economic crisis.

On the basis of the theoretical arguments of OCA theory the US academic antipathy towards the EMU took flesh and bones. The stance of the majority of US economists towards the euro was nicely summarised by Dornbusch (2001) in his famous dictum: 'It can't happen, it's a bad idea, and it can't last.' Jonung and Drea (2009) offer an excellent but partisan (trying to vindicate the EMU) survey of US economists' opinions. They meticulously plot both the different stances (e.g. OCA theory prone academics versus the practically oriented FED economists) and the evolution of the US debate. The general conclusion is that the US debate underwent significant changes, continuously evolving in response to actual events, starting in the early 1990s from a rather sceptical view of the EMU as being unlikely to happen, or at least not according to schedule, to an acceptance of the euro in the late 1990s, sometimes combined with the prediction that it would not last very long. But as soon as Jonung and Drea were ready to declare the victory of European political voluntarism over US skepticism,[6] the eruption of the European sovereign debt crisis put a sudden brake. As already shown, US criticisms returned with vengeance (accompanied with the increasing conflicts between the US and the EU).[7]

Actually, the OCA theory is the closest thing Mainstream economics have to the Marxist disproportionality (or uneven development) thesis. The latter argues that capitalism is characterised by the uneven development of either the regions within a single economy or between different countries. As such it is the exact opposite of the convergence thesis that is derived by definition from the Neoclassical growth model.[8] Marxist Political Economy argues that convergence is a utopia and capitalism is inherently prone to uneven development. This unevenness refers primarily to the production sphere and is then expressed in the sphere of circulation. Mainstream economics cannot have this production-centred emphasis as they are by construction economics of the exchange sphere. The OCA theory is the closest possible notion to the disproportionality argument. It essentially states that unless there is a production-based convergence then any circulation-based unification is futile. And as such it has been vindicated regarding the EMU. The European integration project, particularly regarding its monetary unification, has proceeded from failure to failure through acute political voluntarism. Each previous monetary unification project ended in failure; beginning with the Werner plan, following with the 'snake in the tunnel', the European Monetary System and the European Currency Unit (ECU). Each failure was responded with an even more ambitious leap forward. The EMU and the euro are by far the most ambitious leap. However, it is faced with far more serious problems from its predecessors (which unlike it had provisions for an organised dissolution mechanism in case of failure) and the prospects of an ever more disastrous failure. The gist of its problems is capitalism's inherently uneven development and the concomitant inability to create a unified state behind the economic integration.

Concluding, this mainly Anglo-Saxon explanation of the Greek crisis while sharing the fiscal profligacy argument of the first explanation recognises a rather 'weak' structural cause. It concerns mainly the sphere of circulation (i.e. how the common currency is related to diverse national economies) and has not much to do with the sphere of production per se. Concomitantly, Greek and the Eurozone crises have to do mainly with the architecture of the European monetary system.

IV The Greek problems have national origins exacerbated by errors in EMU's structure but all these can be rectified

The third Mainstream explanation of the Greek crisis is a 'middle-of-the-road' blend. It can be branded as *policy-driven (national disease) cum EMU's rectifiable structural flaws*. It is arguing that the Greek crisis has been caused by a combination of national policy errors (high FDs and debt) coupled with problems created by the incomplete economic unification of the EMU. Consequently, it is argued that a deepening of the economic and political unification of the EU will solve these problems. Essentially, this explanation comes from mainly European analysts that are in favour of European unification but have ideological and/or practical reservations regarding the actual process of this unification. To a great extent these views have Keynesian (or even post-Keynesian) origins.

De Grauwe features prominently among this stream. In De Grauwe (2010a: 1), he argues that the major responsibility for the Greek crisis 'rests with the Greek authorities who mismanaged their economy and deceived everybody about the true nature of their budgetary problems'. Then he adds:

> The crisis has exposed a structural problem of the Eurozone that has been analyzed by many economists in the past. This is the imbalance between full centralization of monetary policy and the maintenance of almost all economic policy instruments (budgetary policies, wage policies, etc.) at the national level. Put differently the structural problem in the Eurozone is created by the fact that the monetary union is not embedded in a political union.
>
> (p. 4)

In another paper he explicitly rejects the fiscal profligacy argument for Spain and Ireland (but not for Greece): 'Are such difficulties due to irresponsible fiscal policies? This could be the case for Greece, but not for Spain and Ireland, so fiscal profligacy cannot be identified as the in-depth source of eurozone problems' (De Grauwe (2010b)). The same argument is voiced by Lane (2012): 'Although Greece (and Italy) has a debt profligacy record' (Lane (2012): 51), 'the origin and propagation of the European sovereign debt crisis can be attributed to the flawed original design of the euro' (Lane (2012): 65). Thus, 'the main flaw is that the monetary union was not accompanied by a banking and fiscal union' (Lane (2012): 49).

Similar concerns are being advanced by explicitly post-Keynesian economists. Botta (2012: 3) argues that 'Actually, the current eurozone crisis seems to have been decisively aided by the original institutional setup of the eurozone and its *incomplete* nature with respect to a fully developed federal union.'

Again from the post-Keynesian camp, Hein *et al.* (2011) emphasise the existence imbalances in the euro area as the root cause of the euro crisis. They explicitly reject the first Mainstream explanation: 'The current euro crisis is considered by many observers – above all by the dominating economic policy makers and advisors in Germany and also in the European Commission – as a crisis of government deficits and debt' (p. 3).

> The current euro crisis can better be interpreted as the consequence of preceding private debt and current account imbalances and not as a result of excessive public deficits. In the four countries outlined above, the private sector obviously tended to spend more than its income. This was associated with government surpluses (Ireland, Spain) or amplified by government deficits (Portugal, Greece), which led to very high and rising current account deficits in the four countries.
>
> (p. 9)

This post-Keynesian emphasis on EMU's imbalances and particularly those associated with the balance of payments (hence the current account) is quite interesting. As such it points to a structural characteristic of the EMU which sometimes has been branded as neo-mercantilism: the Eurozone is structured in such a manner as to merit the trade surpluses of the Northern countries against the trade deficits of the Southern countries. This argument can be found also, as we will explain later, in the more radical post-Keynesian 'financialisation' explanations of the crisis. Tellingly, several of the post-Keynesians belonging to this third middle-of-the-road explanation of the Greek crisis participate also to the radical 'financialisation' thesis (e.g. E. Hein). On the other hand, the current account imbalances argument has been taken up by more conservative theorists that do not ascribe to the 'financialisation' thesis but aim for a more unified European integration (e.g. Merler and Pisani-Ferry (2012)).

There are a number of problems with this third mainstream (and quasi-mainstream in its post-Keynesian variant) perspective. The first has already been mentioned. It offers a structural explanation but this is a 'weak' one. It attributes the structural problems to the sphere of circulation and neglects the sphere of production. It agrees with the second mainstream explanations with regard to EMU's problems pointed out by the OCA theory. But it believes that a more unified economically and politically EU can overcome these problems. In this belief it departs from the harder versions of the second explanation which believe that an economic and political unification of the EU similar to that of the US is impossible. This is the second major problem of this perspective. Its political and economic voluntarism goes against historical wisdom. Europe has been the main ground where capitalism was born on the basis of the nation-state and the national economy. Almost every inch of the borders of each state has been soaked in blood in wars against its neighbours. Hence national political and economic identities are deeply entrenched. Moreover, the current Eurozone crisis has already torn apart whatever feeble pretext existed of a 'common European identity' and a European solidarity. In stark contrast, national interests have resurfaced with vengeance. This makes this aim of a politically and economically unified Europe a utopia unless a major European power (or a bloc of them) achieves overpowering dominance over the other members of the EU. But, whatever the power of Germany and its allies is, there is a long and precarious road to go till it succeeds in this endeavour.

V Mainstream explanations: a critique

Over time Mainstream explanations of the Greek crisis evolved from monistic explanations to a more eclectic mix. The more articulate of them usually attribute its origins at two sets of causes (e.g. Nelson *et al.* (2011)):

a *internal causes*: exorbitant public expenditure, weak tax collecting mechanism, corruption and clientelism (even sometimes cronyism), over-regulated labour and product markets, high wages, a non-market friendly institutional environment, deteriorating competitiveness, etc.;
b *external causes*: EMU's deficiencies, the repercussions of the 2007–8 crisis, etc.

Notwithstanding, this eclecticism hides behind it versions (or combinations) of the three previously delineated explanations. Moreover, the great majority of mainstream explanations, irrespective of their differences, ultimately understand the internal causes of the Greek crisis through the lenses of the TDH.[9] This is their hardcore analytical device since all of them identify the Greek crisis as simply a (fiscal) debt crisis which evolved in an external debt crisis (i.e. *in toto* as simply a *debt crisis*). The adoption of this analytical argument by even vehement neoliberals is quite interesting given its Keynesian origins. Of course, some explanations may add a bit of salt here and there; especially by stressing the importance of clientelism and the institutional framework. Some might even extend clientelism not only to the working class and the middle strata (which is the typical argument) but also to Greek capital. These accounts add to clientelism the upper-class cronyism of Greek capitalism; i.e. the close crony relations existing between the systemic political parties and Greek capitalists. Cronyism is accused of falsifying free competition and thus hinders growth by receiving rents. Notwithstanding, the gist of Mainstream explanations rests upon the TDH.

Then wages are posited as the factor triggering both the FD and the CAD (and even irrespectively of the controversy between the Twin Deficits and the Ricardian Equivalence Hypotheses). The typical argument is that Greek (nominal) unit labour costs increased faster than those of the other European countries. Thus they worsened both the budget deficit and the current account deficit. To be frank they could be other analytical choices. For example, as some Radical (e.g. Stathakis (2010)) but also Marxist explanations (Mavroudeas (2010a)) argue, FD's deterioration can be rightfully attributed to the upper-class' notorious tax evasion and cronyism. The former depresses public revenues and the latter augments public expenditure; thus, in conjunction, derailing the FD. However, the Mainstream explanations stick, for obvious reasons to the supposedly high wages as the main cause of the big and persistent FD. There is a wealth of evidence proving this point. Starting from the high bodies of the EU and the Greek government and moving to the groups of neoconservative economists this argument is reiterated almost verbatim. For example, the first EAP states:

> Real wage growth consistently outpaced productivity gains over the past decade, in part reflecting spillovers from very high public wage increases. The resulting increase in ULC (unit labour costs) eroded external competitiveness, not least with respect to the rest of the euro area.
>
> (EC (2010): 3)

Even those emphasising the deterioration of competitiveness over the worsening of fiscal deficits put the blame on the wages. For example, Ioannides (2012) argues that the basic cause of the Greek crisis has been the deterioration of its competitiveness, mainly due to the rise of unit labour costs, but also due to the existing non-market friendly regulatory framework.[10]

There are a number of well-known problems with the Mainstream logic.

The TDH: a Columbus egg dilemma

The adoption of the TDH by the Mainstream explanations of the Greek crisis is a matter of political expediency rather of analytical principle. The TDH is basically a Keynesian argument that hardcore Neoclassicals reject in favour of the Ricardian Equivalence Hypothesis (REH) that contends that increasing FDs do not affect the CAD.[11] The reason for its adoption is overtly political. It enables putting the blame for the crisis on the public sector (and especially public employees rather than state support to capitalist profitability). This facilitated Greek capitalism in dividing public from private sector employees and pass piecemeal the initial measures of the first EAP (see section II).

In analytical terms the TDH suffers from the fundamental deficiency of Orthodox economics (i.e. of being economics of simply the sphere of circulation). It cannot grasp properly what is happening in the real economy (production processes, industrial structures, productivity increases, etc.) and understands this through the deformed lenses of circulationist accounting relations. Consequently, it ends up with a Columbus egg dilemma: is the FD worsening the CAD or vice versus? Unless you accept the highly dogmatic and unrealistic REH, it is unquestionable that FD and CAD are related. The question is the direction of causality. Because of their deformed lenses Orthodox economics cannot solve convincingly this puzzle. Thus, it is relegated to empirical investigation. Unsurprisingly empirical studies offer inconclusive and mixed results.

This is the Greek case also. Empirical examinations of the TDH for the Greek economy produce contradictory results. Vamvoukas (1999) tests the TDH through various trivariate causality tests for the trade balance, the FD and either real output or inflation rate for the 1948–94 period. He discovers a unidirectional relationship from the FD to the trade deficit in the short and the long run. Similarly, Pantelidis *et al.* (2009) using a VAR and an Error Correction Model for the period 1960–2007, find also a unidirectional causal effect running from FD to trade deficit, in both the short and the long run. However in a following paper, Katrakilidis and Trachanas (2011) adopt a more sceptical view about TDH's validity but at the same time they do not give evidence to the REH. They criticise both Vamvoukas (1999) and Pantelidis *et al.* (2009) for not taking into account significant structural brakes which could alter the integration properties of the examined series. Furthermore, they argue that such omission leads to misspecified dynamic relations and spurious findings. For Katrakilidis and Trachanas this significant structural brake is Greece's accession in the EEC in 1981 which decisively changed the dynamics of the Greek economy. So, they split the period 1960–2007 into the pre-accession (1960–80) and the post-accession (1981–2007) period. Then, applying the Autoregressive Distributed Lags cointegration methodology and Granger causality tests, they find that TDH holds only for the pre-accession period. For the post-accession period the relationship is reversed since long-run causality runs from the trade deficit to the FD. These empirical outcomes are quite interesting since they reveal that the loss of competitiveness because of the accession to the Common Market is one of the reasons for the aggravation of the FD. In a similar manner, Nikiforos *et al.* (2013) posit this structural brake at the 1992 creation of the EMU. Using quarterly data they discriminate into pre-Maastricht Treaty (1980–94) and post-Maastricht Treaty (1995–2010) period. Then applying Granger Causality tests and a VAR model, Nikiforos *et al.* find that for the first period it is the FD that drives the trade deficit whilst for the second period this relationship is reversed. This change is attributed to (a) the 'hard drachma' policy of the period preceding Greece's accession in the EMU and (b) the euro's high exchange rate in the subsequent period. Both of these dampened exports.

Concluding, the TDH is an analytically problematic and empirically unverified thesis. These are well-known problems within Orthodox economics. However, Mainstream explanations of the Greek crisis stick with it because it offers a neat and powerful propagandistic tool.

ULC and competitiveness: a partisan analysis

The next step of the Mainstream analyses (increasing ULCs as the cause of falling competitiveness)[12] is equally problematic; again in both analytical and empirical terms.

Regarding the analytical aspect, ULCs suffer from well-known problems. First, there is an extensive literature disputing whether ULCs are a convincing measure of competitiveness.[13] As Lall (2001) – among others – accurately argues, ULCs consider only cost competitiveness. However, competitiveness goes well beyond cost and price and depends on structural and technological factors and the qualitative dimension of the production process (e.g. productive specialisations, special market conditions). On the contrary ULCs are terribly myopic by looking only at short-run developments and inordinately projecting a micro behaviour to the macroeconomy.[14]

Second, this theoretical myopia leads to serious conceptual problems. The most important of these (as Turner and Van't Dack (1993) accurately argue) is that the two variables that define ULC (productivity and the wage rate, see Note 12) are interrelated as productivity is endogenous and responds to changes in wages. For example, if an economy faces sharp wage increases it might respond by minimising the use of labour and exiting sectors most exposed to labour-cost competition. This will result in increased productivity which obscures the rising labour cost and denotes a deceivingly modest increase in ULCs.

Last but more important, ULC is a partisan concept: it by construction puts the burden of competitiveness on labour but not on capital. Even if structural competitiveness is left aside, price competitiveness does not depend solely on labour cost but also on capital's profit margins (see also Felipe (2007)). Orthodox economics consciously neglect this aspect and equate competitiveness with labour costs. As it can easily be shown, ULCs are related with the wage share and thus with income distribution between capital and labour. By focusing solely on ULCs, Orthodox economics equate competitiveness with wage restraint and engineer a 'race to the bottom' as different economies compete to reduce wages in order to increase their competitiveness.

These analytical deficiencies lead also to serious empirical problems. Kaldor (1978) compared the growth in ULCs and the growth in value in market shares for exports for 12 countries for 1963–75. He found that for several of these countries, the relation between the two variables was positive: this is the famous 'Kaldor paradox'. Fagerberg (1996) made the same study for the period 1978–94 and replicated the same evidence. A crucial corollary of the 'Kaldor paradox' is that competitiveness depends not only on costs and especially wage costs (costs competitiveness) but also on other factors (structural competitiveness). In general, several studies have shown that there is no simple, consistent relationship between trends in the trade balance and trends in ULCs.

In the Greek case all the above-mentioned problems of the ULC perspective are manifested.

To begin with, the data do not support the hypothesis that because of the increased ULCs Greece's export performance deteriorated. As Gros (2011: 1) shows, Greece's share of the exports of goods and services in overall EU27 exports is essentially stable for the pre-crisis period; thus denoting that increasing ULCs had not affected exports. Second, as Malliaropoulos and Anastasatos (2013: 6) show, the increase of Greek ULCs was not as extraordinary as the official mantras argue. They rose by 22 per cent against those of 35 trading partners in the period 2000–9. This compares favourably to an average 36 per cent increase for the EU27 and a 30 per cent increase for the EU-17. The reason for the relatively better performance of Greek ULCs is that, while nominal wages in Greece grew quickly, productivity growth was also higher than the EU average.

The official mouthpieces simply concealed these results and continued their propaganda.

However, more sophisticated Orthodox analyses tried to surpass the problem. They argued that it was the increase of ULCs in the non-tradables sector of the Greek economy that led to a wage-price spiral and ultimately affected competitiveness through the inflation differential between Greece and the EU. Gaulier and Vicard (2012) argue that current account imbalances within the euro area were not driven by export performance. Unit labour costs were de-correlated from export growth: the bulk of their appreciation comes from price developments in the non-tradables sector, with the effect being largest in the crisis countries. In a similar vein Malliaropoulos and Anastasatos (2013: 1) maintain that the falling competitiveness of the Greek economy is primarily related to the increase in relative labour costs and prices of non-tradable goods and services relative to tradables, and secondarily to the increase in ULCs in the export sector (like a reverse Balasa–Samuelson effect).[15] This has harmed price competitiveness by drawing resources away from the tradables sector, thereby reducing the export sectors' productive capacity in favour of the non-tradables sector and increasing the general price level. Then they reject a uniform wage reduction and suggest a wage reduction only for the non-tradables sector.

This moderate position recognises shyly that Greek wage increases were not exorbitant in general but only partly. However, they still toe the line and argue for a discreet austerity coupled with bits of growth measures. This is also an erroneous position in that it mentions but subsequently neglects to examine the role of price increases. Malliaropoulos and Anastasatos (2013: 7) argue that the inflation spiral begins as firms fully pass increases in labour costs on prices. Then inflation feeds to wage increases, leading to even higher inflation as companies pass on the increased wage costs on prices to maintain their profit margins. It is silently bypassed the fact that wages might increase exactly because of increases in the firms' profit margins.

The Mainstream mantra that Greek wage increases caused the CAD flies in the face of reality. Wages steadily lagged behind productivity increases (see Chapter 3 of this volume). It is true that wages increased quickly but productivity also grew rapidly so that increases in the Greek ULCs were actually smaller than the EU27 average. Thus, there was not an aggressive redistribution of GDP in favour of labour. This can be easily seen if we consider not ULCs but RULCs. As Figure 1.1 shows RULCs (i.e. the wage share) are falling for the whole period 1960–2013. If there was a redistribution of GDP in favour of labour, then ULC's increase should go hand in hand with an increase in the wage share (i.e. RULC). The opposite is being observed. Hence, there was a long-term redistribution in favour of capital.

It can easily be discerned – and indeed Malliaropoulos and Anastasatos (2013) accept it – that the deterioration in the ULC since the mid-1990s was to a great extent caused by higher than the European average rates of inflation.[16] But this inflation differential had not as its initiating cause wage increases coming from nowhere (as Malliaropoulos and Anastasatos (2013) appear to argue) but

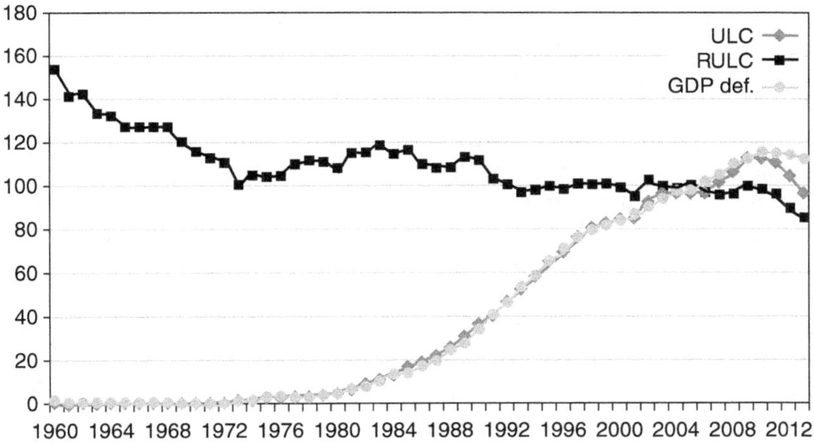

Figure 1.1 ULC, RULC and the GDP deflator, 1960–2013 (source: AMECO).

the fact that capital increased exorbitantly its profit margins in the case of mass consumption goods (i.e. wage goods).

When Greece entered the EMU, drachma was substituted by euro at a rate of approximately 340 drachmas to €1. The change in the price denomination of goods was huge compared to most other EMU economies. The huge gap between the purchasing power of the old and the new currency unit facilitated exorbitant price increases in mass consumption goods. Both anecdotal evidence and some studies (e.g. Zografakis and Mitrakos (2005)) show that, while the average consumer (particularly old agers) lost sense of the real purchasing power of the new currency unit, firms marked-up prices exorbitantly particularly in mass consumption goods. Successive Greek governments consciously took no precaution against this event. They referred to the (traditionally unreliable) official consumer price index, which appeared normal and neglected the fact that firms increased particularly the prices of mass consumption goods. This boosted capital profitability by increasing its profit margins.

These faster price increases of relatively low-priced items with a high purchase frequency (or small-item tickets such as clothing, food, etc.) had to be expected. Indeed, the ECB (2003) had observed this phenomenon after the euro changeover. As a result, there appeared to be a significant discrepancy between inflation rates measured by the Harmonised Index of Consumer Prices (HICP) and the Perceived Inflation Balance Statistic (PIBS). Indeed, Greece belongs to the forerunners in perceived inflation after the euro changeover.

Most Mainstream accounts tend to either reject the problem (as 'euro-illusion') or downgrade it as a short-term phenomenon. For example, it is argued that mass consumption goods are justifiably assigned a small weight in the HICP (because of their low prices). But, because of their higher frequency of purchase, their prices are more easily memorised and thus are given a greater importance in the formation of perceived inflation compared to high-priced rarely purchased items (large-item tickets). Additionally, while the HICP assesses price increases and drops symmetrically, because of consumers' risk aversion, price increases tend to be perceived as being stronger than equivalent price reductions. Consequently, consumers are magnifying their inflation perceptions whereas in reality inflation is lower. A more moderate Mainstream approach maintains that this is a passing phenomenon that over time will be smoothened. In reality, however, significant inflation differentials continue to exist between different categories of consumption goods. This negates the Mainstream expectation that it is a fleeting phenomenon.

Mainstream accounts fail to acknowledge the class character of these inflation differentials. Mass consumption goods (and particularly small item tickets) represent the great bulk of working class' consumption pattern. Moreover, these goods belong to both the tradables and non-tradables sectors;[17] thus surpassing the limits of the Balasa-Samuelson effect. Consequently, increased inflation in mass consumption goods implies: (a) a redistribution from labour to capital and (b) a necessary in retrospect (as price increases are recognised with a time lag) struggle by labour to clutch back at least a part of its lost purchasing power. Hence, capital's profit mark-up in mass consumption goods led to lagged and incomplete wage increases. This is evidenced by the post-euro novel phenomenon of increasing workers' indebtedness in order to sustain their living standards (see Chapter 5 of this volume).

In a nutshell, capital's profit mark-up in mass consumption goods led to (smaller) wage increases and to a significant inflation differential with the other EMU economies. The increase of Greek ULC – setting aside its limited importance regarding competitiveness – was mainly caused by these price increases.

Last, but not the least, if Mainstream explanations want to discern the true causes of deteriorating Greek competitiveness they have to look at some other annoying structural factors. For example, even an ECB (2008: 92) report at the beginning of the crisis had argued that the data on labour compensation and productivity suggest that the weakness of the external accounts of several EMU countries comes from the international specialisation of their economy, rather than from the 'faulty management' of the labour market. Then it claims that during EMU's first ten years the member economies with an overweight in labour-intensive sectors lost positions in favour of emerging economies with a relative comparative advantage, whereas member economies specialised in the higher-price and higher-quality segments of mature industries and products even gained market shares. Gaulier and Vicard (2012) go even further and put the blame not only on emerging economies but on Germany and the euro-centre itself. They argue that the lack of competitiveness of the peripheral countries vis-à-vis Germany is not due to the fact that they are expensive (their wage rates are substantially lower), or that labour productivity has not increased. The problem is that they are stuck at middle levels of technology and they are caught in a trap. Mainstream approaches are well aware of these arguments but shy away from adopting them because of the class interests that direct their analyses.

VI In place of conclusions

Apart from the abovementioned analytical and empirical problems, Mainstream analyses have also broader explanatory problems.

To begin with, they totally underestimate the role of the 2007–8 global capitalist crisis. As already said, they unanimously consider it as a mere financial crisis without origins and causes in the sphere of real accumulation. Initial talks were about a solely US financial crisis and about Europe's, for example, 'decoupling' from it (i.e. being insulated from it). When the crisis spread to the rest of the world 'decoupling' was forgotten but the insistence on its financial character remained. Only when the fears of a 'double dip' materialised (i.e. a return of the crisis that was supposed to have been surpassed in 2009) then attention was paid to the impact of the crisis on real accumulation. But again the line of causality was from the financial sector to the sphere of production. However, if this crisis is so significant and lengthy as it appears to be, it must surely have some initial basis on the main sphere of economic activities (the sphere of production). This is shown by the chapters in Part II of this volume. Mainstream analyses, because of their production-less and circulationist nature, are unable to understand this.

Consequently, Mainstream explanations, in the beginning, considered the Greek crisis as independent of the 2007–8 crisis. This is a point on which both international and Greek pundits agreed. Most international reports (those of the EU, ECB and IMF included), before the onset of the Greek crisis, maintained that the Greek economy was insulated from the 2007–8 crisis and that, once the crisis erupted, it was left unattached. Indicatively, in a pre-election debate in 2009 both G. Alogoskoufis and N. Christodulakis[18] agreed that the Greek economy is insulated from the crisis because its banking sector is better capitalised than those of the West. But as the Greek crisis deepened and went along with the Eurozone crisis Mainstream explanations changed course. This time it was recognised that the 2007–8 crisis has an impact on the Greek crisis; but this is solely an exogenous one. The global crisis affected the Greek one by worsening the international economic environment and setting off grey expectations about sovereign debts.

Because of their analytical deficiencies and their ideological preoccupations all Mainstream explanations *fail to appreciate the fundamental structural dimensions* of the problem at hand and instead relegate it either to policy errors and/or to weak structural origins. They revolve around TDH's misleading Columbus egg dilemma. And they furiously try to convince that wages are the main culprits for both the FD and the CAD. Regarding the FD, they consciously shy away from recognising the catastrophic impact that the notorious crony relations between the state and big capitalist conglomerates have on public revenues and expenditure. Regarding the CAD and the deteriorating competitiveness they consciously disregard the role of structural factors and relations of uneven exchange between the euro-centre and the euro-periphery. Once again, Orthodox economic and Mainstream analyses have exhibited their explanatory inefficiency and their apologetic character.

Notes

1 The first EAP set as a short-term objective the fiscal consolidation and as a medium-term objective the improvement of competitiveness and altering the economy's structure towards a private sector-driven and export-led growth model. However, in practical terms only the short-term objective was pursued. This was done by the PASOK government but in full knowledge of the troika (despite their later bickering).

2 A typical example is offered by Arghyrou and Kontonikas (2010) in a vehemently pro-EAP article: 'the majority of EMU countries have experienced contagion from Greece, most prominently Portugal, Ireland and Spain'.

3 It is a weak argument because, apart from expectations (and the mythical properties attributed to them by mainstream economics), the only way that Greece could contaminate other EU members was through its private creditors (banks and financial organisations). This channel, however important it may have been, has, after the PSI, been checked as the great majority of Greek debt is in the hands of official lenders (practically the troika).

4 Labour mobility within the EU is relatively low. According to an ECB report, in 2000 only 0.1 per cent of the total EU-15 population (or 225,000 people) changed official residence between two member countries (Heinz and Ward-Warmedinge (2006)). Additionally, most of this labour mobility reflected the influx of Eastern European migrants. In a marking contrast, labour migration between US states was 5.9 per cent of its total population in 2000 (Heinz and Ward-Warmedinge (2006)).

5 Only 1.24 per cent of EU's total GDP is being used for fiscal transfers (McDougall (1992)).

6 In a similar vein, De Grauwe (2003: 58), while accepting the OCA theory and pointing out certain EMU deficiencies, he rejects US scepticism: 'The traditional theory of optimal currency areas tends to be rather pessimistic about the possibility for countries to join a monetary union at low cost.'

7 For an analysis of the intra-imperialist contradictions between the US and the EU see Mavroudeas (2010a, 2010b, 2012).

8 For a review of the convergence thesis see Mavroudeas and Siriopoulos (1998).

9 Only the post-Keynesian variant of the third explanation might differ with regard to the TDH by stressing the current account imbalances as an independent factor causing the Greek problem.

10 There are some dissenters on this point. For example Hardouvelis *et al.* (2010) and Malliaropoulos (2010) do not appear to agree, at least wholeheartedly, that increased wages are the main cause of the deterioration of competitiveness.

11 The Ricardian Equivalence Hypothesis was first stated by D. Ricardo and it was elaborated by Barro (1974). It maintains that it is irrelevant for consumers whether an increase in public expenditures will be financed by taxation or public borrowing. Consumers anticipate that an expansionary fiscal policy through public borrowing will be financed by future tax increases. So, in order to response to future tax burdens, they will increase their savings instead of consumption leaving demand and thus the CAD unaffected.

12 *Nominal ULCs* are defined as total wage compensation per unit of real output. This is equal to the nominal wage rate per worker divided by labour productivity:

$$ULC = \frac{wage\ compensation}{output} = \frac{wL}{y} = \frac{w}{\lambda}$$

where w stands for the nominal wage rate, L for number of workers, y for real output and λ for labour productivity.

Real ULCs are derived by dividing nominal ULCs by the price level and are therefore identical with the wage share in *GDP*:

$$RULC = \frac{wage\ compensation}{GDP} = \frac{wL}{Py} = \frac{wage\ compensation}{GDP}$$

where *P* stands for the *GDP* deflator.

13 For a literature review see Turner and Van't Dack (1993).

14 See also Felipe and Kumar (2011) for the technical contradictions of this projection.

15 The Balassa–Samuelson effect argues that productivity growth differs among sectors, while wages tend to be less differentiated. Productivity is supposed to grow faster in the tradables sector. The subsequent sectoral wage increase spills over to the whole economy increasing wages in all sectors. Thus, the prices of non-tradable goods relative to those of tradable goods rise leading to the increase of the general price index. Given that productivity growth is typically faster in developing countries, this effect implies that their real exchange rate will tend to rise over time.

16 *ULC* can be broken down in its two components: labour's share in *GDP* (wage-to-*GDP* ratio) and the *GDP* deflator:

$$ULC = (W / GDP) \times P = (\text{wage-to-}GDP\text{ ratio}) \times (GDP\text{ deflator})$$

17 Since Greece's accession to the European Common Market imports have made significant inroads in the mass consumption goods market.

18 They are both academic economists which have served as finance ministers the former of ND and the latter of PASOK.

References

Arestis P. (2009), 'New consensus macroeconomics: a critical appraisal', Levy Institute Working Paper 564.

Arghyrou M. and Kontonikas A. (2010), 'The EMU sovereign-debt crisis: a call and an opportunity for a Greek supply-side revolution', http://greekeconomistsforreform.com/financial-system/the-emu-sovereign-debt-crisis-a-call-and-an-opportunity-for-a-greek-supply-side-revolution/.

Azariadis C. (2010), 'Development is the only solution: seventeen proposals for a new development strategy', http://greekeconomistsforreform.com/wp-content/uploads/A-I-P-DEVELOPMENTw.-abs-10-06-10.pdf.

Barro R. (1974), 'Are government bonds net wealth?', *Journal of Political Economy* 82(6).

Booth P. ed. (2013), *The Euro: The Beginning, the Middle … and the End?* London: IEA.

Botta A. (2012), 'Conflicting claims in the Eurozone? Austerity's myopic logic and the need for a European federal union in a post-Keynesian Eurozone center–periphery model', Levy Institute Working Paper 740.

De Grauwe P. (2003), *Economics of Monetary Union*, Oxford: Oxford University Press.

De Grauwe P. (2010a), 'The Greek crisis and the future of the Eurozone', EuroIntelligence, March.

De Grauwe P. (2010b), 'The financial crisis and the future of the Eurozone', European Economic Policy Briefings no. 21, Bruges, Belgium: College of Europe.

Dellas H. (2011), 'Greek wages and international competitiveness', http://greekeconomistsforreform.com/wp-content/uploads/Dellas_competitiveness.pdf.

Dornbusch R. (2001), 'The Euro controversy', MIT Department of Economics Editorial.

EC (2010), 'The economic adjustment programme for Greece', European Economy, Occasional Papers 61.

EC (2012), 'The second economic adjustment programme for Greece', European Economy, Occasional Papers 94.

ECB (2003), 'Recent developments in Euro area inflation perceptions', *Monthly Bulletin*, July.

ECB (2008), 'Monitoring labour cost developments across Euro area countries', *Monthly Bulletin: Tenth Anniversary of the ECB*.

ECB (2012), 'A fiscal compact for a stronger economic and monetary union', *ECB Monthly Bulletin*, May.

Fagerberg J. (1996), 'Technology and competitiveness', *Oxford Review of Economic Policy* 12(3), Special issue on competitiveness.

Feldstein M. (1997), 'EMU and international conflict', *Foreign Affairs*, November/December.

Feldstein M. (2010a), 'Let Greece take a holiday from the Eurozone', *Financial Times*, 17 February.

Feldstein M. (2010b), 'The euro's fundamental flaws: the single currency was bound to fail', *International Economy*, Spring.

Felipe J. (2007), 'A cautionary note on the interpretation of unit labor costs as an indicator of competitivenes, with reference to the Philippines', *Philippine Journal of Development* 63(2).

Felipe J. and Kumar U. (2011), 'Unit labor costs in the Eurozone: the competitiveness debate again', Levy Institute Working Paper 651.

Gaulier G. and Vicard V. (2012), 'The signatures of Euro area imbalances', Banque de France.

Gibson H., Hall S. and Tavlas G. (2012), 'The Greek financial crisis: growing imbalances and sovereign spreads', *Journal of International Money and Finance* 31(3).

Gros D. (2011), 'Competitiveness pact: flawed economies', *CEPS Commentary*, 18 March.

Hardouvelis G., Malliaropulos D., Monokroussos P., Anastasatos T., Stamatiou T. and Sampaniotis T. (2010), 'The Greek economy and its stability programme', *Economy and Markets* 5(3), Eurobank.

Hein E., Truger A. and van Treeck T. (2011), 'The european financial and economic crisis: alternative solutions from a (post-)Keynesian perspective', IMK Working Paper 9.

Heinz F. and Ward-Warmedinge M. (2006), 'Cross-border labour mobility within an enlarged EU', ECB Occasional Paper Series 52.

Ioannides Y. (2012), 'Greece, the Eurozone and the debt crisis', http://greekeconomistsforreform.com/wp-content/uploads/Ioannides-Presentation-Fletcher-Oct-28-11-Text+Figs3.pdf.

Jonung L. and Drea E. (2009), 'The euro: it can't happen. It's a bad idea. It won't last. US economists on the EMU, 1989–2002', European Economy, Economic Papers 395, December.

Kaldor N. (1978), 'The effect of devaluations on trade in manufactures', in N. Kaldor, *Further Essays on Applied Economics*, London: Duckworth.

Katrakilidis C. and Trachanas E. (2011), 'Has the accession of Greece in the EU influenced the dynamics of the country's 'twin deficits'? An empirical investigation', *European Research Studies* XIV(1).

Kosters W. (2009), 'Common Euro bonds: no appropriate instrument', *Intereconomics* 44(3).

Krugman P. (2012a), *End This Depression Now*, New York: W.W. Norton & Co.

Krugman P. (2012b), 'The revenge of the optimum currency area', *New York Times*, 24 June.

Lall S. (2001), *Competitiveness, Technology and Skills*, Northampton, MA: Edward Elgar.

Lane P. (2012), 'The European sovereign debt crisis', *Journal of Economic Perspectives* 26(3).

McDougall D. (1992), 'Economic and monetary union and the European Community budget', *National Institute Economic Review* 140(1).

McKinnon R.I. (1963), 'Optimum currency areas', *American Economic Review* 53.

Malliaropulos D. (2010), 'How much did competitiveness of the Greek economy decline since EMU entry?' *Economy and Markets* 5(4), Eurobank.

Malliaropulos D. and Anastasatos T. (2013), 'The improvement in the competitive position of the Greek economy and prospects for an export-led growth model', *Economy and Markets* VIII(1), Eurobank.

Mavroudeas S. (2010a), 'Greece and the EU: capitalist crisis and imperialist rivalries', Paper presented in the 1st conference of IIPPE (International Initiative for Promoting Political Economy) and Greek Scientific Association of Political Economy, University of Crete, 10–12 September 2010.

Mavroudeas S. (2010b), 'The Greek external debt and imperialist rivalries: "one thief stealing from another" ', *Monthly Review Zine*, www.mrzine.monthlyreview.org/2010/mavroudeas200210.html.

Mavroudeas S. (2012), 'The crisis of the European Union and the failure of its salvation plans', *Spectrezine*, www.spectrezine.org/crisis-european-union-and-failure-its-%E2%80%98salvation-plans%E2%80%99.

Mavroudeas S. and Siriopoulos C. (1998), 'Testing convergence and divergence: the data from Greece', *Journal of Applied Business Research* 14(1).

Meghir C., Vayanos D. and Vettas N. (2010), 'The economic crisis in Greece: a time of reform and opportunity', http://greekeconomistsforreform.com/wp-content/uploads/Reform.pdf.

Merler S. and Pisani-Ferry J. (2012), 'Sudden stops in the euro area', Bruegel Policy Contribution 2012/06.

Mundell R.A. (1961), 'A theory of optimum currency areas', *American Economic Review* 51(4).

Nelson R., Belkin P. and Mix D. (2011), 'Greece's debt crisis: overview, policy responses, and implications', Congressional Research Service, www.fas.org/sgp/crs/row/R41167.pdf.

Nikiforos M., Carvalho L. and Schoder C. (2013), 'Foreign and public deficits in Greece: in search of causality', Levy Economics Institute, Working Paper 771.

Panetta F. (2011), 'Life in the Eurozone with or without sovereign default?' in Allen F., Carletti E. and Corsetti G. (eds), *Life in the Eurozone with or without Sovereign Default?* Philadelphia, PA: FIC Press.

Pantelidis P., Trachanas E., Athanasenas L.A. and Katrakilidis C. (2009), 'On the dynamics of the Greek twin deficits: empirical evidence over the period 1960–2007', *International Journal of Economic Sciences and Applied Research* 2(2).

Stathakis G. (2010), 'The fiscal crisis of the Greek economy', Paper presented in 1st conference of IIPPE (International Initiative for Promoting Political Economy) and Greek Scientific Association of Political Economy, University of Crete, 10–12 September 2010.

The Economist (2010), 'A very European crisis', *The Economist*, 6 February.

Turner P. and Van't Dack J. (1993), 'Measuring international price and cost "ompetitiveness"', BIS Economic Papers 39, Bank for International Settlements.

Vamvoukas G. (1999), 'The twin deficits phenomenon: evidence from Greece', *Applied Economics* 31.

Weidman J. (2012), 'Rebalancing Europe', Speech at the Chatham House Members Event, Rebalancing Europe, London, 28 March.

Zografakis S. and Mitrakos T. (2005), 'Inflation's redistributive effect in Greece', Economic Bulletin 24, Bank of Greece [in Greek].

2 The fiscal crisis in Greece

Whose fault?

Thanasis Maniatis

I Introduction

One of the most visible aspects of the deep crisis that has plagued the Greek economy for six years now is the fiscal crisis which is manifested in extremely large public deficits and a record high public debt. Furthermore, it is the service of this enormous debt which has forced the successive Greek governments of the last three years to adopt harsh pro-cyclical fiscal measures, that is to raise taxes and cut public spending during a serious recession, turning it to a Great Depression for the Greek economy and society.

We have argued elsewhere that the Greek crisis stems from a combination of three distinct but interrelated processes, first, the world economic crisis and the subsequent stagnation in the major capitalist economies, second, the Greek economic crisis, both of them having to do with the low profitability of capital due to the law of the falling rate of profit and, third, the fiscal crisis of the Greek state, which has been aggravated by the first two processes.[1]

In this chapter we concentrate on the fiscal aspect of the crisis from a class perspective and we examine empirically the net fiscal position of the working class in Greece for the entire post-war period (1958–2011) with a special emphasis on the last years of the period, since 1995.

The empirical estimation of the net social wage helps in clarifying further two important issues in the Political Economy literature. First, the nature and role of the state in advanced capitalism and especially the redistributive role of the welfare state vis-à-vis the income and the standard of living of the working class. In this way it informs us also about the appropriateness of the term welfare state to the extent that this refers to the well-being and the standard of living of workers and other similar social strata. Second, it sheds light on the impact of state fiscal and social policies on the current and previous crisis episodes through their effect on the profitability and accumulation of capital. In short, the level and fluctuations of the net social wage are crucial issues for the processes of reproduction (of labour power and capital in general), profitability and accumulation.

The previous crisis experienced by the capitalist world economy during the late 1960s and the entire period of the 1970s was attributed by mainstream and certain radical authors primarily to excessive wage growth (Glyn and Sutcliffe (1972), Weisskopf (1979), Armstrong *et al.* (1991)) and in many cases to generous social benefits for workers as well (Bowles and Gintis (1982), Gintis and Bowles (1982), Glyn (1975, 2006), O'Connor (1984)). According to the logic of this argument, the increases in the market wage and the 'social wage' undermined directly or indirectly profitability and eventually ended the post-war boom. This argument was disputed empirically later (see Moseley (1987), Shaikh (1987), Shaikh and Tonak (1994) for the refutation of 'wage squeeze' argument, Shaikh and Tonak (1987) for the 'social wage-induced profit squeeze' argument respectively) albeit after the crisis had bottomed down and the neoliberal period had already begun.

In Greece, the latest crisis is still underway and running its course. The overall assessment of the origins of crisis, its fundamental cause and its economic and social effects has not been done yet. It is still debated whether it was a rupture in the financial sector which led to a crisis in the 'real' economy, or a case where a stagnating 'real' economy due to the incomplete recovery of profitability, led to financial overexpansion and then, when the financial bubbles broke, to a serious crisis in the 'real' and the whole economy. It is clear, however, that the unprecedented fiscal stimulus which was applied during the initial stages of the crisis and especially the public expenditures undertaken for the bailout of the financial sector institutions, have exacerbated the fiscal imbalances from which many states were suffering even before the onset of the economic crisis. It is evident though from Figure 2.1 that when the crisis started, the public deficit was on a downward trend since 2000 and public debt as a percentage of GDP was more or less constant around the value of 100 per cent since the

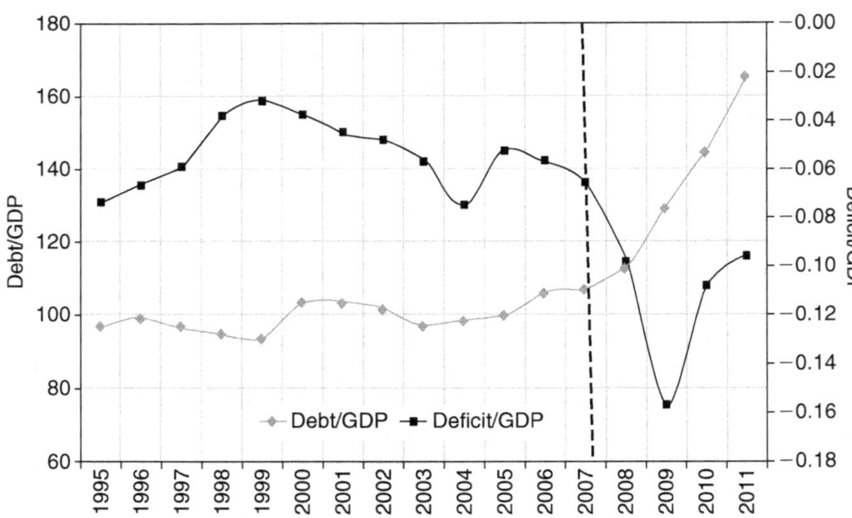

Figure 2.1 Public deficit and public debt as a percentage of GDP, 1995–2011.

beginning of the 1990s. It is obvious that something else triggered the acute fiscal crisis of the last five years. In any case, most countries and especially Greece and other Southern European economies have found themselves in the midst of a fiscal crisis with huge public deficits and a non-sustainable public debt, and in many cases and certainly in Greece this fiscal crisis tends to overshadow the underlying economic crisis.

This is a period where the costs of the crisis are distributed to the different social classes as the governments adopt certain economic measures in order to lift the economy out of the deep recession. After many years of stagnating or even falling real wages it is not easy for the ruling elite to blame high labour costs as the cause of crisis, as happened in the 1970s. However, as the turn of events has brought to the forefront the fiscal difficulties and the 'sovereign debt crisis' of many countries, the terrain of the ideological battle has changed for the worse for wage and salary earners in both the private and the public sectors. During the first stage of the crisis, the negative role of the greedy and myopic financial capitalists, or the ill effects of the increased inequality of the era were emphasised. Now all this has been forgotten in ruling circles, and it is fiscal profligacy and generous social policies which are presented as the main culprit of the current economic malaise. In many countries, the 'fiscal excesses' have been used as an excuse for the attack first on the wages of public employees and subsequently on the wages and social benefits (especially on pensions but practically on all entitlements like unemployment benefits, healthcare benefits, etc.) of workers in general. Behind this attack lies the often implicit claim that somehow workers and pensioners are responsible for the fiscal crisis. Demographic reasons (increases in life expectancy, low fertility rate, etc.) in general are also cited as responsible for the fiscal austerity implemented against the majority of the population. However, the victims of those hostile policies regarding people's welfare and standard of living are predominantly workers, the elderly and the poor. Thus, the fiscal crisis is being used by the ruling classes as an opportunity to strengthen the dominance of capital over labour. The ideological hegemony of capital appears as strong as ever. Somehow, the response to both crises (the current one and the crisis of the 1970s) by the system has been similar; it even seems that the attack on wages and social benefits is stronger in the present crisis relative to what happened at the initiation of the first neoliberal period in the late 1970s.

The claim that the working class is to blame for the fiscal imbalances and the accumulated public debt in Greece calls for an examination of the class aspect of the public budget, and therefore of the budget deficits and public debt in this country. The answer to this question is provided in the radical and Marxist Political Economy literature by the empirical investigation of the social wage issue. In simple terms, the measurement of the net social wage for labour in one country involves the estimation of the net benefits wage and salary earners receive from the state expenditures directed at them when all kinds of taxes that are paid by those workers are subtracted.

We will discuss briefly the methodology of estimating the net social wage below, and we will present our results for the Greek economy. But before that, it is illuminating to look at the overall picture of the Greek public finances for the most recent, 1995–2012, period. It could be argued that at least as far as Greece (currently the country with the biggest fiscal problems) is concerned, it is so obvious where the source of the fiscal imbalances lies, so as to almost predetermine the results of the estimation of the net social wage for labour.

II Comparing the fiscal structure in Greece and EU-15 (1995–2012)

Table 2.1 presents in summary form the fiscal structure of the Greek state compared to that of the EU-15 as a whole, during the past 18 years. It is evident there, that despite arguments about profligate state spending in Greece, the state spends about the same percentage of GDP as the EU-15 average. In fact, even the small positive difference of 0.6 per cent of GDP was created in the few years after 2008 when all ratios of public expenditures and public revenues as shares of GDP in Greece increased significantly due to the dramatic fall in the national output. On the contrary, public revenues as a share of total economic activity (and especially taxes as we discuss below) were much lower (3.6 per cent of

Table 2.1 Public expenditures, taxes and budget deficits as a percentage of GDP in Greece and EU-15, 1995–2012, average values

Categories	*EU-15*	*Greece*	*Difference*
1. Government expenditures (1995–2012)	48.1	48.7	0.6
2. Government revenues (1995–2012)	45.0	41.4	–3.6
3. Budget deficit (1995–2012)	–3.0	–7.3	4.3
Public expenditures (1995–2011)			
4. Government employee compensation	10.9	11.6	0.7
5. Education	5.1	3.5	–1.6
6. Health	6.6	5.5	–1.1
7. Social protection expenditures	18.8	17.0	–1.8
8. Interest payments	3.5	6.9	3.4
9. General public expenditures	7.0	12.2	5.2
10. Defence expenditures	1.6	2.9	1.3
Taxation/GDP (1995–2012)			
11. Total receipts from taxes and social contributions	41.0	35.2	–5.8
12. Total tax receipts	26.9	22.1	–4.8
13. Total (actual and imputed) social contributions	14.2	13.2	–1.0
14. Current taxes on income, wealth, etc.	13.3	8.5	–4.8
15. Taxes on income	12.4	7.8	–4.6
16. Taxes on individual or household income including holding gains	9.6	4.8	–4.8
17. Taxes on the income or profits of corporations including holding gains	2.8	2.8	–
18. Taxes on production and imports	13.3	13.4	0.1

Source: Eurostat, government finance statistics.

GDP) than the European average. Hence, the main reason for the larger deficits by 4.3 per cent of GDP than the European average in Greece seems to be not heavy spending but inadequate state revenues.

Looking further at the structure of public expenditures, we observe on the one hand that in Greece the wages of public employees (a usual target of neoliberal attacks in almost all countries) as a percentage of GDP are again very close to the EU average especially until 2008. On the other hand, Greece was lagging seriously behind the European average in spending for all three categories in the traditional fields of social welfare expenditures (health, education and social protection, i.e. pensions, unemployment benefits, etc.). Looking at the major public expenditure categories which are not related to the welfare and income of the working class (interest payments, general public expenditures and defence) we see that Greece is above the European average in all of them since it pays a significant amount (almost double that of the European average) of its product (6.9 per cent of GDP) to its (mostly foreign) creditors in the form of interest. It is interesting to note that interest payments were almost equal to the budget deficits for the entire period meaning that the primary budget was in balance on average all those years. Since interest payments are included in the category of general public expenditures (general administration, courts, etc.) the same picture emerges for this category as well. Finally, Greece is a well-known heavy defence spender easily surpassing the European average.

On the side of taxes we observe that the main reason for Greece lagging so much behind the EU average (by 5.8 per cent of GDP) appears to be the relatively low taxes on income and wealth especially on households; since taxes on corporate profits are quite low across Europe to allow for significant divergence from the average in individual countries, indirect taxes are close to the European average and social security taxes are 1 per cent lower for Greece. This is a common pattern in the tax structure in Southern European countries due to the fact that their labour force includes great numbers of independent professionals (doctors, lawyers and mechanics), farmers, small employers and shopkeepers. Favourable tax treatment for those social strata who are also political allies of the upper classes, and the fact that wage and salary earners are the only category which cannot exercise tax evasion practices, results in systematically low state revenues, this being the main reason behind persistent public budget deficits.

In short, it is obvious that relatively low social spending and high spending for state bureaucracy, interest, waste and armaments, combined with reliance on social security taxes, consumption taxes and low taxes on profits and incomes of non-workers suggest that a certain bias exists in the Greek fiscal structure which calls for a class based analysis of public spending and taxes. It appears that the question of who pays for the social expenditures in Greece is not so difficult to answer even with this cursory look at the structure of its public finances. We turn to this issue next, namely to the estimation of the net social wage ratio for labour in Greece.

III The empirical method of the net social wage measurement

In general, when the public budget process is viewed from a social class perspective, there are four fundamental reasons for the creation of systematic budget deficits:

- excessive benefits and transfers for the working class;
- excessive benefits, transfers and subsidies for capital and non-workers;
- relatively low taxation of workers;
- relatively low taxation of capital and non-workers.

The estimation of the net social wage reveals the net fiscal position of the working class, namely the balance of social benefits directed at workers and taxes deducted from their gross income and therefore helps in the evaluation of the claim that the subsidisation of wage earners and pensioners (former workers) is responsible for the fiscal crisis of the state.

Over the last twenty-five years, a number of studies have appeared in the literature, which try to estimate the net benefit received by workers when both state expenditures directed at workers, and taxes paid by them are taken into account (Shaikh (1978, 1984), Shaikh and Tonak (1987, 1994, 2000), Tonak (1987), Miller (1989, 1992), Guerrero (1992), Sepehri and Chernomas (1992), Akram-Lodhi (1996), Fazeli (1996), Maniatis (2003), Shaikh (2003), Freeman (1991), Fazeli and Fazeli (2010), Reveley (2006)). Even though there are still some inconsistencies in the empirical methodology applied in the studies for certain countries, by and large, a common methodological framework has been established.

3.1 Measuring the net social wage

Table 2.2 summarises the net social wage terminology.

3.1.1 General methodology

In measuring the net social wage we follow the methodology developed by Shaikh and Tonak (1987, 1994, 2000) adjusted for the treatment of indirect tax

Table 2.2 Net social wage terminology

Net Social Wage = Labour Benefits − Labour Taxes N = LB − LT
Labour Benefit Ratio = Labour Benefits / GDP lb = LB / GDP
Labour Tax Ratio = Labour Taxes / GDP lt = LT / GDP
Net Social Wage Ratio = Net Social Wage / GDP n = lb − lt = N / GDP

class incidence in order to make our results comparable with those of similar studies in other developed capitalist economies. Shaikh and Tonak (2000: 248) note:

> Our primary focus is on the extent to which the state's involvement in taxation and expenditures serves to redistribute a portion of the nation's surplus product to, or from, the working class. In keeping with our focus on class, we define the category of 'working population' as consisting of those members of the population not having ownership of capital as a principal income source. Our task is to assess the impact of government activities on the income and consumption of this population by properly accounting both the expenditures directed toward them and the taxes deducted out of their income stream.

More specifically, if we think of society as consisting only of capital (property owners) and labour[2] (wage and salary earners), the net national income is divided into a labour portion (wages and salaries) and a capital portion (property income). The state modifies this original division as it taxes all market incomes and uses some of those revenues in order to create and provide health, recreational, cultural, education services, and also to pay for pensions, unemployment benefits and other transfers which form part of the overall standard of living of active and retired labourers. The net social wage defined as the difference between labour benefits and labour taxes expresses the way in which the original labour portion is affected by those activities. Therefore, in order to gauge the net impact of state spending and taxation on gross labour income or total economic activity, we calculate three ratios. The labour benefit ratio, defined as labour benefits received from the state divided by the GDP, the labour tax ratio defined as labour taxes divided by the GDP, the net social wage which is defined as labour benefits minus labour taxes, and the net social wage ratio defined as the net social wage divided by the GDP (see Table 2.2).

It is obvious from the above that there are three crucial issues in measuring the net social wage; (a) the definition of what Shaikh and Tonak call the 'working population', which is used in this literature as a proxy for labour or the working class, (b) the estimation of the part of total state expenditures that becomes labour benefits in the form of monetary income (i.e. unemployment benefits, pensions, etc.) and collective consumption (i.e. education, health services, etc.) and (c) the estimation of the part of total taxes that is paid by labour.

The working population. Our definition of the working population includes all wage and salary earners and their dependants, as well as the pensioners who were wage and salary earners in their economically active life. In effect, this definition of labour includes the persons who currently depend, had depended or will depend mainly on the sale of their labour power for their reproduction. The net effect of fiscal policies on the market income of this population (i.e. the net social wage), and its magnitude relative to GDP (i.e. the net social wage ratio) express the state impact on the standard of living of this population. This is exactly the definition of labour adopted in all similar studies (see Shaikh and Tonak (1994: 356), Akram-Lodhi (1996: 181), Sepehri and Chernomas (1992: 75)) since they focus on how the state changes the market distribution of net national income between capital and wage labour.

Allocation of state expenditures to workers. Greek National Accounts classify total state expenditures into public consumption expenditures, subsidies, net transfers to households, net transfers abroad, public investment expenditures and interest paid on the public debt. We can distinguish three groups of state expenditures according to how they relate to labour income and consumption.

Group I includes government spending for transfers and social consumption that are directed towards the whole population, namely health, education, social security and welfare from public consumption expenditures and health and education transfers from the category net transfers to households. In order to determine the portion of those expenditures that becomes labour income and consumption, we multiply them by the Labour Share, defined as the proportion of employed and unemployed wage and salary earners in the total economically active population.

Group II includes state expenditures that are directed exclusively towards labour, subsidising its income and consumption. Those include pensions for former wage and salary earners, unemployment allowances, industrial injury allowances, family allowances and transfers to non-profit institutions from the category net transfers to individuals, and housing expenditures from the category public investment.

Group III includes all those state expenditures that cannot be considered labour income or consumption such as public consumption expenditures for general administration, justice, police and defence. All of them represent costs for the reproduction of the system, and along with transfers such as war pensions, net transfers abroad, subsidies to firms and interest paid on the public debt are excluded from the benefits received by the working population.

The sum of labour benefits derived from state expenditures in Group I and Group II gives us the total labour benefits (LB) for each year.

Allocation of total taxes to workers. Total state revenues fall mainly into six categories: personal income taxes (at the state and local government level), social security contributions and payroll taxes, corporate income taxes, property taxes, indirect or consumption taxes and other direct taxes for local government and public funds.

We can distinguish again three groups of taxes according to how they relate to gross labour income. Group I includes taxes that flow entirely out of labour income (total employee compensation and labour pensions) such as personal income taxes paid by wage and salary earners and pensioners and their social security contributions.

Group II includes taxes that fall on the entire population like direct taxes for local government and other public institutions and indirect or consumption taxes as well as public monopoly revenues. In order to estimate the portion that is paid by labour we multiply the first category by the Labour share as defined above and the second category by the share of total wages in private consumption expenditures.

Group III includes taxes which are not paid by labour, like corporate income taxes that are paid out of profits, property taxes that until very recently were paid by wealthy individuals, personal income taxes paid by farmers, merchants, industrialists, independent professionals and rentiers.

The sum of Group I taxes and the estimated portion of taxes paid by labour from Group II gives us total labour taxes for each year.

Net social wage and net social wage ratio. The difference between total labour benefits received from the state and total taxes paid by labour, is equal to

Table 2.3 Allocation of benefits from state expenditures to wage labourers

Categories of public expenditures classified by economic function	*Labour benefits*
A. Public consumption	
1. General public services	–
2. Defence	–
3. Public order and safety	–
4. Education	Labour share
5. Health	Labour share
6. Social security and welfare	Labour share
7. Housing and community services	100%
8. Recreation, culture and religion	Labour share
9. Economic services	–
9a. Fuel and energy	
9b. Agriculture, forestry and fishing	
9c. Mining, manufacturing and construction	
9d. Transportation and telecommunications	Labour share
9e. Other economic services	
10. Other functions	
B. Subsidies	
Subsidies to firms	–
C. Current transfers to households	
1. Pensions	100% or labour share
2. Unemployment compensation	100%
3. Family allowances	100% or labour share
4. Sickness allowances	100% or labour share
5. Welfare transfers	100%
D. Public investment	
1. General public services	–
2. Defence	–
3. Housing	Labour share
–	
–	
E. Property income paid	
1. Interest	–
2. Rent	–

Table 2.4 Allocation of taxes to wage labourers

Tax categories	*Labour taxes*
1. Personal income tax	Labour share
2. Local government taxes	Labour share
3. Corporate income taxes	–
4. Social security contributions of wage earners	100%
5. Payroll taxes	100%
6. Property taxes	–
7. Indirect business taxes (consumption taxes)	Labour share
8. Other taxes	Labour share

the net social wage. This net transfer is the net contribution of the state to the standard of living of labour and it can be positive or negative; in the latter case it is a net tax on labour. It is also useful to express the net social wage as a percentage of some measure of market labour income like total employee compensation or the total product (GDP) of the economy. This is the *net social wage ratio* and it indicates the significance of the net impact of the state budget compared either with the market income of labour or with the total economic output of the country.

IV The net social wage in Greece

Our results for the net social wage ratio (n) and its constituent parts, the labour benefit ratio (lb) and the labour tax ratio (lt) are presented below. First, we concentrate on the most recent period 1995–2011.

In Figure 2.2 we observe that the share of labour in total taxes is much higher than its share in state expenditures. This share remained more or less constant around 65 per cent until 2000 and then rose to 70 per cent until the end of the period examined here. On the contrary, the low share of labour in state expenditures (reflecting among other things the relatively low percentage of wage labourers in total employment which was around 65 per cent at the end of the period) rose steadily from 30 to 45 per cent reflecting a rise in social expenditures and especially pensions as we discuss below.

As a result of the class struggles around the formation of the two sides of the public budget, the labour benefit ratio and the labour tax ratio ended up as shown in Figure 2.3 and Table 2.5. The labour tax ratio after an initial rise until 2000 fell slightly afterwards and then it was stabilised around its average value of 24 per cent for the entire period. The labour benefit ratio stayed constant around 16 per cent until 2000, and then rose significantly until the end of the period to the value of 23 per cent. It is obvious that despite widespread notions about the withdrawal of the state from the fields of social welfare during the period of neoliberalism, labour benefit and labour tax ratios were still rising albeit at a slow pace.[3]

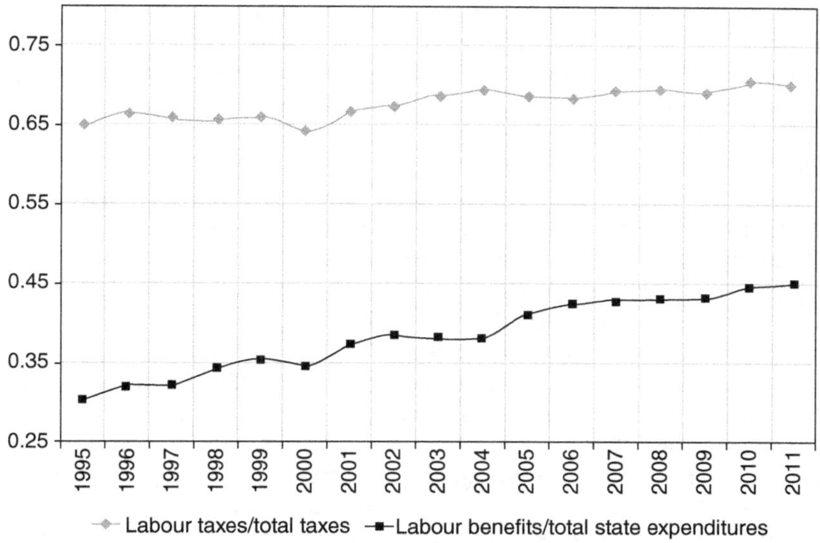

Figure 2.2 The share of labour in total taxes and state expenditures, 1995–2011.

Table 2.5 Social expenditures as a percentage of GDP, OECD countries

	1980	*1985*	*1990*	*1995*	*2000*	*2005*	*2007*	*2009*	*2011*
Australia	10.3	12.2	13.2	16.2	17.3	16.5	16.4	17.8	18.1
Canada	13.7	17.0	18.1	18.9	16.5	16.9	16.8	19.2	18.3
Denmark	24.8	23.2	25.1	28.9	26.4	27.7	26.5	30.2	30.0
France	20.8	26.0	25.1	29.3	28.6	30.1	29.7	32.1	32.1
Germany	22.1	22.5	21.7	26.6	26.6	27.3	25.1	27.8	26.2
Greece	10.3	16.1	16.6	17.5	19.3	21.1	21.6	23.9	23.5
Ireland	16.5	21.1	17.3	18.1	13.4	16.0	16.7	23.6	23.5
Italy	18.0	20.8	19.9	19.8	23.1	24.9	24.7	27.8	27.6
Japan	10.2	11.1	11.1	14.1	16.3	18.5	18.7	22.4	–
Holland	24.8	25.3	25.6	23.8	19.8	20.7	21.1	23.2	23.7
New Zealand	17.0	17.6	21.5	18.6	19.0	18.1	18.6	21.2	21.5
Norway	16.9	17.8	22.3	23.4	21.3	21.6	20.5	23.3	22.6
Portugal	9.9	10.1	12.5	16.5	18.9	23.0	22.7	25.6	25.2
Spain	15.5	17.8	19.9	21.4	20.2	21.1	21.3	26.0	26.0
Sweden	27.1	29.5	30.2	32.0	28.4	29.1	27.3	29.8	27.6
UK	16.5	19.4	16.7	19.9	18.6	20.5	20.4	24.1	23.9
USA	13.2	13.2	13.6	15.5	14.5	16.0	16.3	19.2	19.7
OECD-30	15.6	17.3	17.6	19.4	18.9	19.8	19.2	–	–
OECD-34	15.5	17.2	17.6	19.5	18.7	19.7	19.2	22.1	21.7
EU-21	18.5	20.6	20.5	22.8	21.6	22.7	22.1	25.4	24.9

Source: OECD Social Expenditures.

In fact, we see in Table 2.5 that Greece – being a laggard in welfare state development – was among the few countries that raised social spending significantly between 1995 and 2007 (after that year social expenditure as a share of GDP increased everywhere due to the crisis that lowered GDP and triggered an increase in social spending). And as shown in Table 2.6 it was mostly spending on pensions that raised social spending in general in Greece and in other Southern European countries.

As shown in Table 2.7 the net social wage ratio was negative for the entire period except for one year[4] indicating that the working class as a whole was actually subsidising the state budget; the average value of this subsidy or net tax for workers was 5.1 per cent of GDP. Furthermore, we can deduce from Figure 2.4 that the net social wage ratio first fell slightly until 1999 then rose slightly until 2002 and then it rose considerably until 2011.

As shown in Figure 2.3 its average value for the first half of the period examined here was –7.4 per cent and it was much lower than that, namely –3.1 per cent during the period 2003–2011.

Table 2.8 brings together the average values of the public deficit, interest paid on the public debt and the net social wage, all expressed as a percentage of GDP for the period 1995–2011. It is evident there, that it is the interest paid on the public debt which is responsible for the public deficits; at least for the last eighteen years. Workers contribute positively with their net taxes (i.e. the negative net social wage) to public finances helping the state to run a balanced primary budget that is when interest charges are deducted from total state expenditures.

Table 2.6 Old age pensions as a percentage of GDP, OECD countries

	1980	*1985*	*1990*	*1995*	*2000*	*2005*	*2007*	*2009*
Australia	3.6	3.4	3.0	3.6	3.8	3.3	3.4	3.5
Canada	3.0	3.7	4.2	4.7	4.3	4.1	4.1	4.5
Denmark	4.8	4.7	5.1	6.2	5.3	5.4	5.5	6.1
France	9.4	10.5	10.6	12.0	11.8	12.4	12.5	13.7
Germany	10.4	10.3	9.7	10.5	11.1	11.4	10.6	11.3
Greece	5.4	8.7	9.9	9.7	10.8	11.8	12.1	13.0
Ireland	5.1	5.5	4.9	4.3	3.1	3.4	3.6	5.1
Italy	8.9	11.1	10.1	11.3	13.5	13.9	14.0	15.4
Japan	3.9	4.7	4.8	6.1	7.3	8.7	8.9	10.2
Holland	6.4	6.2	6.7	5.8	5.0	5.0	4.7	5.1
New Zealand	7.1	7.6	7.4	5.7	5.0	4.3	4.3	4.7
Norway	4.5	4.7	5.6	5.5	4.8	4.8	4.7	5.4
Portugal	3.7	4.1	4.9	7.2	7.9	10.3	10.7	12.3
Spain	6.2	7.5	7.9	9.0	8.6	8.1	8.1	9.3
Sweden	7.1	7.6	7.7	8.2	7.2	7.6	7.2	8.2
UK	5.5	5.6	4.8	5.4	5.3	5.6	5.3	6.2
USA	6.2	6.2	6.1	6.3	5.9	6.0	6.0	6.8
OECD-34	5.8	6.4	6.4	6.9	6.9	7.0	7.0	7.8

Source: OECD Social Expenditures.

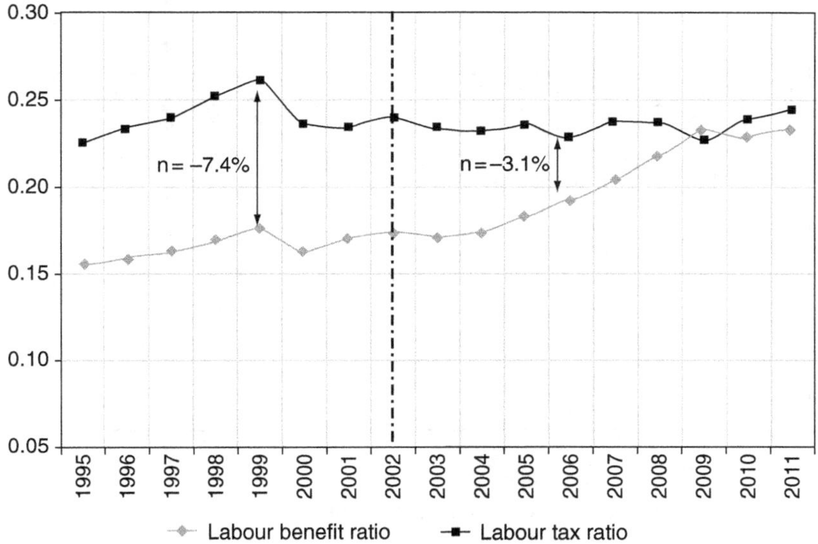

Figure 2.3 The labour benefit ratio and the labour tax ratio in Greece, 1995–2011.

Table 2.7 The labour benefit ratio (lb=LB/GDP), the labour tax ratio (lt=LT/GDP) and the net social wage ratio (n=N/GDP) in Greece, 1995–2011

Year	*Labour benefit ratio*	*Labour tax ratio*	*Net social wage ratio*
1995	0.155	0.226	–0.070
1996	0.158	0.233	–0.075
1997	0.163	0.240	–0.077
1998	0.169	0.252	–0.083
1999	0.176	0.261	–0.085
2000	0.162	0.235	–0.073
2001	0.170	0.234	–0.064
2002	0.174	0.241	–0.067
2003	0.170	0.234	–0.064
2004	0.173	0.231	–0.058
2005	0.183	0.236	–0.053
2006	0.192	0.229	–0.037
2007	0.203	0.237	–0.034
2008	0.218	0.238	–0.020
2009	0.233	0.227	0.006
2010	0.228	0.238	–0.010
2011	0.233	0.244	–0.011
Average	0.186	0.237	–0.051

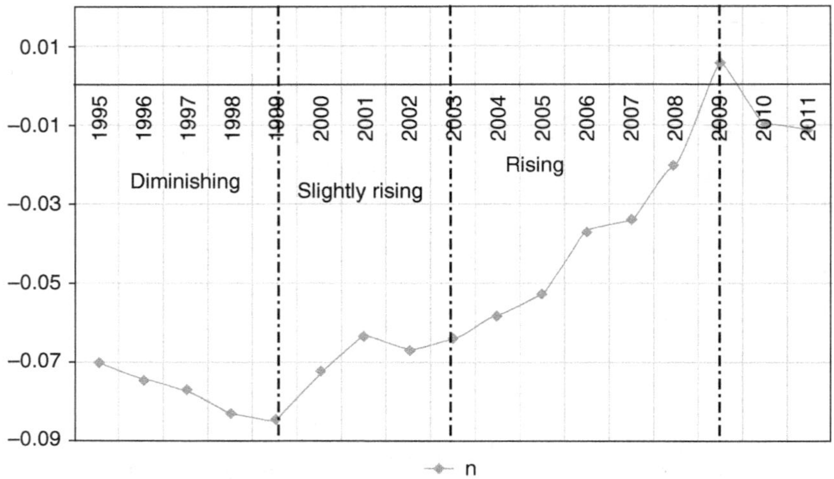

Figure 2.4 The net social wage ratio in Greece, 1995–2011.

Table 2.8 Net social wage, budget deficit and interest paid on public debt as a percentage of GDP, 1995-2011. Average values.

Year	*Greece*
Public deficit/GDP	–0.073
Interest paid/GDP	0.069
Net social wage ratio	–0.051

In Figure 2.5 we can see the standard negative relation between military and net social spending (here for workers only) at least for the first two phases of the period until 2006. Then, the rise in social spending is so great that military and social spending rise together, until the heavy austerity measures in 2010 and 2011 when both fall together.

In Figure 2.6 we present the estimation of the net social wage ratio for the entire 1958–2011 period. Based on the behaviour of the net social wage ratio we can distinguish four different phases of welfare state development in Greece. During the 'golden age' of capital accumulation and growth which lasted from the beginning of the period until the mid-1970s the net social wage ratio was negative and falling as initially the taxes of active workers easily overmatched low social spending for health and education services and pension spending for the relatively few retired workers. The military dictatorship of 1967–74 by slowing down social spending and suppressing labour unions and political parties lowered even further the net social wage ratio. Even after the fall of the military dictatorship the net social wage ratio continued to fall until 1980 as increased military spending due to the conflict with Turkey crowded out social

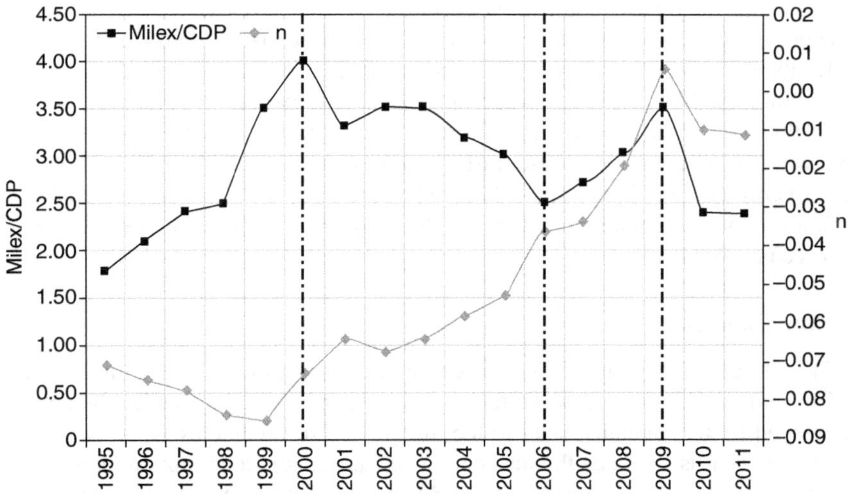

Figure 2.5 Military spending and the net social wage ratio in Greece, 1995–2011.

spending. Then, during the 1980s the first social democratic government in Greece increased significantly social spending and the net social wage ratio started to rise even though it remained negative. By the start of the decade of the 1990s the neoliberal ideology and policy were firmly established in the Greek economy and society and as in other advanced capitalist economies there were serious efforts from both right wing and social democratic governments to reduce the role of the state in the overall economic reproduction process. As a

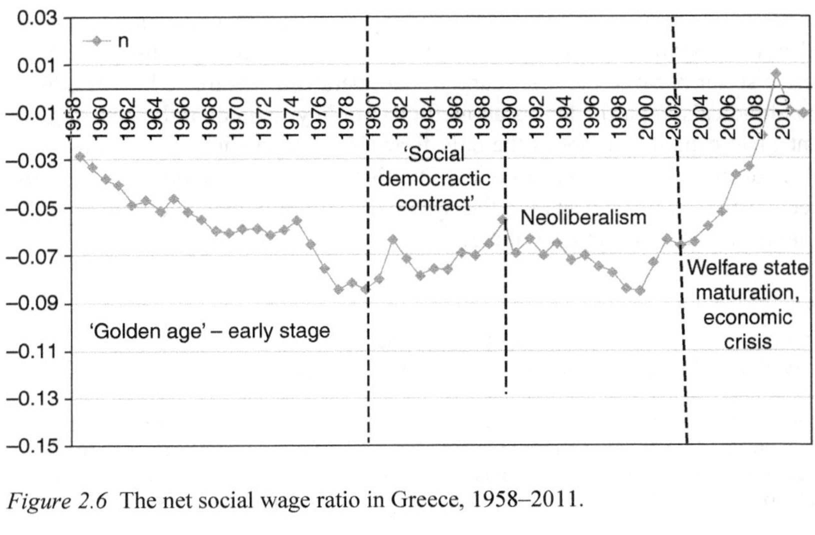

Figure 2.6 The net social wage ratio in Greece, 1958–2011.

result, the rising trend of net social wage ratio was interrupted and only in 2000 the net social wage ratio resumed its upward trend.

Then, as we saw above, the maturation of welfare state arrangements especially about retirement from active work and the devastating economic crisis after 2008 raised the net social wage ratio pushing it even in positive territory in 2009; the only such case for the entire post-war period before it resumed its downward trend as the dramatic austerity measures were first implemented by the government in 2010 and after. The pressing need of re-establishing profitability at a reasonable level for capital made necessary the attack even on a negative net social wage.

V Conclusions

Taking into account the results of our empirical investigation along with those of similar studies, it appears that the term welfare state is a misnomer for the actual role played by the capitalist state in the distribution of income as far as labour is concerned. That is so, since the net social wage is actually a net tax on labour. As Shaikh and Tonak (1987) noted in the 1980s, the welfare state and the social wage were a 'myth' and they remain so three decades later.[5] This fact does not imply that labour should not fight against attempts for cutbacks in social spending, increases in retirement age and increases in labour taxes, which will lower even further the net social wage ratio. Those attempts by the state and capital do not stem exclusively from the fiscal difficulties encountered by governments all over the world. The reduction in the market income share and the post-fiscal income share of labour is even more necessary nowadays for the system. That is so, because the performance of capitalist economies during the neoliberal period and especially during the current crisis lags seriously behind the experience of the 'golden age' period, not allowing any wage or social wage concessions. On the contrary, the survival of the system in this era of diminished productive potential requires further attacks on the income and the standard of living of a class that was already losing ground in the distributive battle. The fight against neoliberal capitalism has been ineffective so far because the first round of neoliberalism was treated by its adversaries and radicals in particular, as an inefficient policy regime on the part of governments, and capital, and not as the only form that current capitalism can assume given its current productive capabilities. The fight against neoliberalism can only be effective if it is a fight against the system as a whole and not against some presumably erroneous or unjust policies.

Notes

1 See Maniatis (2012) and Maniatis and Passas (2013).
2 That is, abstracting from intermediate social strata like self-employed professionals and small farmers.
3 Harman (2007) made the point that class struggle and the needs of the system for a healthy and functional labour force prevent the state from making drastic cuts in social spending. Of course, our empirical analysis shows that these expenditures, the bulk of which goes to retired labourers as pensions, are paid by (active) workers themselves.

4 In 2009 GDP fell by 3.6 per cent and many deferred government obligations especially for healthcare services were allocated to the budget of that year, hence the enormous deficit of 15.6 per cent of GDP and the significant rise in the labour benefit ratio which made the net social wage positive.
5 Even non-Marxists were sceptical about the supposed benevolent role of the state vis-à-vis the standard of living of the working class. As Mishra (1984: 85, emphasis in the original) noted early on:

> In any case we may point out in this connection that to treat social welfare provision as a 'social wage' (as some Marxists seem to do) could be very misleading. For this suggests that the 'social wage' is an *addition* to the 'economic wage' of the working class, whereas the fact of the matter is that part of the economic wage is taken away from the workers and then returned (to the workers and others) in the form of social services.

References

Armstrong P., Glyn A. and Harrison P. (1991), *Capitalism since 1945*, Oxford: Basil Blackwell.
Akram-Lodhi H. (1996), 'The public finances of the United Kingdom: a re-interpretation', *International Review of Applied Economics* 10(2).
Bowles S. and Gintis H. (1982), 'The crisis of liberal democratic capitalism: the case of the United States', *Politics and Society* 11(1).
Eurostat, epp.eurostat.ec.europa.eu/portal/page/portal/government_finance_statistics/data/Database (accessed 8 June 2013).
Fazeli R. (1996), *The Economic Impact of the Welfare State and the Social Wage: The British Experience*, Avebury: Brookfield.
Fazeli R. and Fazeli R. (2010), 'The impact of the welfare state and social policy on the working population: the recent British experience', *Forum for Social Economics* 39(2).
Freeman A. (1991), 'National accounts in value terms: the social wage and profit rate in Britain, 1950–1986', in Dunne P. (ed.), *Quantitative Marxism*, London: Polity Press.
Gintis H. and Bowles S. (1982), 'The welfare state and long-term economic growth: Marxian, neoclassical and Keynesian approaches', *American Economic Review* 72(2).
Glyn A. (1975), 'Notes on the profit squeeze', *Bulletin of the Conference of Socialist Economists* 4(1).
Glyn A. (2006), *Capitalism Unleashed*, Oxford: Oxford University Press.
Glyn A. and Sutcliffe T. (1972), *British Capitalism, Workers and the Profit Squeeze*, Harmondsworth: Penguin.
Guerrero D. (1992), 'Labour, capital and state redistribution: the evolution of net taxes in Spain (1970–1987)', *International Journal of Political Economy* 22(3).
Harman C. (2007), 'Theorising neoliberalism', *International Socialism* 117(winter).
Maniatis T. (2003), 'The net social wage in Greece, 1958–1995', *International Review of Applied Economics* 17(4).
Maniatis T. (2012), 'Marxist theories of crisis and the current economic crisis', *Forum for Social Economics* 41(1).
Maniatis T. and Passas C. (2013), 'Profitability, capital accumulation and crisis in the Greek economy, 1958–2009: a Marxist analysis', *Review of Political Economy* 25(4).
Miller J. (1989), 'Social wage or social profit? The net social wage and the welfare state', *Review of Radical Political Economics* 21(3).
Miller J. (1992), 'A negative net social wage and the reproduction crisis of the 1980s', in

Moseley F. and Wolff E. (eds), *International Perspectives on Profitability and Accumulation*, London: Edward Elgar.

Mishra R. (1984), *The Welfare State in Crisis*, New York: St. Martin's Press.

Moseley F. (1987), 'The profit share and the rate of surplus-value in the United States 1975–1985', *Cambridge Journal of Economics* 11(4).

O'Connor J. (1984), *Accumulation Crisis*, New York: Basil Blackwell.

OECD (various editions), *National Accounts*, Paris.

OECD (2012), 'Government social spending', www.oecd-ilibrary.org/social-issues-migration-health/government-social-spending-2012_socxp-gov-table-2012-1-en.

Reveley J. (2006), 'Taxing times: state-led income redistribution in New Zealand's "golden age" ', *Australian Economic History Review* 46(3).

Sepehri A. and Chernomas R. (1992), 'Who paid for the Canadian welfare state between 1955–1988?' *Review of Radical Political Economics* 24(1).

Shaikh A. (1978), 'National income accounts and Marxian categories', mimeo, New York: New School for Social Research.

Shaikh A. (1984), 'On the social wage', mimeo, New York: New School for Social Research.

Shaikh, A. (1987), 'The falling rate of profit and the economic crisis in the US', in Cherry R., D'Onofrio C., Kurdas C., Michl T., Moseley F. and Naples M. (eds), *The Imperiled Economy*, New York: Union of Radical Political Economists.

Shaikh A. (2003), 'Who pays for welfare in the welfare state? A multi-country study', *Social Research* 70(2).

Shaikh A. and Tonak E.A. (1987), 'The welfare state and the myth of the social wage', in Cherry R., D'Onofrio C., Kurdas C., Michl T., Moseley F. and Naples M. (eds), *The Imperiled Economy, Book I*, New York: Union of Radical Political Economists.

Shaikh A. and Tonak E.A. (1994), *Measuring the Wealth of Nations: The Political Economy of National Accounts*, New York: Cambridge University Press.

Shaikh A. and Tonak E.A. (2000), 'The rise and fall of the US welfare state', in Baiman R., Boushey H. and Saunders D. (eds), *Political Economy and Contemporary Capitalism: Radical Perspectives on Economic Theory and Policy*, New York: M.E. Sharpe.

Tonak E.A. (1987), 'The US welfare state and the working class, 1952–1980', *Review of Radical Political Economics* 19(3).

Weisskopf T. (1979), 'Marxian crisis theory and the rate of profit in the postwar U.S. economy', *Cambridge Journal of Economics* 3(4).

3 Explaining the rising wage–productivity gap in the Greek economy

Thanasis Maniatis and Costas Passas

I Introduction

The nature of the relationship between real wages and productivity has been receiving much attention recently, as both the effects of possibly rising unit labour costs in the context of a fixed exchange rate regime and of rising inequality have been of much interest in the contemporary world on both sides of the Atlantic. This, though, is hardly something new as the relationship between wages and productivity is firmly embedded in mainstream microeconomic theory, but empirically shown not to hold particularly well in the long run and especially for the period after the mid-1970s.

The increasing gap between the rate of growth of labour productivity and the rate of growth of real hourly wages, i.e. the wage–productivity gap, is considered one of the characteristics of the neoliberal period and, particularly by the under-consumptionist and distributional genres of Heterodox economics, as one of the prime causes of the current economic crisis at the end of the neoliberal period. The latter, having started at the second half of the 1980s in Greece and almost a decade earlier in advanced capitalist countries such as the USA and the UK, is the period that followed the stagflation crisis of the 1970s after the end of the so-called 'golden age' era of capital accumulation and growth of the first post-war period.

Since Ferguson's (1996) influential work, a number of econometric models have been proposed for the estimation of the determinants of the rising wage–productivity gap. Among the determinants proposed, a prominent role is reserved for the decline of union density during the neoliberal period, with the argument focusing on the diminished ability of labour to control both the pace of work and thus productivity and also its ability to achieve gains in real wages. Moreover, a number of additional determinants of the wage–productivity gap have been proposed such as the degree of openness in the economy, the unemployment rate, the pace of technological change.

Investigating the explanatory factors of the wage–productivity gap is particularly relevant for contemporary Greece, as often the discourse is limited only to the dramatic decline of wages brought by the attack on labour during this crisis and not to developments in productivity. It should be noted, that in a situation of a dearth of investment, productivity increases are achieved almost exclusively as the result of the increased intensification of the production process. Wage labourers in this situation face a defeat in two fronts. They lose as consumers, as their purchasing power is lowered together with their income and they also lose as producers since they are forced to use more intensively their labour power during the same working day.

The appropriate definition of variables is critical for the estimation of the wage–productivity gap. In particular, labour productivity, despite its deceptively easy general definition as a measure that relates output produced to the input of labour can be specifically measured in a number of ways depending on the theoretical paradigm adopted. The numerator can be value added, gross or net of depreciation, or gross output, that is, also including intermediate inputs. It can also be either Marxian value added (see Shaikh and Tonak (1994), Maniatis and Passas (2013)) or conventional value added.[1] The denominator can be hours worked, or persons employed. More importantly, if we use the distinction between productive and unproductive labour developed in Classical Political Economy and Marx, then since only productive labour creates new value and wealth, our estimates of productivity and real wage growth change significantly compared to the case where we use their conventional counterparts.

The rest of this chapter will be structured as follows. In the second section we will present a brief survey of the literature on the divergence between productivity and wages. Then, in the third section we will focus on the significance of the proper measurement of the variables involved. In particular, we discuss two specific issues. The first has to do with the choice of deflators for productivity and real wages, and the second with the distinction between productive and unproductive labour for the proper measurement of the labour input. Finally, we will estimate a Vector Error Correction Model (VECM) incorporating the determinants of the wage–productivity gap and we will present our conclusions.

II Theories of distribution

Basic microeconomic theory suggests that in the short run – when firms choose only the amount of employment having no choice over the employment of capital stock that is therefore considered fixed – the profit maximisation behaviour of the firms is such that they determine their output at the point where marginal cost (labour cost) is equal to marginal revenue. The equalisation of marginal wages and marginal labour productivity determines equilibrium output. Therefore, assuming that the economy is in equilibrium, wages and productivity should change by an equal amount over time, with the causation running from productivity to wages. In the medium and long run, when firms choose both the amount of employment of labour and the amount of capital stock used in the production process, the simplistic framework described for the short run changes in some important ways. First, the role of wage bargaining in general and of labour unions in particular comes into play, thus allowing wages to deviate from productivity (Blanchard (2006), Calmfors *et al.* (1988)). In this context one should also add the effects of wage rigidities, changes in work intensity as opposed to general changes in labour productivity, entry or mobility restrictions, sex and age discrimination in the workplace and also the effect of differences in the skills of employees. Second, international competition may erode the power of unions therefore limiting their impact on wage setting (Danthine and Hunt (1994)). Third, by allowing investment in capital stock to take place, firms may decide to substitute labour with capital or vice versa, therefore changing the capital–labour ratio and having as a result a divergence of total factor productivity (TFP) from labour productivity. However, as mainstream theory simply assumes that factors in the production process in a perfectly competitive equilibrium are paid their marginal product, there can be no systematic long-run wage–productivity gap.

Contrary to mainstream theory, in Marx there is no law of diminishing marginal productivity of labour since technological advancement is central in the Marxian theoretical system. In the Marxian analysis of distribution, wages are the price of labour-power, or the ability of the worker to perform useful labour. In normal times, the price of labour-power is understood to be independent of labour supply, i.e. the labour supply is perfectly elastic, since unemployment or the systematic presence of a reserve army of labour forces the workers to seek work at any wage rate offered in the market, the latter depending on the rate of capital accumulation and the demand for labour. As Marx notes in Volume I of *Capital* the rate of accumulation is the independent variable and the real wage is the dependent variable. In episodes of strong growth where unemployment is nearly eliminated, wages tend to rise above the subsistence level (which is supplemented by a 'historical and moral element'), profits are squeezed, accumulation slows down, unemployment rises and therefore wages revert back to a new historically given 'subsistence' level. At this level of abstraction surplus-value and profit is the residual of the total output as determined by the state of technology and productivity less wages of productive labour. Summarising, according to the Marxian theory, wages depend primarily on the pace of capital accumulation and the resulting demand for labour and also on the outcome of the struggle of labour with capital for the division of newly produced value. However, as far as the long-run pattern of class distribution of income is concerned, since no capitalist firm or sector could survive surrendering wage increases larger than productivity growth, classical Marxian analysis posits a rising wage–productivity gap and a falling wage share for productive labour (which may result in a falling profit share if the ratio of unproductive labour compensation and other similar costs over productive labour increases sufficiently) which does not necessarily give rise to a rising profit rate when the capital–output ratio rises.

The predictions of two influential Marxist currents developed during the twentieth century and especially during the stagflation crisis of the 1970s about the long-run pattern of distribution are based on a falling profit share and a rising profit share respectively. The first one is associated with the 'profit squeeze' theory which regards productivity growth and real wage growth as determined simultaneously by a more or less common set of factors[2] ('social' and 'technical') and claimed that in the conditions of the post-war 'golden age', low levels of unemployment rate, diminished 'cost of job loss' and worker protection stemming from the arrangements of the welfare state, changing class power relations led to systematically larger increases of wages than productivity and a falling profit share. This approach despite becoming dominant during the 1970s and the 1980s has receded during the period of neoliberalism as productivity growth clearly exceeded real wage growth. This development in class income distribution was more in line with the other major Marxist tradition that of the underconsumption-monopoly capital approach which believes that technologically advanced big units of capital (monopolies) have achieved high levels of productivity which greatly exceed real wages (restricted in a social system based on class and exploitation of direct producers) thus creating a wage–productivity gap and a rising (potential) profit share which furthermore causes realisation problems.

It could be argued therefore that two out of three main currents of Marxist theory predict an increasing wage–productivity gap over the medium or long run as a normal development and we turn now to the econometric identification and estimation of some of the variables that might have caused the widening of this gap in the Greek economy during the neoliberal phase of its post-war period of development.

III Determinants of the wage productivity gap

In trying to discuss possible determinants of a rising wage–productivity gap it is helpful to express it in a more detailed form. By definition, the wage–productivity gap – if wages and output are deflated by the CPI (Pc) and the GDP deflator (Py) respectively – can be decomposed into: (a) labour's terms of trade, i.e. the ratio between the price of products that labour consumes as measured by the consumer price index (CPI) over the price of output as measured by the GDP deflator, and (b) the nominal labour share of output, since both total wages and total output are divided by hours worked.

$$w-y=(W/GDP)-(Pc/Py)$$

That is, the wage–productivity gap is translated into either a fall in the nominal labour share or to a deterioration in labour's terms of trade or some combination of the two.

Capital–labour ratio

The relation between capital deepening, as reflected by a rising capital–labour ratio and labour productivity growth is well documented in the literature on the determinants of productivity, with an increase in the capital–labour ratio resulting into an increase in productivity (Englander and Gurney (1994), Syverson (2011)). On the other hand, new investment in capital affects wages via changes in the composition of the labour force, as new capital equipment requires more skills, so the wages of unskilled workers tend to be depressed relative to those of highly skilled, and via a substitution effect between capital and labour although wage bargaining institutions play a significant role in the final outcome (Krugman (1994), Koeniger and Leonardi (2007)). Therefore, an increase in the capital–labour ratio should result in an increase of labour productivity without necessarily a similar increase in hourly wages, thus most probably resulting in an increase of the wage–productivity gap.

Consumer price index (CPI)

The impact of consumer inflation on productivity is subject to debate in the literature as evidence exists for both a positive and a negative relationship. Bulman and Simon (2003) propose a negative relationship with inflation partially destroying the information encoded in prices, thus causing a number of allocation inefficiencies which result in a productivity growth slowdown, and also affecting productivity through distortions in the tax system. Contrary to these arguments, others such as Wakeford (2004), propose a positive relation, with higher wage inflation both outright increasing the 'cost of job loss' for workers and also creating a substitution of labour with capital thus increasing productivity. Empirically, the impact of inflation on real wages is found to be negative at least in periods of high inflation (Braumann 2004), although others (Hendry 2001) indicate that the opposite case can be possible. Thus, an increase in inflation should more likely result in an increase of the wage–productivity gap, although this is not an unambiguous result.

'Cost of job loss' – unemployment

Within the heterodox tradition and especially in the Social Structures of Accumulation school, the 'cost of job loss', i.e. the combined effect of the level of the unemployment rate, the duration of unemployment periods, the level of unemployment benefits and net wages before and after unemployment spells, is found to have a significant impact on productivity growth. Empirical research on the field (Weisskopf *et al.* (1983), Rebitzer (1987)) shows that increased cost of job loss exerts a positive impact on productivity growth. Other studies though (Weisskopf (1987)) indicate a more complex relationship, as unemployment is found to have the inverse impact on productivity especially in situations where the socio-economic institutional environment of a country is based on cooperative capital–labour relations and worker security.

Union density

Ferguson (1996: 79) indicates that declining union power from the 1980s onwards resulted in the elimination of labour's ability to achieve real wage gains parallel to productivity increases. Ferguson's analysis reveals that declining union density affects positively the wage–productivity gap in two distinct ways: first by failing to protect the employment level in industries with falling unionisation rates and second by failing to keep wages at the level of productivity growth in those industries. In partial contrast to Ferguson's argument, Zavodny (1999: 51) concludes that although declining union power has probably played a role in the increasing wage–productivity gap, this role is probably of lesser importance as industries with declining unionisation rates do not tend to have significantly faster increasing wage–productivity gaps. Thus, there is reason to believe that decreasing union power should tend to increase the wage productivity gap.

International competition (import penetration)

Trade openness is generally considered to positively affect productivity (Syverson (2011)). In such an argument, trade openness exerts pressure in industries subject to international competition to innovate, and obviously this in turn is translated into increases in productivity. In addition, there is evidence that trade openness results in increasing downward pressure to wages (Stone and Cepeda (2011)) mainly exerted by reducing the power of labour unions especially in advanced capitalist countries. Therefore, international competition in general and trade openness in particular is expected to have a positive impact on the wage–productivity gap, as it tends to increase productivity and reduce real wages.

Labour force composition (age, sex. education)

The increased participation of young workers and women in the labour force as a result of low rates of unemployment has been considered that brought into the labour force an echelon of workers that had lower skills, thus driving productivity growth downward. This view was initially held by Nordhaus (1972) and others regarding the 'productivity slowdown' of the 1970s. According to this argument the influx of labour from agriculture to manufacturing lowers productivity growth because of inefficiencies stemming from the qualitative characteristics of the new members of the labour force. In addition, labour characteristics such as age, sex and race have been found in a number of studies to influence earnings, with younger and female workers being paid less than older and male workers. Therefore, age and sex affect wages and productivity in the same direction and thus these variables are expected to affect the wage–productivity gap only because of their scale and not necessarily in a particular direction. That said, in a number of studies (Ilmakunas and Maliranta (2002)) the effects of age and sex variables have been found to have a positive impact on the wage–productivity gap.

In the mainstream literature aggregate macro models of endogenous growth with explicit treatment of 'human capital' (see for example Mankiw *et al.* (1992)) provide the theoretical underpinnings for the establishment of a relation between 'human capital' and growth. Within this tradition, formal educational attainment (Benhabib and Spiegal (1991)) and informal on the job skill acquisition (DeJong and Ingram (2001)) were identified as factors positively correlated with productivity growth. However, in a number of studies the importance of human capital has been found to be minimal in comparison to capital deepening (Schwerdt and Tuunen (2007)). On the other hand the positive relation of education and wages is one of the most well-known and tested aspects in the labour economics literature either based on a 'human capital' approach or on an incentive model or in other similar models (Mincer (1958, 1974), Lazear (1979)). The main argument here is that earnings are a function of human capital accumulated through schooling and work experience that increases with age. Thus, since an increase in accumulated human capital increases both productivity and wages the effect on the wage–productivity gap is not predetermined.

IV Real wage, productivity, deflators and the ratio of unproductive to productive labour

Having presented a short survey of the literature we now turn to the empirical investigation of the relationship between wages and productivity in the Greek economy. We note that in what follows, both labour productivity and wages refer to constant value measures per hour worked for the total private economy.

Figure 3.1 presents the evolution of labour productivity in the post-war Greek economy, measured as gross real value added to total hours worked, and real hourly wages. Since a common argument found in the literature (see for example

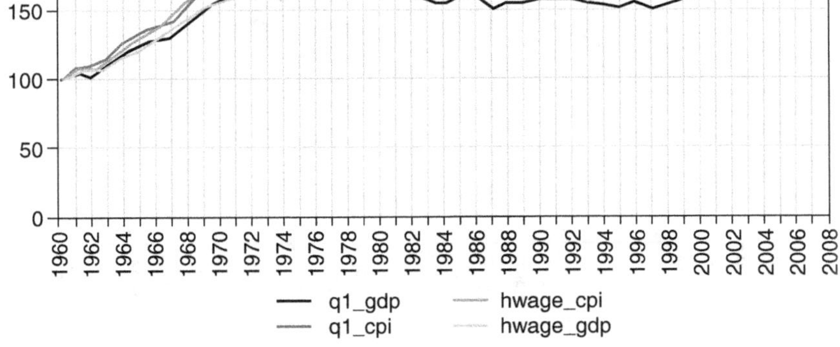

Figure 3.1 Labour productivity and real hourly wages, total private economy, 1960–2008.

Bosworth and Perry (1994), Feldstein (2008)) has been that the existence of a wage–productivity gap is merely a statistical artefact of differences arising from the evolution of the output (GDP) deflator and the CPI, we deflate both productivity and hourly wages with both deflators. In particular, for the aggregate private economy we can deduce that since 1985 and certainly after 1990[3] productivity growth clearly and systematically exceeds real wage growth signifying the advent of the neoliberal period for Greece.

In Figure 3.2 we substitute total wages and productivity of total employment with the respective variables when the distinction between productive and unproductive labour is used. Output is Marxian real value added, wages are the wages of productive labour or variable capital and the labour input in the productivity variable is hours worked by productive labour. In this case also, wages are found to lag systematically behind productivity growth despite differences that still arise from the choice of deflators. In Figure 3.3 we present a graphic depiction of the gap between Marxian labour productivity and wages of productive labour. This variable is measured as the difference between the Marxian productivity index and the index of the real wage of productive labour index with base year 1960 = 100. Thus an increase in the gap is understood as an increase in the rate of exploitation. This graph makes obvious the gap that exists when both variables are deflated by the same price index (CPI) and the fact that it starts to increase systematically from the mid-1980s, the time period when the neoliberal period started in Greece.

It should be noted here that the distinction between productive and unproductive labour affects the measurement of labour productivity via two distinct channels.

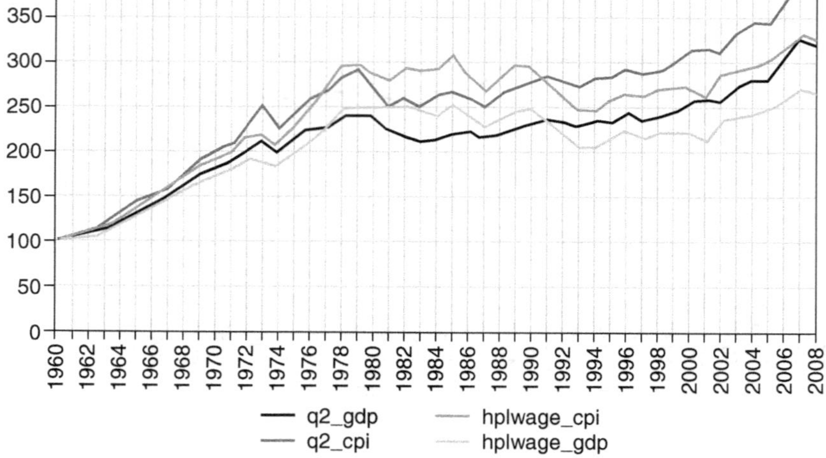

Figure 3.2 Labour productivity and real hourly wages, productive labour, 1960–2008.

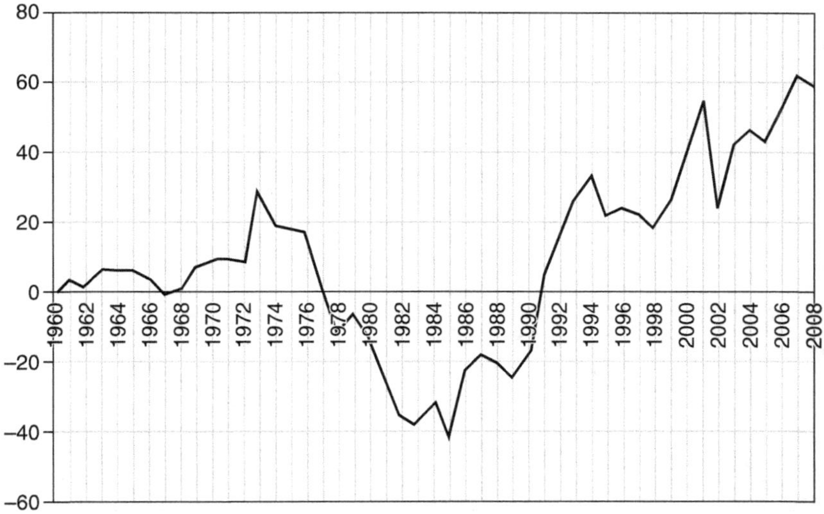

Figure 3.3 Wage–productivity gap, productive labour, CPI deflator.

First, the denominator of productivity, labour input, is restricted to productive labour hours worked, instead of hours worked by the total labour force. The reason for this is that whereas in the mainstream tradition output is the result of the total labour input, in the Marxian and generally in the Classical tradition of Political Economy, value and surplus-value are exclusively the result of the labour activity of the section of the labour force classified as productive labour, if we abstract from production of value by self-employed independent commodity producers. In other words in the Classical and Marxian tradition only productive labour input results in value and surplus-value creation available for accumulation, whereas unproductive labour is considered a cost and a barrier to accumulation. Unproductive labour thus consumes instead of increasing surplus-value produced by productive labour. Second, the numerator of labour productivity is Marxian Value Added, a measure that is defined as the sum of intermediate inputs of the trade sector and the value added of production, trade and finance and insurance sectors (Shaikh and Tonak (1994)). We note that in Marxian Value Added we do not include fictitious components of value added found in mainstream National Accounts and in particular we do not include the value added reported for Public Administration and Compulsory Social Security, and the real estate sectors. The relationship between the Marxian and the mainstream measures of productivity can be seen in Figure 3.4. Marxian labour productivity has by default a higher level than its mainstream counterpart both because of a larger numerator and a smaller denominator, with differences in growth rates arising because of the evolution of the ratio of unproductive labour to total labour and of the ratio of intermediate inputs of trade to mainstream value added.

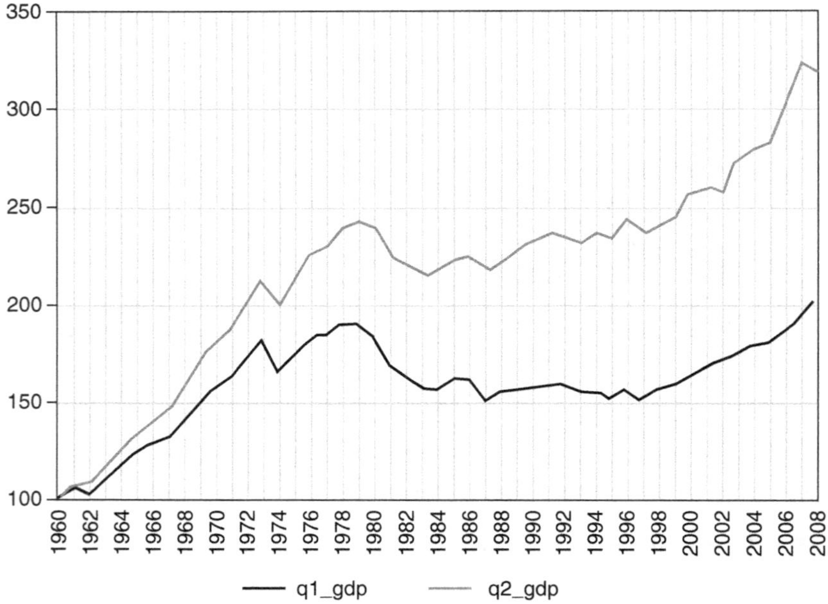

Figure 3.4 Mainstream (q1) and Marxian (q2) labour productivity, index 1960 = 100.

V Econometric estimation of the determinants of the wage–productivity gap

The hypothesis that we want to test is that the wage–productivity gap is influenced by the capital–labour ratio, the unemployment rate, unionisation, import penetration and inflation. The capital–labour ratio is expected to have a positive impact on the wage–productivity gap, since an increase in the means of production per worker should *ceteris paribus* increase productivity without necessarily increasing wages. An increase in the unemployment rate is also expected to result in an increase of the wage–productivity gap as labour pressed by higher unemployment levels should be less likely to be successful in gaining wage increases in line with productivity changes. Unionisation is expected to have a negative impact on the wage–productivity gap, as higher levels of unionisation are expected to allow labour to increase wages without necessarily equally increasing productivity growth at the same time, or to reduce work effort, labour extraction and thus productivity growth without a similar reduction in wages. Import penetration is expected to increase the wage–productivity gap via increased international competition and thus a lowering of the wages or productivity increases that are not reflected on wage growth. Finally, increases in the CPI are expected to have a positive impact on the wage–productivity gap since wages are not indexed to changes in the price of consumption goods and generally their purchasing power can be protected less efficiently in a situation of significant inflation rates.

Equation 1 presents the relationship that we want to test:

$$GAP_t = \alpha + \beta[(KL_p]_t) + \gamma[(UNEMP]_t) + \delta(UNION_t) + \varepsilon(IMP_t) + \zeta(CPI_t) + \varepsilon_t \tag{1}$$

where α is a constant, *GAP* is the wage–productivity gap defined as the difference between the index of Marxian productivity and the index of real hourly wages of productive labour, KL_p is the fixed private capital to productive labour ratio, *UNEMP* is the unemployment rate, *UNION* is union density, *IMP* is a measure of import penetration measured as imports over *GDP*, and *CPI* is the logarithm of the consumer price index. Subscript t denotes time. Both value added and wages are deflated by the *CPI*. We note that we estimate Equation 1 for the period after the wage–productivity gap started to rise; that is for the period after 1986 when as we mentioned above the first efforts for the establishment of a neoliberal regime were undertaken in the Greek economy.

To estimate Equation 1 we will proceed in the following steps. First, we will perform unit root tests on the variables so as to know their order of integration and avoid spurious results. Second, if the variables are found to be integrated of order one, [I(1)] we will perform cointegration tests to test for the existence of possible cointegrating relationships. Finally, if the variables are found to be cointegrated we will estimate the relationship using a Vector Error Correction Model (VECM).

In order to test for the presence of unit roots in the variables we perform an Augmented Dickey–Fuller Test (ADF) with lag selection based on the Schwarz Information Criterion and a maximum of four lags. Results presented in Table 3.1 indicate that all variables were found to be difference stationary, with the exception of the logarithm of CPI that was found to be stationary also in levels.

Since variables were found to be I(1) and I(0), we perform a Johansen test for cointegration assuming a lag length of one in first differences. The reason for the latter is that our series are annual. Results of both the trace and eigenvalue tests in Tables 3.2a and 3.2b indicate that no more than two cointegrating equations exist at the 0.05 level of confidence. Since cointegrating relationships were

Table 3.1 ADF unit root tests

ADF test	*Level*		*First difference*	
Variable	t-*statistic*	*5%* p *value*	t-*statistic*	*5%* p *value*
GAP	–1.263305	0.6274	–5.186109	0.0005
KLp	1.885843	0.9996	–3.978205	0.0066
UNEMP	–1.489343	0.5192	–3.182915	0.0356
UNION	–0.818194	0.7940	–3.463480	0.0206
IMP	–1.523306	0.5025	–2.884746	0.0641
log CPI	–3.936511	0.0076	–4.207516	0.0049

found to exist for any trend specification that we tested, we employ the Pantula (1989) principle and select a specification of no trend and no intercept.

Having established that the variables are cointegrated we proceed with the estimation of the VECM for one lag in first differences and one cointegrating relationship. Table 3.3 presents the estimation result for the long-run coefficients and the error correction term (ECT). In the estimation results of Equation 1 presented as Model 1 in Table 3.3 all variables were found to be highly significant and with the expected sign except for unemployment that was found to be insignificant and with an unexpected sign. Therefore, we re-estimate Equation 1 excluding unemployment. Before that of course we perform again a Johansen test on this smaller number of variables with identical results as reported above. Results of the VECM estimation are presented as Model 2 in Table 3.3. All variables retain their significance and their sign therefore also providing a first indication of the robustness of estimation.

Substituting the coefficients of the VECM Model 2 to Equation 1 we obtain the relationship:

$$GAP2\_CPI = 23.73 * KLP - 339.58 * UNION + 212.88 * IMP + 45.328 * CPILOG$$

It is important to note that the variable for union density has the highest coefficient value indicating the very important impact of unionisation on the wage–productivity gap.

Also, Standard tests on VECM residuals for autocorrelation, normality and heteroscedasticity were performed (not reported for brevity), with results

Table 3.2a Johansen trace test, Model 1

Hypothesized no. of CE(s)	*Eigenvalue*	*Trace statistic*	*0.05 critical value*	*Prob.***
None*	0.990605	178.0051	83.93712	0.0000
At most 1*	0.888372	79.98566	60.06141	0.0004
At most 2	0.521209	33.94137	40.17493	0.1840
At most 3	0.439772	18.47507	24.27596	0.2261
At most 4	0.259114	6.307438	12.32090	0.3995
At most 5	0.000445	0.009345	4.129906	0.9370

Table 3.2b Johansen eigenvalue test, Model 1

Hypothesized no. of CE(s)	*Eigenvalue*	*Max-Eigen statistic*	*0.05 critical value*	*Prob.***
None*	0.990605	98.01945	36.63019	0.0000
At most 1*	0.888372	46.04429	30.43961	0.0003
At most 2	0.521209	15.46630	24.15921	0.4674
At most 3	0.439772	12.16764	17.79730	0.2864
At most 4	0.259114	6.298093	11.22480	0.3170
At most 5	0.000445	0.009345	4.129906	0.9370

Table 3.3 VECM estimation results, dependent variable Marxian productivity wage gap: CPI deflator

Variable	*Value*	*Standard error*	*Value*	*Standard error*
	Model 1		*Model 2*	
ECT	−0.355347	(0.18878)	−0.268853	(0.15568)
KLp	−32.80058	(6.28031)	−23.72771	(10.6474)
UNEMP	43.33339	(69.9865)		
UNION	258.7982	(27.4553)	339.5837	(28.2047)
IMP	−159.5406	(21.0697)	−212.8846	(30.0873)
CPI (log)	−45.51548	(2.49080)	−45.32779	(3.43017)
R^2	0.441342		0.416048	
adj R^2	0.201917		0.221398	
AIC	7.802882		7.751924	
SBIC	8.151056		8.050359	

indicating that our model passes those standard tests. Finally impulse responses of the wage–productivity gap to one standard deviation innovations are presented in Figure 3.5.

V Conclusions

One of the most defining features of the period of neoliberalism is the bias in the class distribution of income in favour of capital. All measures of distribution, the rate of surplus-value, the profit–wage rati, and statistics of income dispersion like the Gini coefficient of inequality moved in the direction of capital and the wealthy during this period. The exact mechanisms and the fundamental causes of this movement have not been explored thoroughly, especially in countries like Greece. Our empirical results for the 1986–2008 period indicate that the arguments derived from the Classical and Marxian Political Economy analysis of distribution relations hold reasonably well in the case of the Greek economy. Mechanisation and capitalisation of production, i.e. expulsion of living labour from the production process in a period of slightly rising unemployment, while raising productivity at the same time affect negatively the bargaining power of labour, thus increasing the wage–productivity gap, the rate of exploitation and possibly the profit share. As the 'globalization process', i.e. the intensification of capitalist competition on a global scale proceeds and less productive (on average) national capitals like the Greek ones are exposed more and more to international competition (and especially with virtually no protection within the Eurozone) they are more likely to increase the rate of exploitation of workers especially in an environment of falling profitability. Moreover, probably due to the effect of this increasingly competitive environment, it appears that workers could not protect effectively their purchasing power in the face of price increases in consumption goods as they did in the inflationary period of the 1970s when the wage–productivity gap was narrowing. Finally, and perhaps most importantly

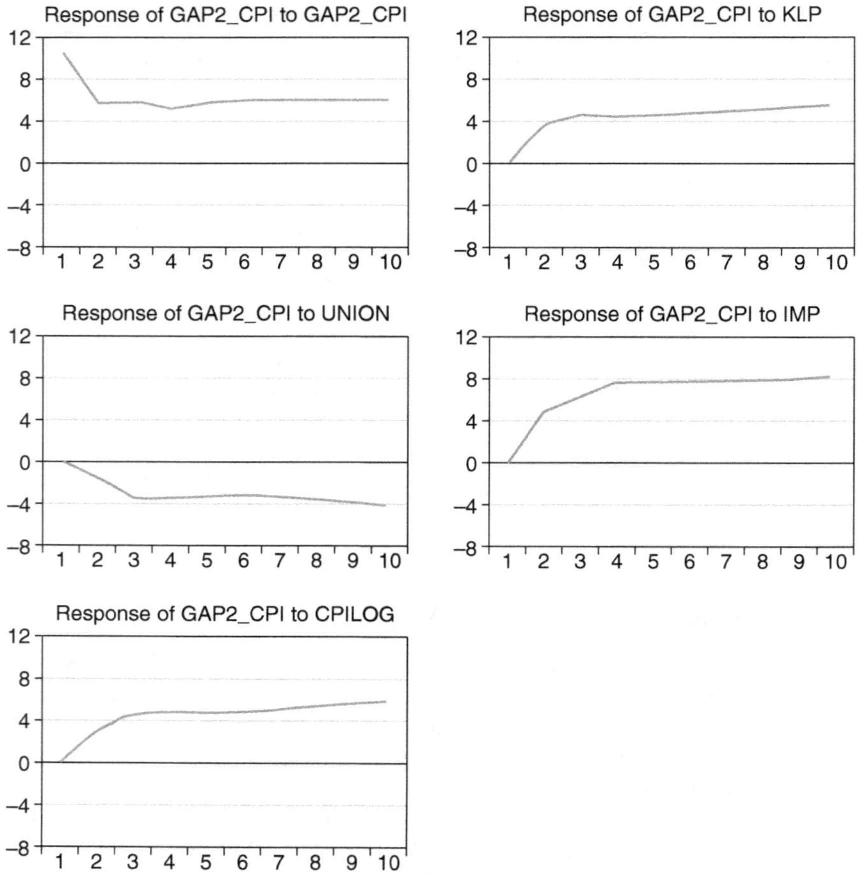

Figure 3.5 Impulse responses.

as expected by the Political Economy approach the (declining) unionization rate during the neoliberal period contributed significantly to the stagnation of real wages and the increase in the wage–productivity gap, i.e. in the fall of the wage share of productive labour and the increase in the rate of surplus-value.

Notes

1 According to the scheme developed by Shaikh and Tonak (1994), Marxian value added differs from conventional value added as it appears in official National Accounts in that it includes intermediate inputs of the trade sector and revenues paid to the royalties sector by the production and trade sectors, while it does not include the value added of the public sector and other imputations of the conventional methodology.

2 See Gordon (1987) for a review of Marxist distribution theories.

3 See Chapter 6 for the periodisation of the post-war era of Greek capitalism on the basis of the behaviour of the profit rate. The neoliberal period starts first around 1985 and becomes firmly established after 1990.

References

Benhabib J. and Spiegel M. (1991), 'Growth accounting with physical and human capital accumulation', Working Papers 92–24, C.V. Starr Center for Applied Economics, New York University, New York.

Blanchard O. (2006), 'European unemployment: the evolution of facts and ideas', *Economic Policy* 21(45).

Bosworth B. and Perry G. (1994), 'Productivity and real wages: is there a puzzle?' *Brookings Papers on Economic Activity* 1994(1).

Braumann B. (2004), 'High inflation and real wages', *IMF Staff Papers* 51(1).

Bulman T. and Simon J. (September 2003), 'Productivity and inflation', RBA research discussion papers rdp2003–10', Reserve Bank of Australia.

Calmfors L., Driffill J., Honkapohja S. and Giavazzi F. (1988), 'Bargaining structure, corporatism and macroeconomic performance', *Economic Policy* 3(6).

Danthine J.-P. and Hunt J. (1994), 'Wage bargaining structure, employment and economic integration', *Economic Journal* 104(424).

DeJong D. and Ingram B. (2001), 'The cyclical behavior of skill acquisition', *Review of Economic Dynamics* 4(3).

Englander S. and Gurney A. (1994), 'OECD productivity growth: medium-term trends', *OECD Economic Studies* 22.

Feldstein M. (2008), 'Did wages reflect growth in productivity?' NBER Working Paper Series 13953.

Ferguson W. (1996), 'Explaining the rising wage–productivity gap of the 1980s: effects of declining employment and unionization', *Review of Radical Political Economics* 28(2).

Gordon D. (1987), 'Distribution theories', in Eatwell J., Milgate M. and Newman P. (eds), *The New Palgrave: Marxian Economics*, New York: W.W. Norton & Co.

Hendry D. (2001), 'Modelling UK inflation, 1875–1991', *Journal of Applied Econometrics* 16(3).

Ilmakunnas P. and Maliranta M. (2002), 'Labour characteristics and wage–productivity gaps', *New Zealand Economic Papers* 36(1).

Koeniger W. and Leonardi M. (January 2007), 'Capital deepening and wage differentials: Germany versus US', *Economic Policy* 22.

Krugman P. (1994), 'Past and prospective causes of high unemployment', *Economic Review*, Issue QIV.

Lazear E. (1979), 'Why is there mandatory retirement?' *Journal of Political Economy* 87(6).

Maniatis T. and Passas C. (2013), 'Profitability, capital accumulation and crisis in the Greek economy 1958–2009: a Marxist analysis', *Review of Political Economy* 25(4).

Mankiw G., Romer D. and Weil D. (1992), 'A contribution to the empirics of economic growth', *Quarterly Journal of Economics* 107(2).

Mincer J. (1958), 'Investments in human capital and personal income distribution', *Journal of Political Economy* 66(4).

Mincer J. (1974), *Schooling, Experience, and Earnings*, New York: Columbia University Press.

Nordhaus W. (1972), 'The recent productivity slowdown', *Brookings Papers on Economic Activity* 3(3).

Pantula S.G. (1989), 'Testing for unit roots in time series data', *Econometric Theory* 5.

Rebitzer J. (1987), 'Unemployment, long-term employment relations, and productivity growth', *Review of Economics and Statistics* 69(4).

Schwerdt G. and Tuunen J. (2007), 'Changes in human capital: implications for productivity growth in the euro area', *Ifo Working Paper Series* 53.

Shaikh A. and Tonak A. (1994), *Measuring the Wealth of Nations*, Cambridge: Cambridge University Press.

Stone S. and Cepeda R. (October 2011), 'Wage implications of trade liberalisation: evidence for effective policy formation', *OECD Trade Policy Papers* 122.

Syverson C. (2011), 'What determines productivity?' *Journal of Economic Literature* 49(2).

Wakeford J. (2004), 'The productivity–wage relationship in South Africa: an empirical investigation', *Development of Southern Africa* 21(1).

Weisskopf T. (1987), 'The effect of unemployment on labour productivity: an international comparative analysis', *International Review of Applied Economics* 1(2).

Weisskopf T., Bowles S. and Gordon D. (1983), 'Hearts and minds: a social model of U.S. productivity growth', *Brookings Papers on Economic Activity* 14(2).

Zavodny M. (1999), 'Unions and the wage–productivity gap', *Economic Review* Q2.

4 The Greek EU–IMF Memoranda

A problematic strategy for Greek capitalism

Demophanes Papadatos

I Introduction

Today Greek capitalism is at the epicentre of international developments. Its economic crisis is related and significantly affects the global capitalist crisis and the associated Eurozone crisis.

Since 2009, capitalism has been in the midst of a global crisis. This crisis, as it is well known, started in the US as the crisis of the so-called sub-prime mortgage asset backed securities. Both the current Greek crisis and the Eurozone crisis are a continuation of the 2007–9 crisis which, in turn, is the continuation and culmination of a whole series of previous crises. The latter erupted with an unusually high frequency after the 1987 NYSE (e.g. crises of the Mexican peso, the Russian ruble crisis, the Turkish Lira and the Asian and Argentine crises). All these crises have as common root the 1973 global economic crisis and its falling profitability cause and repercussions. The subsequent capitalist restructuring waves succeeded only partially in restoring capital's profitability. In other words, the profit rate never managed to reach its prior 1973 levels.

Greek capitalism's response to its current crisis is the instigation of a sweeping restructuring aiming to transform it from a capitalism that its driving force was the state and the public sector to one led by the private sector. This strategy is applied via the troika Memoranda. It has a serious 'external' constraint: this ambitious restructuring has to take place amidst the unfavourable environment of the global economic crisis.

This chapter begins with a brief description of the context of the global capitalist crisis within which and because of which Greek capitalism is experiencing its own crisis. Then, the general theoretical framework of the Greek Memoranda is analysed in comparison to the standard IMF neoliberal structural adjustment models applied around the world. Subsequently the specific characteristics and the peculiarities of the Greek Memoranda are exhibited. Finally, the reasons for their systematic failures and the broader historical, economic and social constraints that are making the Memoranda strategy infeasible are exposed.

II The theoretical and political background of the Memoranda: the neoliberal approach to export-led growth

The theoretical and political background of the strategy of the Memoranda has its roots several decades back in the late 1970s and early 1980s. At that period the so-called debt crisis in the less developed countries occurred, as a result of the 1973 global capitalist crisis. The falling profitability in the main imperialist economies and the subsequent decline in economic activity had consequences that led to serious deficits in the balance of payments especially in the less developed countries. At the same time the revision of US monetary policy in order to tame inflation through the implementation of the monetarist doctrines suddenly placed additional burdens on those economies borrowing in dollars. It obliged them to pay huge interest on their loans while at the same time their exports (and the incomes generated from them) started falling. This led to debt crises that began with the 1982 Mexican crisis and spread rapidly throughout the developing world; particularly in Latin America and many African and Eastern European countries. At the same time the collapse of the so-called socialist countries removed all barriers for Western imperialism in imposing the neoliberal policies on a global scale. The IMF and the World Bank were instrumental in formulating and imposing these policies. Thus, many developing countries – that previously denounced such policies as new imperialism – were obliged to succumb to their 'assistance' and adopt, in exchange for loans, their policy and structural prescriptions.

For neoliberal theory, the debt problem in many countries was considered as a *solvency problem* (i.e. they could not pay the interest on their debts without a commitment to major economic and structural reforms) and much less a *liquidity problem* (that could be solved by the granting of short-term loans to them and the adjustment of policy). Before the crisis 2007–9, the dogma of neoliberal structural adjustment was based on what J. Williamson called 'Washington Consensus'. This term encapsulates the broad agreement between officials and neoliberal intellectuals both in industrialised economies and in international institutions on the main guidelines of the neoliberal structural adjustment prescription: free market reign, trade liberalisation, unrestricted capital flows, privatisations and downsizing of the public sector, etc. (see Mavroudeas and Papadatos (2007)).

The imposition of this agenda on a global scale facilitated greater international economic integration under the dominance of Western capitalisms. The specific nature of this international integration favours interests of the most aggressive fractions of international and internationalised capital, as predominantly expressed by the Western multinational enterprises. Consequently, an alliance was forged between business elites and conservative intellectuals in order to promote the neoliberal corporate 'globalisation'. One of its primary tools is the extension of the then GATT, leading in 1996 to the creation of the World Trade Organization (WTO).

A crucial element of the neoliberal prescription of internal and external liberalisation is the adoption by the less developed economies of an export-oriented strategy. The logic behind this is that less developed economies are characterised by lower Organic Compositions of Capital and have the potential for higher rates of surplus-value. Consequently, when Western multinationals can invest without restrictions and risks in these economies they can reap extra-profits. According to the neoliberal prescription, export-orientation must be coupled with prudent fiscal and monetary government policies. Particularly, a balanced budget is required in order to eliminate rampant inflation; which distorts entrepreneurial plans and expectations. Moreover, inflation is considered an indirect tax reducing capital's profitability. This follows suit from the neoliberal conception that 'prices should be determined correctly' and governments should not be allowed to distort them. It is claimed that the implementation of these reforms is likely to spark private initiatives that would lead to an additional 'growth dividend'. Finally, neoliberalism emphasises the necessity of institutional reforms. Essentially this implies that previous institutional arrangements favouring national capitals (through cronyism) and/or workers' rights should be removed. These institutional restructuring has to be imposed irrespective of democratic and constitutional constraints. Supposedly 'incorruptible' economic technocrats (preferably with a previous service in international organisations and corporations) are preferred in running these new processes.

The main elements of the neoliberal strategy as encapsulated in the IMF adjustment programmes are the following:

a The integration of the national economy in the global economy by opening it to international capital.
b The depreciation of the exchange rate in order to improve competitiveness and avoid excessive recession in the short run.
c Labour market liberalisation to improve competitiveness.
d Fiscal consolidation in order to downsize the public sector and reduce the public social costs (e.g. health insurance, education, quality of life) and relinquish these areas to private capital exploitation.
e Public debt's 'haircut' – in case this is not sustainable – so as to facilitate the programme's implementation without excessive recessionary burden on the economy.

The strategic objective is to strengthen the long-run international competitiveness so that the country can become attractive for multinational enterprises as a destination for foreign direct investment in order to produce products (goods and services) for exports. Thus the developmental strategy of the neoliberal agenda emphasises the outward orientation of countries with particular attention on export growth and on attracting foreign direct investment.

This strategy is best epitomised in the Mexican experience (Palley (2011): 6–7). In the Mexican case the main change is that structural adjustment has transformed it into a kind of 'production platform' for exportable goods and services of the globalised transnational corporations. This means that the Mexican industrial infrastructure does not follow primarily the needs of its own internal division of labour. Instead the new industrial infrastructure corresponds to the requirements of 'globalised' production and finance promoted by transnational corporations.

Nevertheless, this neoliberal strategy is highly disputable. If the neoliberal view that outward-oriented economies really grow faster is correct then exports and FDI should increase total investment (or, at least, not reduce it). According to Weeks (2007: 116–17) for developing countries, although both exports and FDI grew faster in the 1980s and 1990s than previously, it was not always accompanied by faster GDP growth. Additionally, in UNCTAD's 1992 *World Investment Report* some doubt was expressed on the role of foreign investment, both in its investment-enhancing role and its function as vehicle for export growth. The report points out that FDI's share in domestic investment of developing countries was very small (below 5 per cent). It also argues that in many cases the activities of transnational corporations do not always contribute to the long-term sustainability of growth through trade. Moreover, sometimes transnational corporations abuse their market power in ways which prevent the growth of local investments (UNCTAD (1992): 14).

The South African experience is also characteristic (Geld and Black (2004): 179–203). South Africa is a middle-income semi-industrialised economy with an established industrial base, a segmented labour market with very high unemployment, and real exchange rate depreciation during the 1990s. It engaged in an economic policy to promote export-led growth through FDI attraction and integration into global production networks in order to address saving shortages, which were identified as the underlying reason for poor fixed investment rates. Nonetheless, most new FDI in South Africa has not been part of a process of globalisation of production, in the sense of output being exported into global production networks. Instead new FDIs focused on domestic and regional markets. Many investors mitigated risk by limiting the irreversibility of their investment, by outsourcing production or focusing on service provision rather than more capital-demanding manufacturing operations. Most firms entered for market-seeking purposes, though the relevant market encompasses both the domestic economy and neighbouring countries. Integration of domestic production processes into global networks remains limited. Overall, FDI levels in South Africa for the 1990s period have been low, so that policy objectives of increased output and employment from FDI have not been met.

Another issue is that until 1980, FDI for all the practical purposes of balance of payments accounting was equivalent to capital formation. After 1980, with the liberalisation of capital account and privatisation associated initially with the Washington Consensus, the FDI's nature underwent substantial change. Privatisation took the form of debt-equity 'swaps' as public assets were sold to foreign firms. These changes in the nature of FDI had important consequences. After 1980 FDI flows have a different meaning from before, as it is no longer valid to infer that FDI in terms of balance of payments accounting would result in capital formation. It could no longer be assumed that all or even a portion of FDI results in the creation of new assets. With capital account deregulation and its associated domestic asset acquisition by international firms, the emphasis on FDI's advantages shifted from the straightforward contribution to capital accumulation to more speculative outcomes. These include the possibility that the FDI might generate: (1) technologies and skill not otherwise available; (2) access to new export markets; and (3) spread effects with an industry that raises the managerial or technical efficiency of domestic firms (UNCTAD (1999): 34–5). However, empirical evidence suggests that no general conclusion could be drawn about these outcomes, which seemed to depend on the specifics of each country.

III The Greek Memoranda strategy

The Greek Memoranda follow, with significant modifications, the guiding lines of IMF's structural adjustment programmes (SAPs). The typical IMF programmes had to be modified in the Greek case because it was the first time in IMF's history, that such a large programme was imposed on a developed economy. In addition, it was also the first time that such a programme was imposed on an economy that is a member of a monetary union such as the EMU. These facts pose several technical and political difficulties. It should also be noticed that the Greek EAP is a four-years plan as contrasted with the typical three-years IMF SAPs. This reflects the magnitude and complexity of the Greek adjustment.

In common with standard IMF programmes, fiscal consolidation and labour market liberalisation are key pillars of the Greek Memoranda. Opening the economy to international capital was not something to take significant action since the economy as an EU member was already open.[1] What is really missing from the Greek programme is the initial devaluation of the currency as the country is a member of the Eurozone and cannot devalue its currency by itself. This is where problems start to arise as a vital element of standard IMF procedures is missing; thus generating additional burdens for the other pillars of the programmes. Particularly, the inability of exchange rate devaluation lead to even tougher austerity measures in order to restore competitiveness.

Another element of the Greek Memoranda that stands out is that the programme is not only pro-cyclical but also front-loaded, meaning that the bulk of painful measures was implemented in the first year (Weisbrot *et al.* (2009), Weisbrot and Montesino (2012)). As has been publicly made known this was demanded by the EU and in contrast to IMF's views. The IMF argued that an overly front-loaded programme combined with the missing currency devaluation element aggravated the recession more than it should. But the EU, aiming to contain the Greek problem as soon as possible in order to avoid contagion to other countries (something which of course for a series of reasons, occurred),[2] demanded a front-loaded programme.

The declared aim of the Greek Memoranda is to tackle a crisis seen as a crisis of debt; primarily attributable to excessive FDs and unconnected to the 2007 global capitalist crisis. At the same time the programme aims to structurally transform the Greek economy in accordance with the standards of the IMF's

SAPs. More specifically, it aims to transform Greek capitalism from a system where the state is its driving force to a system where the private sector takes the wheel of the economy. Therefore, the strategy is twofold: (a) to face the immediate liquidity problem (due to the excessive public debt) and (b) to implement a structural transformation of Greek capitalism (something schematically expressed with the objective to increase competitiveness). However, what is undeclared is the fact that all this effort takes place in the midst of a global capitalist crisis associated with the wider EU crisis. Literally this is an extremely difficult task (which is also true for every problem of capitalism), the burden of which falls on the working people.

The Memoranda strategy is organised through two EAPs and their numerous interim revisions. The first EAP was launched in March 2010. It issued €110 billion loans (80 billion from EU countries and 30 billion from IMF) with 5.5 per cent interest rate, for the service of the external debt and the needs of the Greek economy with a time horizon (in terms of its loans) until 2013. Then it was assumed that Greece would not be needing support and could borrow directly on the international markets. This means that the loan programme was planned for the three-year period of 2010–13. Moreover, it was planned that BD in 2014 would be less than 3 per cent of GDP. It was also predicted that for the first two years of the programme the economy would shrink by about 6.6 per cent and that cumulative growth of 5.3 per cent would follow in 2012–14 (Table 4.1).

But the forecasts of the first EAP proved to be tragically unrealistic even from its first review. So in July 2011 the second EAP followed which gave €130 billion in loans (from the newly created EFSF and the IMF) at instalments up to 2014 (that is the programme's duration extended to a four-year programme: 2010–14). Again it was envisaged that at the end of 2014 the economy, after a deeper recession, would have returned to growth, BD and the debt would be under control, and the country could return to borrowing from the international markets (Table 4.2).

After the interim reviews these forecasts were also dashed quickly so the troika was forced in February 2012 to accept the 'haircut' of the Greek debt to the private sector (PSI) and to supply an additional small loan to Greece to

Table 4.1 The macroeconomic framework of the first MoU

	2009	*2010*	*2011*	*2012*	*2013*	*2014*
			(Yearly change %)			
Real GDP growth	–2.0	–4.0	–2.6	1.1	2.1	2.1
Contribution of domestic demand	–2.5	–7.5	–5.9	–0.7	0.8	1.0
Net trading contribution	0.7	3.5	3.2	1.7	1.4	1.1
Unemployment	9.5	11.9	14.8	15.3	14.9	14.6
HICP inflation (average)	1.3	1.9	–0.4	1.2	0.7	0.9

Source: Greek Authorities and Services of the European Commission.

Table 4.2 Macroeconomic scenario of the second Greek MoU (main features)

	2009	*2010*	*2011*	*2012*	*2013*	*2014*
Real GDP (growth rate)	–3.2	–3.5	–6.9	–4.7	0.0	2.5
Fiscal domestic demand contribution*	–3.6	–7.0	–10.0	–7.2	–1.4	1.5
Net trade contribution	3.1	3.1	2.8	2.3	1.4	1.2
Employment (growth rate)	–0.7	–1.9	–6.3	–4.8	–0.2	1.6
Unemployment rate (% of labour force)	8.9	11.7	15.9	17.9	17.8	16.7
Compensation of employees, private sector per head	0.6	–0.3	–3.2	–13.0	–3.8	–2.2
Unit labour cost (growth rate)	4.3	–1.6	–1.0	–7.8	–1.3	–1.9
HICP inflation	1.3	4.7	3.1	–0.5	–0.3	0.1
HICP inflation at constant taxes	1.1	1.4	1.2	–1.2	–0.8	0.1
Current account balance (% of GDP)	–14.3	–12.3	–10.3	–6.9	–5.3	–4.6
Net borrowing vis-à-vis RoW (% of GDP)	–13.3	–10.6	–8.3	–4.8	–3.1	–2.4
Net external liabilities (% of GDP)	–112.9	–101.9	–116.0	–88.1	–90.0	–89.6
General government deficit (% of GDP)	–15.8	–10.6	–9.3	–7.3	–4.6	–2.1
General government primary surplus (% of GDP)	–10.6	–5.0	–2.4	–1.0	1.8	4.5
General government debt (% of GDP)	129.3	144.9	165.3	161.4	165.4	162.1

Source: European Commission.

Note

* Excluding change in inventories and net acquisition of valuables.

allow the country to manage the internal impact of the 'haircut'. The new benchmark is 2020 during which it is assumed that the debt/GDP ratio will be 120.5 per cent of GDP and that this will be a sustainable debt level from the point of view of the international markets which they will resume lending to Greece. Of course the magnitude of 120 per cent is of 'political' nature since it is empirically known that a debt is sustainable if it is of the order of 60–80 per cent of GDP. The 120 per cent figure was chosen because it is corresponding to Italy's debt level ratio and the EU by no means wants to involve Italy in a rescue programme as the EU cannot dispose the necessary funds for a 'rescue' of this magnitude.

IV The systematic failures of the Memoranda strategy

As discussed above, the implementation of the Memoranda strategy systematically fails regarding its forecasts and its time schedules. Indicative of this failure is that from May 2010 to May 2013 their forecasts for GDP growth had to be revised downwards eight times. Correspondingly, the troika had to revise downwards seven times its own forecasts for the required fiscal adjustment: the initial fiscal austerity measures were €25 billion while the most recent estimate revises their cumulative amounts upwards to €66 billion. There is a similar failure to forecast the government debt, the ratio of foreign debt to GDP, the level of unemployment, etc. These results are at least unacceptable. What are the reasons behind these failures?

Recently, an official debate ignited after a study by Blanchard and Leigh (2013) that argued that the Greek EAPs underestimated the fiscal multiplier. This meant that the planners of the programme thought the structural changes (i.e. the transformation of the private sector into the driving force of the economy) and the shrinkage of the public sector would not have such a big recessionary effect on the economy as they finally ended up having. Additionally, although this is something not said in the debate, the substitution of the reduced public activities in the economy by private economic activities did not happen. The reason for this is very simple: in a crisis situation (and in the midst of a global economic downturn), where structural changes with an uncertain outcome are implemented, no private capital (with the possible exception of adventurers and economic condottieri!) invests. Of course soon enough another IMF study came to deny Blanchard's results (Ran *et al.* (2013)).

The interesting thing here is that the concept of the fiscal multiplier is a Keynesian concept and Blanchard himself is a New Keynesian. This shows that, despite Keynesian rhetoric to convince for the opposite, IMF programmes are not purely neoliberal but in reality a mixture of neoliberalism and conservative Keynesianism. In fact, both the Washington Consensus and the post-Washington Consensus (after the various crises of the 1990s and the 2007–9 episode) represent such a mix. As a result, this formal debate between on the one hand 'austerity hawks' and on the other hand the advocates of 'smooth management' and flexible compromises is misleading.

However, the problem is much broader than its technical dimension, such as the size of the fiscal multipliers. The fundamental problem of the Memoranda strategy and its programmes is that it must, simultaneously, manage the immediate short-run problems posed by the crisis (such as FD and the external debt) and, at the same time, to change the structure of the economy, amid a global economic downturn. This is an extremely ambitious undertaking. Both the direct economic measures as well as the structural reforms disrupt the entire post-war architecture of Greek capitalism and have deep political and economic consequences.

First, there is a violent change of the internal structure of Greek capital which affects corporate groups, the structure of sectors and sub-sectors of export and import activities, retail trade, etc. This means that powerful economic groups of the past are at risk while new ones are trying to emerge. As this process is very painful and takes time it makes intra-capitalist rivalries and conflicts extremely brutal. Furthermore, the significance of foreign capital and its range of activities in the Greek economy expand at the expense of domestic capital.

Second, the whole range of activities for small and medium enterprises (SMEs) – because they are primarily associated with the old structure of the economy – is shrinking rapidly as the concentration and centralisation of capital proceeds very intensively. This has a huge social impact as middle classes, which historically for Greece were extremely massive for Western standards, contract dramatically. This development is of high significance as it undermines one of the most fundamental class alliances in Greek society that supported the post-war model of Greek capitalism, economically, politically and socially. This 'proletarisation' of the middle classes poses a serious threat to the social and political stability of Greek capitalism. Moreover, it destabilises crucial economic relations and functions of the system that are not adequately replenished by other, newly created functioning economic relations.

Third, the Memoranda strategy must, in literally no time, turn the living standards of a euro-periphery country to that of a Balkan or even a Third World economy. Only with such a rapid devaluation of the value of labour-power and a corresponding increase in the exploitation of labour can profitability recover. It is only in this way (i.e. through a large depreciation of capital and a simultaneous increase in its profitability), that Greek capitalism can emerge from its crisis and resume the process of capital accumulation (i.e. economic growth). But, as already explained, this requires a deep recession of a long duration. In addition, the restart of economic growth does not mean the end of austerity but the opposite. In order to sustain the capital profitability, austerity should be continued and deepened. Otherwise the recovery of capitalist accumulation will stop again and recession will return. Finally, even when the process of capitalist accumulation restarts, this will happen with the Greek capitalism downgraded and weakened within the international capitalist system.

Summarising, the whole project is very ambitious and risky because economic activities and social balances are violently disrupted. This turns the crisis from primarily economic to social and political, which can lead, at any time (even in a phase where normal economic growth might seem restored), to uncontrolled socio-political explosions. Nevertheless, the Greek and EU ruling classes know there is no alternative. The Keynesian view of anti-cyclical policy and mild austerity – because even Keynesian scenarios (at least the serious ones) provide for some kind of austerity – has already been used at the outbreak of the global crisis and shown that it cannot resolve the crisis. The conservative Keynesian policy of stimulating demand (*á la* Krugman) – which is the only one discussed in official circles and social-democratic circles of the Left – does not provide for any kind of income redistribution towards the working classes of the population (such as the progressive Keynesian policies of the post-war period) but mainly anti-recessionary measures which restrict the devalorisation of capital. These can be useful policies only for the first critical phase of a crisis when its outbreak is sudden; because their implementation facilitates the avoidance of a massive and uncontrollable wave of business bankruptcies that may even lead to an immediate collapse of the economy. Nonetheless, after this first critical phase is over, these policies are no longer useful because they cannot resolve the problem of the overaccumulation of capital (in reality they contribute to its deterioration) as they do not help the sufficient increase of the exploitation of labour and wage reduction. Therefore, the path of pro-cyclical economic policies for the capitalist system in crisis is a unique option.

All these problems are clearly visible in the Memoranda strategy as its technical schedules and timetables continue to fall out, despite multiple revisions and adjustments. The Greek politico-economic block that supports the Memoranda (with the government as its key exponent) argues that 2013 will signify the beginning of recovery and the programme will be a 'success story'. However, even a simple examination of the declared policy targets of the Memoranda can prove the futility of any possible expectations about a 'success story'. Specifically, the primary targets of the programme are:

a To make the public debt sustainable: that is to allow Greek capitalism to return to borrowing on the international markets at realistic rates, meaning at interest rates that can be serviced by the Greek economy. This implies that interest rates should roughly correspond to the rate of growth of the economy.
b To transform the Greek economy to an export-oriented economy (i.e. in an economy with systematic trade surpluses) and so support GDP growth rate from revenues from abroad. This will help manage liquidity problems (especially overseas payments) reflected in the CAD.

As regards the first target, it has already been argued that the 122.5 per cent debt/GDP ratio as a threshold for giving access to international capital markets is arbitrarily assumed because of Italy. But even this prospect is highly unrealistic. Moreover, it is known that sustainable long-term debt management is only feasible at ratios of debt/GDP between 60 and 80 per cent; otherwise exorbitant and unrealistic growth rates of GDP are required. This problem of the long-term viability of the Greek debt is something strongly stressed by all the international competitors of the EU and is certainly reflected in the present objections and reservations of the IMF as regards the viability of the Greek debt. More specifically, according to National Account relationships, fiscal stability (and hence the sustainability of sovereign debt, meaning the capacity to manage it), depends on four factors:

a The initial ratio of debt to GDP. In the Greek case, this is historically given (it started from 120 per cent of GDP at the beginning of the crisis), and it has been rising since then (due to the loans taken from troika). Hence, the aim is to limit it close to 120 per cent of GDP by 2022.
b The rate of the primary surplus relative to the GDP. It is the only factor which is under government control. A primary budget surplus means the public sector is no longer running a deficit and instead of burdening the deficit it starts gradually reducing it through repayment. The government insists that from 2013 onwards there will be a primary surplus. This is done by incredible statistical alchemy which is to the full knowledge (and thus consent) of the lenders. As the target is systematically missed, the government is engaged in various small and large 'tricks' such as: covert tax increases (i.e. increases in the withholding of taxes, taxes collected in advance, hidden consumer taxes), crediting the return from European Central Banks of the profits accruing from the holding of Greek Bonds by the Eurosystem, privatisation-sellouts, the internal default on payments due by the state (overdue payments of the state) as also the tremendous reduction of the Public Investments Programme (PIP). It is surprising that with all these, the government, based on figures announced by the Greek Ministry of Finance celebrates over the artificial achievement of a primary surplus. However, as data coming from the Bank of Greece (which are closer to the actual cash position of the public sector) have shown, the budget deficit continues. The major reason for the continuation is not to be found in public employees' wages (which after all have shrunk dramatically) but to the overt and hidden subsidies given to private companies sometimes even with blatant favourism. Finally, it should be noted that even if, for the sake of the argument, we accept the achievement of a primary surplus this does not mean that there is no FD and therefore a funding problem; because the latter also depends on the overall fiscal balance. The last is dramatically burdened from repayments (i.e. the cost of servicing external debt to which one must include the troika loans).
c The real interest rate paid on public lending. This depends on the troika of creditors and for the whole duration of the Memoranda loans the real interest rate is estimated to be 4.5 per cent. The problem is what happens after the end of the loan instalments in 2014. Then the Greek government should be able to borrow at realistic rates (estimated to be between 5 and 5.8 per cent). Nevertheless, we know very well that this is far from certain. Even if the

pledging of some long-term bond (e.g. ten-year) rumoured succeeds, this will come through special machinations and there is no certainty that this will continue in the future.

d The growth rate of GDP. This is the most important magnitude of the four factors, currently very loosely controlled by the government as the basic tools at its disposal for the control of this magnitude have been eliminated (e.g. the PIP). As regards the expectations for a possible European Marshall plan, they don't seem to be based on any realistic facts as both the EU budget and the so-called National Strategic Reference Framework (NSRF) are shrinking. Also the rate of absorption of the previous NSRF is dramatically low because of the limited national funds available, due also to the successive reductions in the national PIP; even after the silent decrease of the Greek national participation to 5 per cent of the costs of the NSRF programme. Meanwhile, the Greek economy, because of the Memoranda, has sunk in a downward recessionary spiral. There are three main consequences from this recessionary spiral. First, there is a cumulative loss of GDP, which exceeds 24 per cent. Second, even if the recession starts its de-escalation, it will last for at least another two years and the loss will probably surpass 27 per cent of GDP. This has negative consequences for the three of the four parameters of debt sustainability and leads to the need for new austerity measures to the extent that the primary surplus is the only parameter that can be affected by the government. Third, it is empirically known that in order for the debt management to be sustainable, the growth rate of the economy should roughly equal the lending rate. It is obvious that because of the recessionary spiral this is not likely to happen.

In addition, the other fundamental target of the strategy of the memorandum which is the strengthening of exports is in serious trouble. Because of the austerity imposed by the EAPs, there was an improvement of the trade balance. The problem is that this improvement comes almost exclusively from the sharp reduction in imports. By contrast the side of exports shows an extremely unstable path. After the outbreak of the crisis in Greece, there was some weak improvement of exports; but there was not a stable improvement. The sudden recovery in exports was the result of the reduction of domestic consumption due to the EAPs which pushed domestic capital to accelerate its efforts to find markets abroad. Nevertheless, the existing structure of the Greek economy coupled with the effect of a global downturn (which is not over yet) limit the possibility of export-led growth; at least for the short run.

A radical improvement in the export performance of the Greek economy requires groundbreaking structural transformations, which even for the 'shock and awe' EAPs' policies require time. As international experience has shown, this is a long and uncertain process and results occur with significant time lags. So the efforts to achieve export growth of the economy in the short run soon run into serious difficulty. For example much of the Greek exports are dependent on imports of intermediate products, thus they are dependent on imports. The case of petroleum products is typical, as the latter form the main bulk of the recent increase in Greek exports. It is indicative that Greek exports excluding oil in the first four months of 2013 grew just 0.8 per cent compared to 2012 levels. Therefore, the decline in imports is associated with the problems of export growth. In addition, there is financial sluggishness (signifying the inability to obtain private loans, export credits, guarantees, etc. because of the crisis at home and abroad) that also hampers the improvement of export performance.

Finally, there is another extremely important obstacle to the success of the export-led growth strategy in Greece. As already argued in the first section of this study, the structural transformation into an export economy is a strategy which is imposed also to the main competitor economies of Greek capitalism (Economakis *et al.* (2013)). Therefore, it is not enough for the Greek economy to become competitive against the other export-oriented economies if it is to be successful and achieve significant growth. This problem becomes obvious if we consider the issue of wage reduction in order to achieve price competitiveness. Labour took the brunt of the export transformation with staggering wage reductions. However, this seems inadequate as direct competitors also reduce their own wages.

Another problem concerning both the competitiveness of Greek capitalism as well as other aspects of the programme is the relatively weak disinflation of the Greek economy.[3] The strategy of export-oriented economy requires the competitive disinflation of the Greek economy. That is the general decline of prices so that the Greek products can become more competitive abroad. However, while wages have been brutally 'deflated' selling prices either are not dropping or are falling very slowly. It is characteristic that only in the third quarter of 2013 appeared a weak reduction in the general price level. This is another failure of the EAPs. The main reason for this inadequate disinflation is that Greek capital (particularly in sectors related to the mass consumption of the population) organises monopolistic and oligopolistic situations in order to keep its profitability or even to increase it by exploiting the reduction of wages which it does not pass on to prices.

Some other factors, on which the designers of the Memoranda strategy also place some hopes, can be described as 'windfall gains'. The most important of these factors is tourism, finding and exploiting natural resources and foreign investment. Foreign investment is also associated to the export-led growth strategy. To the extent that they will arise such 'windfall gains', it is hoped that they will help to alleviate the pressure of debt and facilitate the structural transformation of the economy. Nevertheless these factors are extremely unstable and dubious. Tourism depends crucially on the international political and economic environment. A global recession (or a recession in basic tourist countries) and events like a military adventure in the Mediterranean can very easily exert a negative effect on tourism. Accordingly, even if confirmed the projected natural resources reserves will require some time before production is commenced. Finally, as regards foreign investment the experience of the privatisation programme is very enlightening. As this experience shows under the present circumstances foreign capital is of course ready to enter the country and acquire domestic assets but only at very low prices and therefore with a very limited economic impact as regards the creation of new assets. So the well-documented negative international experience on FDI after 1980 will most likely be repeated in the Greek case.

All of the above-mentioned technical issues suggest that politico-economic constraints pose the most serious problems to the achievement of the targets of the Greek Memoranda. In addition, these limitations are further enhanced by the fact that the resolution of Greek capitalism's crisis is taking place within the deep global recession that followed the crisis of 2007–9, suggesting that the latter is far from being resolved. All these affect the implementation of the Greek programme in multiple ways. Some of these ways come from the fact the Greek crisis is developing within the wider context of a European crisis. As hegemonic European capitalisms are themselves under pressure, they tend to exert excessive force for the implementation of the programme without the needed flexibility on various social and political issues that arise exactly because of the rigid implementation of the programme. Moreover, as they themselves feel the pressure of economic crisis they are not willing to spend excessive amounts of money on Greece (but also for the other PIIGS) even if the economic crisis threatens their own economic 'backyard'. This drives the EAPs' aims beyond realistic limits (especially if we add to this the inter-imperialistic rivalries), which make an already risky game become even more precarious (Mavroudeas (2013): 307).

V Conclusions

The strategy of the Memoranda is not failing due to some errors in its general logic as a policy of devalorisation and capital destruction, but because of its time-horizon and the extent of destruction of productive forces required for its success; something that from a historical point of view we can say is over-ambitious. The time-horizon of fiscal contraction is too short as a result of the pressures of the EU's hegemonic imperialisms, which are in turn under pressure by the general development of the crisis and the intensification of competition with other major centres of capitalism (USA, China and Japan). This creates a further cost of financing the Greek economy that the European 'partners' of the country do not seem willing to bear to the necessary extent. Both the Greek and European capitalisms try to avoid the destruction of capitals to the extent necessary for the sustainable recovery of profitability and the overcome of the crisis. This means that the entire burden of adjustment falls on the working and middle classes, which implies the depreciation of the value of labour-power even to Third World levels and the massive destruction of these middle classes, a key post-war ally of Greek bourgeoisie. It is a transformation that goes far beyond the social and historical boundaries of Greek capitalism and, therefore, creates the objective conditions for a revolutionary process in Greek society.

Notes

1 However, there is the notorious crony part of the economy where Greek capitals exploit their close 'entanglement' with the political elite in order to keep out international capital. The recapitalisation of the Greek banking sector and its final outcome will prove whether Greek capital will succeed in keeping its crony mechanisms till the end.

2 The fact that EU policymakers thought they could avoid the consequences of breaking a global financial bubble (created by the extremely loose monetary and fiscal policies of the US) via the implementation of restrictive monetary and fiscal policies at home shows they did not sufficiently realise that with free capital mobility there can be no immunity for any country to the suffering of the consequences of bubble-bursting.

3 The reduction in the general level of prices would make the EAPs less onerous for employees as they could keep at least a part of their old standard of living. This would accentuate less social discontent against the Memoranda while it would exert a lesser negative effect on domestic demand.

References

Blanchard O. and Leigh D. (2013), 'Growth forecast errors and fiscal multipliers', IMF Working Paper, No. 13/1.

Economakis G., Androulakis G., Gotsoulias K. and Markaki M. (2013), 'FDI in Greece and Bulgaria: a comparative investigation' [in Greek], in Miltiades J. Kipas (ed.), *Economic and Social Development in Eastern Europe and the Balkans*, Athens: Herodotus.

Geld S. and Black A. (2004), 'Globalisation in a middle-income economy: FDI, production and the labour market in South Africa', in Milberg W. (ed.), *Labor and the Globalisation of Production: Causes and Consequences of Industrial Upgrading*, New York: Palgrave Macmillan.

Mavroudeas S. (2013), 'Development and crisis: the turbulent course of Greek capitalism', *International Critical Thought* 3(3).

Mavroudeas S. and Papadatos D. (2007), 'Reform, reform the reforms or simply regression? The "Washington Consensus" and its critics', *Bulletin of Political Economy* 1(1).

Palley I.T. (2011), 'The rise and fall of export-led growth', Levy Economics Institute, Working Paper No. 675.

Ran B., Haonan Q. and Roaf J. (2013), 'Assessing the impact and phasing of multi-year fiscal adjustment: a general framework', IMF Working Paper, No. 13/182.

UNCTAD (1992), *World Investment Report: Transnational Corporations as Engines of Growth*, Geneva: UNCTAD.

UNCTAD (1999), *World Investment Report: Foreign Direct Investment and the Challenge of Development*, Geneva: UNCTAD.

Weeks J. (2007), 'Exports, foreign investment and growth in Latin America: skepticism by way of simulation', in Shaikh A. (ed.), *Globalisation and the Myths of Free Trade: History, Theory, and Empirical Evidence*, London: Routledge.

Weisbrot M. and Montesino J.A. (2012), 'More pain, no gain for Greece: is the Euro worth the costs of pro-cyclical fiscal policy and internal devaluation?' Working Paper, Washington, DC: CERP.

Weisbrot R., Cordero J.A. and Montesino J.A. (2009), 'IMF-supported macroeconomic policies and the world recession: a look at forty-one borrowing countries', Washington, DC: CERP.

5 Financialisation and the Greek case

Stavros Mavroudeas

I Introduction

The financialisation thesis has been immensely popular within Radical and Marxist Political Economy in recent years. It has acquired a prominent position within explanations of the 2007–8 global capitalist crisis. As such it has also a strong presence among explanations of the Greek crisis. As it is argued in the Introduction to this volume, explanations of the Greek crisis can be categorised in three main groups (Mainstream, Radical and Marxist explanations). Essentially financialisation dominates Radical explanations and has also a significant presence within Marxist explanations aside more classical Marxist approaches (such as those presented in this volume). Its dominance within Radical explanations stems from the fact that more traditional Radical underconsumptionist explanations are obviously irrelevant regarding the Greek case. It is unanimously accepted that the pre-crisis period was characterised with an impressive growth of consumption; thus making unsustainable any argument that it was caused by insufficient demand. This is also true for the 2007–8 global crisis and led to a similar subsumption of underconsumptionist approaches by the financialisation approach (as exemplified in the case of the Monthly Review school).

This chapter criticises the financialisation explanations of the Greek crisis as both analytically problematic and empirically unsound. The next section of the chapter presents and criticises the financialisation thesis. In a nutshell, it is argued that financialisation exaggerates the significance of finance in modern capitalism and its claims about a new phase or stage of 'finance-led' or financialised capitalism are unsubstantiated. Essentially financialisation maintains that money capital is not only autonomised from 'productive' capital and dominates the latter but also that it acquires autonomous from the latter channels of profitability. This chapter argues that this analysis is unrealistic and unjustifiably elevates short-term phenomena to structural systemic transformations. Additionally, regarding the 2007–8 crisis, financialisation theories argue that it is not an *à-la-*Marx crisis (i.e. rooted in the sphere of production) but a financial crisis (a crisis of financialised capitalism). Again this argument is rejected.

The third section presents and analyses the main financialisation explanations of the Greek crisis. Three main versions are distinguished. The first version is proposed by Lapavitsas *et al.* (2010a, 2010b) and follows his own understanding of financialisation. His analysis of the Greek crisis emphasises the problem of competitiveness and accepts the Mainstream analysis of Unit Labour Cost (ULC).[1] However, he reaches opposite conclusions by arguing that EMU is a neo-Mercantilist structure that divides the EU in a trade surplus euro-centre and a trade deficit euro-periphery. Consequently, he suggests a Grexit (i.e. Greece's exit from the EMU). Lapavitsas' approach is criticised for neglecting any reference to the production structure of the Greek and the other EMU economies. Thus he is unable to see the existence of relations of 'broad unequal exchange' between the euro-centre and the euro-periphery (see Chapter 8 of this volume). Consequently, his policy suggestions of Grexit are unsustainable unless they are part of a broader strategy of total disengagement from the EU and its Common Market.

The second financialisation explanation of the Greek crisis is offered by Milios and Sotiropoulos (2010). They differ substantially from Lapavitsas' explanation in that they argue that it was not the loss of competitiveness that gave rise to high indebtedness, but the other way around. More specifically, EMU by bringing together countries with very different rates of growth and profitability, gave rise to euro-periphery's high borrowing (by attracting funds from the euro-centre because of its higher profit rates). On this point they replicate uncritically much of the idyllic success story ('strong Greece') presented before the crisis by the Mainstream academic and official circles. Foreign loans boosted euro-periphery's domestic demand, therefore giving rise to increasing inflation and the deterioration of competitiveness. However, Milios and Sotiropoulos reject the significance of the euro-centre–euro-periphery divide as a problematic Dependency theory argument. Then the eruption of the Greek crisis is attributed to the financialisation of modern capitalism that led, through excess leveraging and financial bubbles, to the 2007–8 crisis which they too understand as a mere financial one. This global financial crisis undermined the till then malevolent euro-periphery's CADs. In order to sustain them FDs were augmented and this led to the euro-periphery's collapse. The EMU played only a peripheral role in this affair. Although Milios and Sotiropoulos accept that EMU is not an OCA and that it is a neoliberal project, they reject Grexit and argue for the EU's progressive restructuring. Milios and Sotiropoulos' financialisation explanation is criticised for uncritically accepting the 'strong Greece' argument and for failing to grasp the relations of imperialist exploitation existing within the EU (see Chapter 8 of this volume). Consequently, their analysis of the EMU and the EU is simplistic and leads to the mythical idea of their progressive restructuring.

The third financialisation explanation is offered by Argitis (2012) and follows Minsky's theory. He argues that Greek capitalism is characterised by (a) retarded technological structure, (b) structurally weak competitiveness and (c) cronyism between capital and the state. Argitis argues that this last feature resembles Minsky's notion of the 'strong state' and was based on a strong central bank. Greece's accession to the EMU undermined this 'strong state' and its ability to functionally manage income distribution and inflation–disinflation and led to the financialisation of the economy (i.e. its growth on the basis of financial leverage). This new feature increased its financial instability. Then Argitis argues that the 2007–8 global crisis dismantled Greek capitalism's traumatised structure and led to its crisis. This Minskian explanation of the Greek crisis is criticised for being phenomenological and failing to consider adequately the real economy. Moreover, the Greek crisis was not caused by exorbitant private debts since these were small; particularly comparing to the Western levels. Consequently, it cannot be argued convincingly that the Greek crisis is the outcome of a failed inflation–disinflation process of the private debt.

The final section of this chapter advances a more general critique of the financialisation explanations of the Greek crisis. It argues that financialisation explanations fail to establish convincingly the channels through which financialisation took in its grips the Greek economy. There are two financialisation main conduits: (a) financial leverage in the economy (both the state and the private sector) and (b) over-indebtedness of private households. It is shown that both these channels are rather weak and short-lived in the Greek economy; particularly compared to their Western equivalents. Thus, financialisation cannot be convincingly discovered within the Greek economy. Hence, it has to be introduced from outside: essentially, in the end, all financialisation explanations bring it in through the exogenous impact of the 2007–8 supposedly financial crisis. Concluding, it is argued that this is a weak and unsustainable analysis.

II The financialisation thesis: a dead alley

The financialisation thesis argues that in modern capitalism finance (i.e. the operation of money capital) assumes an increasing primacy in relation to other main fractions of capital (productive and commercial capital).[2]

With regard to Marxism the origins of this thesis go back to Hilferding's (1910 (1981)) seminal work and his implicit notion (never explicitly stated) that modern capitalism has been radically transformed compared to that known and analysed by both Classical Political Economy and Marx: finance has dethroned productive capital from its dominant position. More specifically, according to Hilferding, a new species of capital (finance capital) dominates the total circuit of capital. Finance capital is the fusion of productive with banking capital under the hegemony of the latter. Despite the fact that Hilferding's analysis essentially left aside the Marxian Labour Theory of Value (LTV), it gained immense popularity within Marxist Political Economy during Hilferding's time. It was adopted not only by his ideological friends but also by his foes (e.g. Lenin). Hilferding's thesis was relaunched later by Sweezy (1942). However, neither of them broke from the classical Marxist relationship between surplus-value and interest. The former is extracted by productive capital at the sphere of production and then it is redistributed between profits (accruing to productive capital), interest (accruing to non-productive money capital) and commercial profits (accruing to non-productive commodity capital).

It should be noted that the empirical validity of the *finance capital* concept has been rightfully disputed (see Bond (2010)). It has been shown that the fusion of productive with banking capital is not empirically verified for the greater part of the capitalist world. For example, especially in the Anglo-Saxon countries, the stock exchange rather than the banking system was and still is the main channel for financing private enterprises. Thus the finance capital mix is neither majoritarian nor hegemonic.

The debate regarding the relationship between productive capital and finance took a major turn by the end of the twentieth century. The significant changes that took place during the last decades of the twentieth century influenced crucially the views on the role of the financial system. The long era of 'silent recession' that followed the 1973 global profitability crisis ushered several waves of capitalist restructuring. These succeeded only partially in counterbalancing the falling profitability and the ensuing overaccumulation of capital (see Part II of this volume). This incomplete capitalist recovery led to a flight ahead: the system vigorously employed fictitious capital[3] operations in order to sustain and invigorate capital accumulation. Thus, from the 1990s onwards began what has been termed financialisation. Finance was rapidly deregulated and internationalised. Furthermore, capitals that were overaccumulated in the productive sectors of the economy migrated to the financial sector in order to reap extra-profits through fictitious capital operations. These developments fomented widespread and popular empirical perceptions (or stylised facts)[4] about the rise of a new epoch for capitalism: finance has broken free from the grips of productive capital and established its self-reliant dominance over the whole capitalist system. Several neo-Marxist and Radical Political Economy theories (e.g. the Regulation Approach) started from the 1990s to sketch this conclusion.

In this way the financialisation thesis was constructed in the beginning of the twenty-first century. The term as such was initially coined by the post-Keynesian and neo-Marxist approaches close to and associated with the Monthly Review School. Sweezy (1994) had already alluded to this direction. Moreover, in his last published article, Sweezy (1997) referred to 'the financialization of the capital accumulation process' as one of the three main economic tendencies at the turn of the century (the other two being the growth of monopoly power and stagnation). But more strictly the term was proposed for the first time in a series of papers (by Krippner (2005),[5] Crotty, etc.) included in an influential collective volume edited by Epstein (2005). The rather curious thing is that subsequently the Monthly Review School did not elaborate further the financialisation thesis as it turned its attention to its traditional underconsumptionist views. But the term was energetically adopted by post-Keynesians who developed the concept and its analyses (e.g. Stockhammer (2004)) and sometimes treated the term as their exclusive property (e.g. van Treeck (2008)). Seldom post-Keynesians posit financialisation within a stage of capitalism theory, arguing that a new stage of capitalism has emerged by the end of the twentieth century. This new stage is characterised as 'finance-dominated capitalism' (Hein (2013)) or 'finance-dominated regime of accumulation' (Stockhammer (2009)); the latter adopting the methodology of the Regulation Approach. The post-Keynesian launch of the term 'financialisation' was based on the Keynesian notion of the *rentier*; i.e. an 'unproductive' social stratum collecting various rents which are being subtracted from profits available for productive investment. Thus, the rentier is a drag on capital accumulation.

The incorporation of the term in Marxist analyses followed a bit later. Its Marxist relaunching did not came from the Monthly Review School, which reused it after it was popularised and in order to explain the 2007–8 crisis since pure underconsumptionism had serious explanatory difficulties (e.g. Foster (2010)). The term started being used within Marxist Political Economy either in a 'loose' descriptive manner or in more ambitious analyses.

Bryan *et al.* (2009) maintain that financialisation signifies an epochal change in capitalist economic relations. The processes of securitisation and financial derivatives, both of which have been growing rapidly from the 1980s, involve the commodification of finance, converting monetary processes into commodity relations. This commodification blurs the distinction between money and capital, giving a range of monetary interactions, once considered simply processes of exchange, a new meaning. Thus, they argue that a reconceptualisation of Marxian categories is required and particularly a new understanding of class and class interactions. They controversially suggest that financialisation is transforming labour into a form of capital. Moreover, they maintain that the reproduction of labour is now a source of surplus-value transfer in the form of interest payments and the 'financialization of daily life'.

On the other side, Fine (2009, 2010) uses the notion of financialisation in a different sense from that of the approaches mentioned before. For him it does not constitute a new stage of capitalism and of course finance capital cannot acquire autonomous channels of exploiting the working class (i.e. it will always be dependent upon the extraction of surplus-value by productive capital). Thus, financialisation is simply a special phase of neoliberalism. New forms of operation of money capital and novel institutional arrangements are policies that are used by capital in order to surpass its problems and contradictions.

Lapavitsas (2008), on the other hand, adopted the notion of financialisation from post-Keynesian analyses and attempted to give it an ambitious Marxist pedigree, which at the same time contradicts basic tenets of Marxist analysis. He, essentially, agrees with those analyses that maintain that financialisation represents a new stage of capitalism (or a new 'social order' in more graphical but less theoretically coherent terms). Till now his argument had nothing original compared to its previous definitions. What gave it its special flavour is the thesis that in this new stage of capitalism finance capital[6] not only dominates productive capital but it also exploits directly the working class through usurious activities. In this, he agrees with Bryan *et al.*[7] More specifically, financialisation does not entail solely the expansion of financial leverage and fictitious capital activities. This channel brings profits to finance capital through the redistribution of surplus-value from productive capital towards the former. Financialisation's brand new element – and what gives it its distinct epochal character – is that it acquires another channel of profit: the direct exploitation of workers through the provision of loans.[8] Lapavitsas considers the expansion of credit to workers' households (or rather its contemporary extent) as truly novel. In this case, finance capital acts usuriously and, thus, appropriates part of workers' income. This second financialisation conduit gives finance capital an independent, from productive capital, profit-accruing mechanism. Thus the term 'financial exploitation' was initially coined. After a series of criticisms (e.g. Fine (2009)) for confusing capitalist exploitation with pre-capitalist usurious exploitation it was cosmetically changed to 'financial expropriation'. However, the essential meaning of the term remained the same.

The financialisation thesis is extremely misleading and leads to analytical, empirical and political dead alleys. First, it succumbs to the deceiving impressionism of short-run and conjunctural phenomena and inordinately elevates them to long-run structural changes. Thus, methodologically it follows the same slippery road that the Radical middle-range theories of the 1980s and 1990s trailed (e.g. Regulation Approach, Social Structure of Accumulation; see Mavroudeas (2012), Ch. 3) with dismal results.

Second, it inordinately declares the post-1990s expansion of fictitious capital operations as an almost non-pre-existing phenomenon. Such expansions are not something new or abnormal during capitalist crises. As already mentioned above, capital – when facing prolonged periods of falling profitability and over-accumulation – resorts often to such activities. What gives to the contemporary phenomenon a distinctive – but not structurally significant – character is the fact that capitalism has learned from its previous crises important lessons in the management of crisis. More specifically, it has constructed a sophisticated toolbox of policy mixes in order to at least alleviate or postpone a crisis; but not ultimately to avoid it (as older and newer theories of 'organised capitalism' tend to believe). The last bastion of this financialisation argument is the financial derivatives. It is true that their contemporary expansion constitutes a novel element. But its extent and its significance is disproportionately overemphasised by the financialisation proponents.

Third, especially regarding Lapavitsas' and Bryan's second financialisation conduit, it argues that capitalism has somehow returned to a pre-capitalist stage: the period when capitalist relations were not yet born but the pre-capitalist figures of the merchant and the banker – as they operated within feudalism – prepared the ground for capitalism's birth.[9] The crucial point of the operation of merchants and bankers in feudalism was unequal exchange and usury as a rule in contrast to equivalent exchange as a rule in capitalism. This functioning on the basis of unequal exchange was possible because of the monopolistic and heavily regulated rules of the feudal system. Once however the primary accumulation of capital took place and capitalism was established, the monopolistic feudal rules were abolished and capitalist competition ruled. Then the operation of money capital took its characteristically capitalist modus operandi. The financialisation thesis argues that this is overturned and that there is a return to the pre-capitalist modes of operation. In other words, financialisation theories maintain that interest ceases to be a part of surplus-value and that it acquires an independent existence. Concomitantly, money capital is not only autonomised from productive capital but also dominates the latter. But, if the latter is the ultimate source of wealth, this domination would necessarily entail – and this is actually a conclusion of many financialisation theories – a stifling of productive investment and thus of the accumulation of capital.

Fourth, the financialisation thesis blurs unrealistically class distinctions and class analysis. Both Lapavitsas and Bryan agree that in financialisation thesis finance capital acquires a separate and independent existence from the other fractions of capital. This is not a serious problem in class analysis for the post-Keynesians as they employ the Keynesian notion of the rentier. It is however critically important for the Marxisant versions of the financialisation thesis; and especially Lapavitsas' 'financial expropriation' and Bryan's surplus-value transfer. The usual argument for this structural separation of finance capital from the other fractions of capital is that financial profits exhibit for a considerable time period a markedly superior performance compared to non-financial profits. This is true indeed and comes from the interplay between overaccumulation and fictitious capital operations analysed before. However, it is far from a permanent, structurally inscribed characteristic of the system. As already said this structural division of the capitalist class is not a problem for post-Keynesian approaches; but it is for the Marxisant ones. As Fine (2009) accurately criticises it, if financialisation is a long-term structural transformation then it denotes that finance capital does not participate in the formation of general rate of profit; as Marxist Political Economy argues. What is it that prevents capitals from flowing to the financial sector and thus equalise the profit rates inter-sectorally? The formation of a general rate of profit is not a simple technical process but is also one of the factors supporting the unity of the capitalist class. If an entrepreneurial fraction is independent from the wage-relation (and the extraction of unpaid labour-time) means of profiteering and also structurally inscribed different profit rates from the other entrepreneurial fractions then the necessary conclusion is that it constitutes a *separate class*. This is a very grandiose and indeed far-fetched position. For these reasons it has not been voiced although, if the two financialisation conduits hold, it should. Some points offered by Lapavitsas ultimately amount to the argument that there is no structural separation because productive capital is becoming also financialised. This is rather a fig leaf (turning everything to financialisation and thus blurring any structural and functional distinctiveness) than a convincing argument. The same problem holds for Bryan *et al.*: reconstituting labour as a form of capital logically leads to questioning the definition of the working class. Again this is a profoundly controversial and unsubstantiated proposition.

Fifth, the financialisation thesis leads to unwarranted analytical fuzziness. Foster (2010) offers a typical example. He argues, commenting on Sweezy, that the great enigma of capital in our time is the 'financialisation of accumulation'. This implies questioning what, in his own words, all traditions of economics, to varying degrees, do: separate analytically the role of finance from the 'real economy'. This tendency is evident in almost all financialisation literature. Almost all activities in capitalism are supposed to be financialised. Thus, new concepts and analytical frameworks have to be devised and old ones must be radically reformed (e.g. the definitions of exploitation and the total circuit of capital). These changes, as can be seen in the case of exploitation, do not clarify but rather blur the understanding of capitalism's fundamental economic and social processes. A corollary of the financialisation mania is that almost everything is vested in financial garb. The production sphere disappears from the centre of attention and fundamental categories of Marxist economics (particularly labour-time) are being conceptually vaporised.

Finally, regarding the 2007–8 crisis, financialisation theories argue that it is not an *à-la*-Marx crisis (i.e. rooted in the sphere of production) but a financial crisis (a crisis of financialised capitalism). In this they agree with Mainstream explanations of the crisis. The chapters of Part II of this volume refute this argument. Furthermore, as Tomé (2011) very aptly points out, financialisation ultimately ascribes to a Keynesian *possibility theory of the crisis*. This is a very weak – at least for their Marxisant variants – theory of crisis. Lapavitsas (2014: 37) is again a typical example. He states that the development of financialisation has nothing to do with Marx's TRPF. Moreover, he asserts that falling profitability in capitalist production was never a key factor behind the rise of finance. In the end, in his totalising financialisation theory of finance penetrates and subsumes nearly everything in capitalism while being unaffected by any other process. This is a strange theory: on the one hand claiming Marxist credentials and on the other dropping out the main Marxist analytical concept (the profit motive and the profit rate). A corollary of financialisation theories' neglect of the profit rate and their infatuation with finance is that they actually pay little or no attention at all to the sphere of production.

III Financialisation explanations of the Greek crisis

Three main financialisation explanations of the Greek crisis have been proposed. The first one is by Lapavitsas and of course it ascribes to his notion of financialisation. The second one is expressed by Milios and Sotiropoulos and has affinities with the post-Keynesian notion of financialisation. Notwithstanding, their main differences have to do with two more practical issues: (a) the North–South divide in the EU and (b) whether Greece should remain in or leave the EMU. The third explanation is proposed by Argitis and follows the Minskian perspective.

Financial expropriation

Lapavitsas *et al.* (2010a, 2010b) argue that the Greek is a debt crisis. In this they agree with the Mainstream explanations. But they add that it 'is symptomatic of a wider malaise' (p. 11). Its roots lay in (a) financialised capitalism and (b) the EMU. Financialised capitalism caused the 2007–8 crisis which is not an *à-la*-Marx crisis but simply a financial crisis. The profit rate played no role in it.

Lapavitsas argues (without any attempt to substantiate it) that 'it did not fall but also it did not grow'. The crisis was caused by the uncontrolled financial leverage that created unsustainable bubbles. The crisis affected the fragile foundations of the EMU. The latter is not an OCA which, according to Lapavitsas *et al.*, is based on three pillars:

a the independent ECB which commands monetary policy;
b fiscal stringency;
c relentless pressure on wages in order to ensure competitiveness.

Lapavitsas accurately points out that ECB's monetary policy follows the needs of the euro-core countries (the North). However, the third point agrees with the Mainstream arguments on competitiveness. He uncritically agrees with the problematic Mainstream ULC theory and considers only cost competitiveness. As it has been shown in Chapter 1 of this volume (a) the ULC theory is problematic and (b) even within this theory the Mainstream arguments about Greek relative wage increases deteriorating competitiveness are erroneous. Thus, Lapavitsas *et al.* argue that the North (and especially Germany) was more competent in pressurising wages and thus acquired a permanent competitive advantage against the South (the euro-periphery). This is simply the Mainstream argument in reverse: it is not the lazy Southerners but the over-prudent Northerners that caused the problem. The result for Greece (and the euro-periphery in general) was a falling competitiveness that aggravated CADs. The Eurozone was polarised in a North with trade surpluses and a South with debts: the North gave loans to the South in order for the latter to buy its products.

At the same time the Greek economy enjoyed a significant growth that was fuelled by its internal financialisation and the external loans. For Lapavitsas *et al.* the internal financialisation took place through both its channels. Financial and non-financial firms were financialised and workers' and middle-classes' households dived deep in debt. Regarding profitability, Lapavitsas and Kouvelakis (2012: 16) make a forceful but unsubstantiated argument:

> In Greece the crisis did not took the form of falling profitability – on the contrary Greek capital's profitability remained very high till 2007–8, on the one hand because labour's exploitation in the private sector intensified during the recent years and on the other hand because capital benefited from tax exemptions.

The eruption of the 2007–8 crisis disrupted this structure as international financial markets questioned the creditworthiness of the South's sovereign debts. Thus, the Eurozone's crisis began. According to Lapavitsas *et al.* the EMU transmitted the world crisis in Europe because of the imbalances that were latent within it. Again, till this point Lapavitsas *et al.*'s analysis does not differ essentially from post-Keynesian analyses which accept a North–South divide argument.[10] The only significant difference is the addition of the mechanism of 'financial expropriation'.

The final conclusion of Lapavitsas' analysis is that the EMU cannot be rectified; although he sometimes refers to a European Marshall scheme as a solution only to immediately discard it as implausible. Thus, he concludes that the only solution for Greece (and indeed the rest of the euro-periphery) is to exit the EMU. Regarding the relationship with the EU after the Grexit he remains agnostic.

Lapavitsas' explanation suffers from the general weaknesses of his financialisation thesis analysed above. Additionally, it is marred by several country-specific problems. First, he neglects any reference to the production structure of the Greek and the other EMU economies (e.g. differences in technological structure, productivity, productive specialisations). Thus he has a limited and problematic understanding of the relations of imperialist exploitation existing between the euro-centre and the euro-periphery. In particular, because of his neglect of the production sphere, he is unable to see the existence of 'broad' unequal exchange between the North and the South.[11] Additionally, as already said, he accepts uncritically the Mainstream ULC theory. Hence, he ends up with a wrong diagnosis for the problem of Greek competitiveness.

Second, because of his financialisation perspective he cannot grasp properly the internal developments in the Greek economy and particularly in its productive structure. Consequently, his explanation hovers around the TDH dilemma: he argues that it is CAD that ultimately deteriorated FD and led to the debt crisis. As it has been argued in Chapter 1 of this volume, this is a misleading perspective that fails to recognise the 'deep' structural causes of the Greek crisis.

Third, his analysis suffers also on the financialisation plain. The Greek financial system was significantly less leveraged than the Western ones. Additionally, Greek workers' private debts are a relatively new phenomenon (they began with the introduction of the euro) and they are smaller than their Western counterparts. Therefore, financialisation cannot be discovered in Greece and has to be imported from outside. Thus, in Lapavitsas' analysis financialisation as the cause of the crisis has to be imported from outside: it was the eruption of the 2007–8 purportedly crisis of financialised capitalism that affected the public external debt.

Finally, Lapavitsas' policy suggestions are disputable. They revolve around the Grexit proposal. He argues that the recovery of a sovereign monetary policy together with the devaluation of the new (national) currency and the restructuring of the foreign debt will suffice to lead to a radical overhauling of the Greek economy that will make it viable and robust. The pivot of his policy proposals is the Grexit. This strategy cannot answer convincingly the 'deep' structural problems of the Greek economy. Its failure lies exactly in its financialisation perspective and its inability to grasp problems stemming from the sphere of production. For example, the damage inflicted on Greek competitiveness by the EMU was lesser than that caused by the Common Market (see Chapter 8 of this volume). Moreover, Greece cannot engineer a radical productive restructuring of its economy on the basis of extensive and far-reaching active industrial policies by leaving the EMU but staying within the EU since these are prohibited. Last, if the Greek crisis is simply a debt crisis then it may be solved not by exiting the EMU but by reforming it towards a full OCA (i.e. by unifying it fiscally and politically). If the crisis is something more profound and has to do with the sphere of production and relations of unequal exchange stemming from it then exiting the EMU and remaining within the Common Market won't suffice. A full exit from the EU is required. But Lapavitsas shies away from this conclusion.

Class struggle and financialisation

Milios and Sotiropoulos' (2010) financialisation explanation of the Greek crisis follows a different path from that of Lapavitsas *et al.* They argue that it was not the loss of competitiveness that gave rise to high indebtedness, but the other way around. More specifically, EMU by bringing together countries with very different rates of growth and profitability, gave rise to high levels of borrowing for the euro-periphery countries. That is because euro-periphery countries have higher profit rates which attract capital from the euro-core. This trend was augmented since Greece's accession to the EMU because the latter facilitated euro-periphery countries to borrow at low interest rates. Foreign loans boosted the euro-periphery's domestic demand, therefore giving rise to increasing inflation and the deterioration of competitiveness. Milios and Sotiropoulos essentially reject the North–South divide as an expression of the problematic dependency theory. For them foreign loans were not a trick to rob Greece but a perfectly natural phenomenon that helped boost growth. On this point they totally agree with the Mainstream arguments in Greece that the EU helped Greece's development. Indeed, the pre-crisis mainstream argument was that CADs were good imbalances because euro-periphery countries with relatively low levels of real GDP per capita were catching up with richer North European economies. Greater growth opportunities and expectations of faster productivity growth justified elevated levels of fixed investment relative to the pool of domestic savings, hence the need for a current account deficit. The reality is different (see Chapter 8 of this volume). Sustained CADs were by and large not used to finance investment in productive assets but to buy euro-core's imported goods. Thus, Greece's productive structure instead of being developed was actually eroded. Because of this error Milios and Sotiropoulos implicitly accept the Mainstream convergence thesis.

Till this point Milios and Sotiropoulos' analysis replicates much of the idyllic success story ('the strong Greece') presented before the crisis by the Mainstream academic and official circles. Then they add the financialisation thesis. They argue that modern capitalism is financialised; leading to extreme leveraging and financial bubbles. When the 2007–8 crisis (which they too understand as a mere financial one) erupted the till then malevolent euro-periphery's CADs were blown apart. In order to sustain them FDs were augmented and this led to the euro-periphery's collapse.

The EMU played only a peripheral role in this affair. Milios and Sotiropoulos accept that EMU is not an OCA. Furthermore, they argue that EMU is a neoliberal project that imposes austerity on the workers by exposing them to international competition. The eruption of the crisis exposed EMU's weaknesses (because of the asymmetric shocks that cannot be contained within it) and its class nature (as the great burden of the EAPs was placed on the working people). However, the solution is not the Grexit since this would imply a return to an era of nationalist economic and political conflicts. Instead, they propose a policy supporting workers' rights, the overturn of the current neoliberal hegemony in the EU through pan-European alliances and the progressive restructuring of the EMU and the EU.

This second financialisation explanation is marred also by the general deficiencies of its perspective. It should be noted, however, that financialisation as such plays a limited role in this approach compared to the previous one. Milios and Sotiropoulos' explanation has also country-specific problems. First, it uncritically accepts the Mainstream argument about the benevolent and growth-friendly nature of flows of foreign capital. In reality (as it is shown in Chapter 8 of this volume) these flows actually eroded the cohesion of the Greek productive structure and the Greek economy as a whole and created grave structural problems. More specifically, as several empirical studies show, the portion of these capital inflows that went into FDI was insignificant. The greater part of them went into financing imports from the euro-centre.

Second, as already mentioned, Milios and Sotiropoulos uncritically accept the bogus 'strong Greece' argument that was preached by official and Mainstream circles. This argument, after the eruption of the Greek crisis, has fallen into justified disrepute.

Third, because of their preoccupation against Dependency theory, they totally disregard the existence of relations of imperialist exploitation between the euro-centre and the euro-periphery. Thus, they fail to appreciate adequately the catastrophic impact on the Greek economy that the accession to the European Common Market and the EMU had.

Finally, their policy proposals are unconvincing. The belief that there can be a pan-European social movement disputing the neoliberal character of the EMU and the EU and substituting it by a 'social Europe' fails to understand the deep national differences and the economic and political 'uneven development' existing in the EU area.

Minskian disinflation

The third financialisation explanation of the Greek crisis follows the Minskian tradition. It has been voiced by studies by researchers associated with the Levy Institute that supports this tradition. These analyses are close to the post-Keynesian perspective and the Monthly Review School but have also their own distinctive character.[12] Argitis (2012) offers a representative version of the Minskian explanation. He argues that Greek capitalism till today has been characterised by three main features:

a A traditionally weak and obsolete technological structure.

b A structurally weak competitiveness causing chronic and significant CADs. The former is caused by the weak and obsolete technological structure. The latter are caused because Greek capitalism is obliged to import a significant portion of either intermediate or final goods.
c There is strong and extensive cronyism between private businesses and the state. According to Argitis (2012) this system resembles the Minskian notion of the 'strong state'. A fundamental function of the state (together with its central bank) is to manage the inflation–disinflation process by using the FD as a means for supporting capitalist profitability. In this sense, the FD was used more as a redistributive tool than as an anti-cyclical one.

The basic cause of the Greek crisis is the fact that Greece's accession in the EMU undermined this traditional modus operandi of the Greek capitalism without being able to substitute it with another equally functional. Specifically, after entering in the EMU, the 'strong state' remained but lost its central bank (as the Bank of Greece followed the ECB directives). Consequently, debt management became dysfunctional and the financialisation of the economy became necessary. That is, the economy's growth was based on financial leverage. This increased the inherent instability of the capitalist economy. The last point is akin to Minsky's (1992) Financial Instability Hypothesis.

The Financial Instability Hypothesis argues that capitalism is a system inherently prone to financial crises. The latter are caused by the system's endogenous tendency to create speculative 'bubbles' in its financial markets. The mechanism of creation of these 'bubbles' is the following. In periods of economic euphoria and boom firms' cash flows increase more than what is required in order to finance their existing debts. This foments a speculative euphoria that leads to excessive new debt that rapidly surpasses the firm's ability to finance it. This process operates cumulatively and rapidly gets out of control leading to a financial crisis. Banks and lenders react spasmodically and restrict lending more than required. When this process is generalised and extended it affects not only insolvent borrowers but also solvent and viable ones. Consequently, because of monetary contraction the whole economy is thrown into crisis.

The specific mechanism that causes, in periods of economic euphoria, the initial overestimation is the following. According to Minsky the key lies in the accumulation of debt in the private sector. He distinguishes three groups of problematic borrowers that contribute to the accumulation of unviable debt. In the first group belong the hedge borrowers that service their debts with payments coming from their current cash flows from their investments. The second group comprises the speculative borrowers that can service their debts but they are obliged regularly to roll over them by extensions or by getting new loans so as to remain solvent. Finally, Ponzi borrowers that constitute the third group borrow expecting that the increase of the value of their assets would be sufficient enough to service their debts because the cash flows from their investments do not suffice. Consequently, Ponzi borrowers can stay afloat only if there is a constant increase of the value of their assets. The problem, for Minsky, is that when their numbers increase too much then, at some point in time, doubts are going to creep regarding the continuous increase of the value of assets. When these doubts are generalised they will lead to a jam and the increase of the value of assets will stop. This will affect immediately speculative borrowers as they will be unable to service their debts through rolling over them. The fall of speculative borrowers will carry with it the hedge borrowers also as the financial system is overestimating the problem and panicking.

Of course Minsky believed that the inherent instability of the capitalist economy can be stabilised through the appropriate economic policy. This is a mix of fiscal and monetary interventions that will support capitalists' nominal profits. Fiscal policy must buttress effective demand through the increase of public expenditure. This process can continue ad infinitum without adverse effects (inflation, excessive deficits) because of the monopolist structure of the economy. In this way it can support both profits and employment. At the same time, monetary policy must be expansionary as central bank's main function is that of 'lender of last resort'.

Minskians maintain that the 2007–8 crisis is exactly such a 'Minskian moment'. It was caused by the neoliberal policy that dethroned the stabilising Keynesian policy suggested by Minsky and, thus, increased financial instability. Following this perspective, Argitis (2012) maintains that the 2007–8 crisis derailed the already unstable (because of EMU) traditional model of Greek capitalism. The 'strong state' without a strong central bank could not manage and control the debt inflation–disinflation process. Hence, the Greek crisis erupted.

The Minskian theory, despite several intriguing intuitions, has been rightfully criticised as (a) phenomenological and (b) focusing excessively on the financial system and neglecting the real economy. It has also been criticised for having a very narrow and poor understanding of the role of fiscal and monetary policy. This poor understanding derives from Minsky's problematic conception about the role and the character of the monopoly in the capitalist system.

Regarding the explanation of the Greek crisis, the Minskian perspective has serious problems. The more significant one is that the Greek crisis was not caused by excessive private debt. On the contrary, the latter is small compared to that of the more developed Western economies. Thus, it cannot be convincingly argued that the Greek problem was born from the inflation–disinflation circle of private debt. It is probably for this reason that Argitis (2012) leaves aside the typical mechanism of the Financial Instability Hypothesis and sticks more to Minsky's (1986) previous work on the significance of the political and institutional framework for securing the stabilisation of the financial system.

His central argument is that the disintegration of the 'strong state – strong central bank' pair led to the inability of functionally managing the inflation–disinflation process. The obvious justification for this is that the ECB's monetary policy followed the needs and prerogatives of the euro-centre and neglected those of the euro-periphery. Hence, monetary policy did not supported adequately and competently the needs of Greek capital accumulation. However, this explanation is disputable. First, it unwarrantedly assumes that the policy of the Bank of Greece was always accommodative during the post-dictatorship period;

this is not true. Furthermore, it implies that, after the accession to the EMU and the relinquishing to it of the monetary and exchange rate policy, the government and the Bank of Greece lost any ability to exert discreet policies. This is also not true. Finally, if Argitis' (2012) explanation is correct, then the obvious policy suggestion is Grexit. But this is something that he rejects.

Another significant problem of the Minskian explanations is the argument that Greek capitalism is traditionally characterised by a technologically obsolete productive structure. Indeed, this reference to the productive structure is one of the positive elements of Minskian explanations. But the sole reference does not suffice. It has to be analysed as such. The easy answer is recourse to a Dependency theory argument (i.e. dependent Greek capitalism); but this argument has well-known analytical and empirical deficiencies. Moreover, it begs the question why this problematic productive structure survived. This requires a more explicit and comprehensive study of the productive structure of the Greek economy that it is missing. This deficiency is a product of the very focus of the Minskian analysis: it is extensively preoccupied with the financial sphere and pays no attention to the sphere of production.

IV Channels of financialisation in Greece?

Financialisation explanations of the Greek crisis usually pay little attention in substantiating their argument. Financialisation is used as a trendy leitmotiv without establishing whether it does exist and, if so, to what extent in the Greek economy. This requires establishing the channels or conduits of financialisation. There is an expanding literature internationally on this issue which however has not concluded common results and indices.

Palley (2007) has proposed his own understanding of the fundamental conduits of financialisation. He discerns three main channels:

1 Changes in the structure and operation of the economy. These concern mainly changes in the structure and operation of financial markets (deregulation, derivatives, etc.).
2 Changes in corporate behaviour. These include managers' disciplining by the prospect of takeover and ouster if they fail to maximise profits, stock option pay, encouragement of debt finance, etc.
3 Changes in economic policy. These include an increasing array of policy measures (e.g. 'small government', labour market flexibility).

Palley's channels are too broad and ambitious. There can be a simpler but equally accurate categorisation of financialisation's main conduits.

First, there must be a consideration of the degree of financialisation of the private and the public sector of the economy. This encompasses the extent of leverage of the banking sector, the indebtedness of the private sector, the indebtedness of non-financial corporations, the proliferation of the so-called new financial products (e.g. derivatives, collateralised debt obligations) etc. This is the area on which most research is being currently conducted. It is also the area with the greater ambiguities and controversies regarding the appropriate measures and indices.

Second, there must be a consideration of the extent of the indebtedness of private households. This is important particularly for those financialisation theories (like those of Lapavitsas and Bryan) that maintain that finance capital has acquired an independent (from productive capital) channel of exploiting the workers. This channel, as has been analysed in the previous sections, is through usury.

We can have an initial broad picture of the conditions in the Greek economy regarding these two areas. The results are not encouraging for the financialisation hypothesis.

Table 5.1 from IMF's (2012) *Global Financial Stability Report* shows the degree of indebtedness and leverage for a group of selected advanced economies. Those are European economies (Greece and the rest of the PIGS included) plus US, Japan and Canada. It is impressive that in almost all relevant measures Greece has the lowest or one of the lowest grades. For example, its bank leverage is low. Equally, the non-financial corporates' gross debt is low. Moreover, private households' debt is also low.

The low degree of financialisation of both the public and the private sector in Greece is well known and is explained by several reasons. For example, traditionally the Greek stock exchange had a small size and a minimal impact on the Greek economy. It was boosted aggressively by government policies in the late 1990s and had a meteoric growth for some years. Then it crashed in 1999 never to recover again till today. Moreover, public and social entities (like the pension funds) had no or limited exposure to the stock exchange and to the 'new financial products'.

There is an area that gives slightly better results for the financialisation hypothesis in Greece. As is shown in Chapter 6 of this volume, in 1985 and 1990 the profit rates of the financial and the non-financial sectors were very close. But after 1990 the financial sector's profit rate increased rapidly and remained at very high levels till one year before the beginning of the crisis. The ratio of the mass of profits of the financial sector to total profits increases from 2 per cent in 1985 and 1990 to 9 per cent by 2000 and stays at this percentage in 2008. However, this performance is lacklustre compared to the high two-digit ratios that exist in Western economies.

Figure 5.1 gives the picture of households' debt from another angle and for the whole period 2005–10. As it can be seen household debt as a percentage of gross disposable income begins from the lowest level compared to those of the other European economies. It starts increasing rapidly, from 2004 and onwards, after the accession to the EMU. It is true that its rate of growth is impressive. However, despite this high growth rate, it remains lower than all other European economies (except for Spain and only for 2010).[13] Moreover, it is logically accepted – and this was also the case in other crisis-ridden economies – that the degree of households' indebtedness is severely reduced as the crisis deepens. The main reason behind this trend is that the Greek banking sector has sternly limited the extension of credit in general. Particularly regarding private households, banks limited credit provision

Table 5.1 Indebtedness and leverage in selected advanced economies

	United States	*Japan*	*United Kingdom*	*Canada*	*Euro area*	*Belgium*	*France*	*Germany*	*Greece*	*Ireland*	*Italy*	*Portugal*	*Spain*
Household debt													
Gross	88	74	99	89	70	53	63	59	70	120	51	105	89
Net	–226	–236	–178	–151	–123	–191	–127	–118	–48	–68	–171	–124	–72
Nonfinancial corporate debt													
Gross	87	143	118	53	138	178	152	63	75	244	112	154	196
Debt divided by equity	82	184	86	45	106	53	85	107	264	84	139	144	149
Financial institutions													
Gross debt	87	177	742	60	142	124	169	97	33	691	97	63	109
Leverage of domestic banks	11	23	22	18	23	27	24	28	15	24	19	16	20
Bank claims on public sector	7	79	8	18	n.a.	23	17	21	29	27	32	19	26

Source: IMF (2012).

not only because of their own problems but also because households' incomes and wealth have been curtailed severely by the recession and the austerity policies; thus their creditworthiness has been reduced radically.

Households' low indebtedness has to do with the post-war structure of the Greek economy. The middle strata but also increasing segments of the peasants and the workers had the ability and the culture to save. This changed with the introduction of the euro when the savings ratio collapsed and households started amassing debts. The covert increase of inflation in mass consumption goods erodes the purchasing power of all these classes (see Chapter 1 of this volume). Hence, in order to sustain their living standards and induced by the relatively low interest rates and the aggressive marketing policies of the banking sector households turned to debt. This explains the very high growth rate of households' debt. However, this process was always significantly weaker than in Western economies and was terminated abruptly by the eruption of the Greek crisis.

Concluding, empirical facts do not verify the hypothesis that Greece is a financialised economy. This is reflected in the inability of all financialisation explanations of the Greek crisis to establish a convincing internal financialisation mechanism as the cause of the crisis. This failure leads them to make a logical leap: financialisation is introduced from abroad. All financialisation analyses agree that the 2007–8 global crisis was a financial one caused by financialisation (at least in the developed capitalist economies). This financialisation crisis affects the Greek economy not through internal mechanisms but by making impossible the Greek state's borrowing in international markets. This is obviously a very weak and problematic argument.

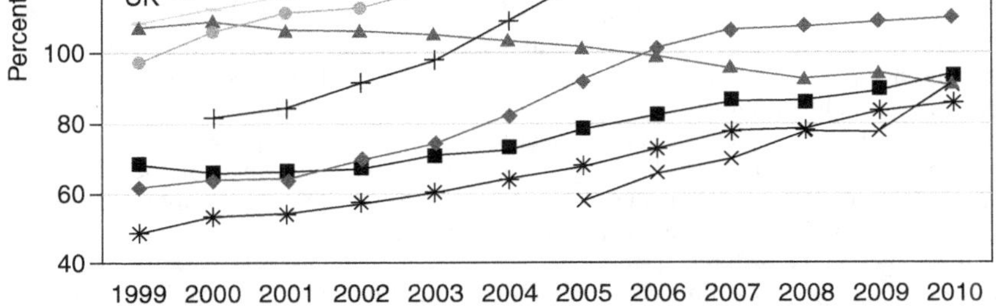

Figure 5.1 Household debt as a percentage of gross disposable income (source: OECD).

Note

Debt of households and non-profit institutions serving households, as a percentage of gross disposable income.

Notes

1 For a detailed analysis of the ULC theory see Chapter 1 of this volume.

2 In fact the notion of 'financialisation' covers a wide range of phenomena: the deregulation of the financial sector and international capital flows, the proliferation of new financial instruments, the shift to market-based financial systems, the emergence of institutional investors as major players on financial markets, etc. However, the definition adopted in this chapter focuses on the politico-economic (and thus macroeconomic) aspect of the term.

3 Marx proposed the term *fictitious capital* in ch. 29 of Vol. III of *Capital*. It is expressed by capital assets (shares, bonds, etc.) whose market value varies according to their expected returns in the future. In recent decades financial derivatives have acquired also increased significance in fictitious capital operations. Fictitious capital differs from productive capital; that is the capital invested in means of production and labour-power. It differs also from typical money capital that represents money funds that are being accumulated or exchanged. Essentially fictitious capital represents accumulated claims and legal titles on future wealth production. Consequently, they practically represent an uncertain bet on value (and surplus-value) that might be produced in the future but which it is being discounted in the present. Its operation is closely related to the expansion of joint stock companies, the negotiation of their assets in the stock exchange and the expansion of credit money (that facilitates to a great extent their transactions and their valuations). Periods of economic euphoria usually foment high expectations about the future and, thus, can engineer waves of robust economic growth (as they influence positively investment). These expectations-led booms have usually the tendency to overshoot; that is to create increasingly over-optimistic future expectations. But as soon as the 'real economy' cannot keep pace with those expectations (i.e. investment does not lead to the expected profits) then its growth starts faltering. In other words, the so-called 'fundamentals' recall to reality the unsustainable growth engineered by fictitious capital. The busts that follow have also the tendency to overshoot; but this time to the downside. These usually lead to the eruption of an economic crisis because of the burst of the so-called 'bubble'.

4 Empirical perceptions or stylised facts are pre-theoretical (i.e. non-verified theoretically and empirically) representations of reality which, however, are considered by their proponents self-proven and undisputable. They, usually, reflect some novel and highly impressive elements which, however, need not be either majoritarian and/or permanent. Theories based on stylised facts are usually middle-range theories with limited explanatory ability (for a more detailed analysis see Mavroudeas (2012), Ch. 3).

5 It should be noted that Krippner (2005: 199) had reservations about whether financialisation constitutes a new phase of capitalism; arguing that it neither necessarily 'represents an entirely novel phase of capitalism … [nor] do these data allow us to draw any conclusions regarding the *permanency* of the trends documented here'.

6 The term 'finance capital' is not identical to Hilferding's concept (which denotes the fusion of 'productive' with banking capital under the dominance of the latter). It refers to capital operating in the financial system (i.e. money and capital markets). Furthermore, it focuses more on capital engaged in the stock exchange rather than on that engaged in the banking system.

7 His initial definition of 'financial exploitation' might be considered equivalent to that of Bryan *et al.* (i.e. denoting the transfer of extra surplus-value from labour to capital). Its subsequent reformulation as 'financial expropriation' tries to side-step the controversial point about surplus-value extracted in the sphere of exchange.

8 Lapavitsas (2009) argues that 'the financial sector has become capable of extracting profit directly out of wages and salaries, a process called financial expropriation'.

9 Lapavitsas (2009) tries to side-step this by arguing:

> These practices are reminiscent of the age-old tradition of usury, but they are now performed by the formal financial system. Financial expropriation represents the generalization on a social scale of financial practices that resemble trucking and usury. It has allowed financial institutions to boost their profits independently of surplus-value generated by the indifferently performing sphere of production. This is a constituent element of financialisation.

10 For example Stockhammer (2011: 90) argues that 'this was not primarily a Greek crisis but a Euro system crisis'. 'The Euro has long been a political project based on dubious economics' (Stockhammer (2011): 94). EMU is part of the global neoliberal pattern which began with the deregulation of finance (the neoliberal mode of regulation) and gave rise to a finance-dominated accumulation regime. This polarised the EU into two groups: a Northern one following export-led growth and a Southern one following credit-led growth (Stockhammer (2011): 86).

11 Emmanouel (1972) distinguishes two categories of unequal exchange in international trade:

a 'Broad' unequal exchange: it is derived from differences in the OCC, i.e. a more developed country (with higher OCC) exploits a less developed country (with lower OCC).

b 'Narrow' unequal exchange: it is derived from differences in the wage rate and the rate of exploitation, i.e. a higher wages country is exploiting a lower wages country.

12 H. Minsky's theory about the inherent instability of capitalist economies was greatly influenced by the views of M. Kalecki and J. Robinson on the issue of the monopoly. It has also a significant analytical proximity with the theory of monopoly capitalism proposed by P. Baran and P. Sweezy.

13 The low indebtedness of Greek households has been consistently verified by several empirical studies. For example, Mitrakos *et al.* (2008) – using the total Greek household bank borrowing to GDP ratio, as calculated on the basis of data submitted by banks to the Bank of Greece – observe that it was and continues to be substantially lower than the corresponding ratio for the euro area.

References

Argitis G. (2012), *Bankruptcy and Economic Crisis: Failure and Breakdown of the Greek Model of Capitalism*, Athens: Alexandreia [in Greek].

Bond P. (2010), 'A century since Hilferding's 'Finanz Kapital': again, apparently, a banker's world?' *Links International Journal of Socialist Renewal*, 19 November.

Bryan D., Martin R. and Rafferty M. (2009), 'Financialization and Marx: giving labor and capital a financial makeover', *Review of Radical Political Economics* 41(4).

Emmanouel A. (1972), *Unequal Exchange: A Study of the Imperialism of Trade*, New York and London: Monthly Review Press.

Epstein G. ed. (2005), *Financialization and the World Economy*, London: Edward Elgar.

Fine B. (2009), 'Financialisation, the value of labour power, the degree of separation, and exploitation by banking', SOAS Research Students, Summer Seminar Series.

Fine B. (2010), 'Locating financialization', *Historical Materialism* 18(2).

Foster J.B. (2010), 'The financialization of accumulation', *Monthly Review* 62(5).

Hein E., Truger A. and van Treeck T. (2011), 'The European financial and economic crisis: alternative solutions from a (post-)Keynesian perspective', IMK Working Paper 9.

Hein E. (2013), 'Finance-dominated capitalism and redistribution of income: a Kaleckian perspective', Levy Institute Working Paper No. 746.

Hilferding R. (1910 (1981)), *Finance Capital*, London: Routledge & Kegan Paul.

IMF (2012), *Global Financial Stability Report: The Quest for Lasting Stability*, Washington, DC: IMF.

Krippner G. (2005), 'The financialization of the American economy', *Socio-economic Review* 3(2).

Lapavitsas, C. (2008), 'Financialised capitalism: direct exploitation and periodic bubbles', SOAS.

Lapavitsas C. (2009), 'Financialised capitalism: crisis and financial expropriation', *Historical Materialism* 17(2).

Lapavitsas C. (2014), *Profiting Without Producing: How Finance Exploits Us All*, London: Verso.

Lapavitsas C. and Kouvelakis S. (2012), *Crisis and Left Vent*, Athens: Livanis [in Greek].

Lapavitsas C., Kaltenbrunner A., Lambrinidis G., Lindo D., Meadway J., Michell J., Painceira J.P., Pires E., Powell J., Stenfors A. and Teles N. (2010b), 'The Eurozone between austerity and default', *Research on Money and Finance*, Occasional Report.

Lapavitsas C., Kaltenbrunner A., Lindo D., Michell J., Painceira J.P., Pires E., Powell J., Stenfors A. and Teles N. (2010a), 'Eurozone in crisis: beggar thyself and thy neighbour', *Research on Money and Finance*, Occasional Report.

Mavroudeas S. (2012), *The Limits of Regulation: A Critical Analysis of Capitalist Development*, Cheltenham: Edward Elgar.

Milios J. and Sotiropoulos D. (2010), 'Crisis of Greece or crisis of the euro? A view from the European periphery', *Journal of Balkan and Near Eastern Studies* 12(3).

Minsky H. (1986), *Stabilizing an Unstable Economy*, New York: McGraw-Hill.

Minsky H. (1992), 'The financial instability hypothesis', Levy Economics Institute, Working Paper No. 74.

Mitrakos T., Simigiannis G. and Tzamourani P. (2008), 'Indebtedness of Greek households: evidence from a survey', *Economic Bulletin* 25, Bank of Greece.

Palley T. (2007), 'Financialization: what it is and why it matters', PERI Working Paper series no. 153.

Stockhammer E. (2004), 'Financialization and the slowdown of accumulation', *Cambridge Journal of Economics* 28.

Stockhammer E. (2009), 'The finance-dominated accumulation regime, income distribution and the present crisis', Department of Economics Working Paper Series, 127. Inst. Für Volkswirtschaftstheorie und -politik, WU Vienna University of Economics and Business, Vienna.

Stockhammer E. (2011), 'Peripheral Europe's debt and German wages: the role of wage policy in the Euro area', *International Journal of Public Policy* 7(1–3).

Sweezy P. (1942), *The Theory of Capitalist Development*, New York and London: Monthly Review.

Sweezy P. (1994), 'The triumph of financial capital', *Monthly Review* 46(2).

Sweezy P. (1997), 'More (or less) on globalization', *Monthly Review* 49(4).

Tomé J.P. (2011), 'Financialization as a theory of crisis in a historical perspective: nothing new under the sun', PERI, Working Paper Series 262.

Van Treeck T. (2008), 'The political economy debate on "financialization": a macroeconomic perspective', IMK Working Paper 01/2008.

Part II

Marxist explanations of the Greek crisis

6 The law of the falling rate of profit in the post-war Greek economy

Thanasis Maniatis and Costas Passas

I Introduction

The Greek economic crisis continues for the sixth year and currently it has reached proportions similar to those of the Great Depression for the advanced capitalist countries of that era. Being such a great crisis, it has naturally generated interest in explaining its origins and nature. In trying to analyse the deeper causes of the Greek crisis, it is obvious that an important part has to be played by the analysis of the world economic crisis which started two years earlier and its exact nature and causes are still debated, especially within the Radical and Marxist Political Economy tradition.

The world economic crisis of the late 1960s and 1970s was debated fiercely in the Radical and Marxist literature. A common element in all approaches was the crucial role played by the behaviour of the profit rate. All alternate approaches pointed to the significant fall in capitalist profitability since the late 1960s and tried to locate its ultimate cause. Thus, three major crisis theories emerged with the first emphasising technical change and the increase in unproductive labour relative to productive labour,[1] the second blaming insufficient effective demand as the cause behind the fall in the capacity utilisation rate and the actual profit rate,[2] while the third approach ascribed the fall in the profit rate to the squeeze in the mass of profits caused by excessive increases in the real wage and/or a slowdown for technical or social reasons in productivity growth.[3]

The situation is quite different regarding the explanations offered for the current crisis. Many authors within the radical and Marxist literature do not consider explicitly the behaviour of the profit rate arguing instead that (a) the crisis was not caused by a fall in profitability, and (b) that imbalances or disproportionalities stemming from the neoliberal arrangements or financialisation in particular, were responsible for the rupture in the workings of the world economy.

Thus, the world economic crisis of 2008 and the subsequent stagnation have been presented and discussed in the literature mostly as either a financial or a sovereign debt crisis. When the analysis does not remain at the financial sphere and tries to trace and locate the roots of crisis in the 'real' economy, then it is usually restricted at the level of distribution and circulation of value and income, neglecting the production sphere. Radical economists and some Marxists blame the institutional arrangements and the consequent results of neoliberalism, but not necessarily capitalism as such, as responsible for the current crisis. Even before the onset of the crisis, emphasis was placed on increased personal income inequality and the bias against wages in favour of profits in the pattern of class or functional income distribution charactersing the neoliberal institutional structure or neoliberal Social Structure of Accumulation (Crotty (2000), Kotz (2003, 2008)). Thus, this structure is considered as a failure now, as it is threatened seriously by an underconsumption crisis. Even though it is not explicitly stated[4] by the proponents of this thesis, this evaluation of the current crisis is the direct opposite to that proposed for the demise of the first post-war 'regulated' Social Structure of Accumulation during the 'golden age' period, which according to this view was ended by a profit squeeze crisis caused by the opposite reason, the increased strength of labour.[5] It has to be remembered though that the neoliberal paradigm was conceived and established as a response to the structural crisis of the 1960s to 1970s. Thus, the current crisis could be regarded and called a 'crisis of neoliberalism' only in the sense of the failure of this social form to repair, to solve the previous structural crisis of accumulation, the stagflation crisis of the 1970s.

In this respect, the current crisis is viewed as the culmination of contradictions inherent in the neoliberal regime (see Kotz (2008, 2009), Harvey (2010)). The latter is considered as that institutional structure which followed the 'Keynesian compromise' of the post-war 'golden age', constructed on the basis of the following constituent pillars: (a) increased class and personal income inequality, (b) financialisation of the economy and (c) accumulation of all types of private and public debt and creation of asset bubbles, to compensate for stagnant or falling wages. It is evident from the above that this view bears many similarities with an underconsumption theory of crisis, since if one goes beyond the financial sphere, the fundamental cause of the crisis appears to be the inequality of income and the consequent low purchasing power of workers.[6]

A somewhat different position is that adopted by Dumenil and Levy (2010) who deny that either insufficient profitability of capital or underconsumption were the fundamental cause of the crisis. In their view this is a crisis of overconsumption by the upper classes and underaccumulation of productive capital (due to the financialisation of the economy) which produced trade deficits and excessive indebtedness for the US economy. This combination formed an 'unsustainable trajectory' which resulted into a crisis of neoliberalism as a distinct social order in the form of the crisis of 'financial hegemony' within the US economy, and then affected the entire world capitalist economy. Dumenil and Levy place emphasis on the successful efforts of capitalists to obtain higher incomes and not on the unsuccessful efforts by capital and governments to increase substantially the profit rate.[7]

On the contrary, for other Marxists this crisis is not just a conjunctural event or the outcome of some policy mistakes[8] but rather a product of the normal function of the capitalist economy, which suffers from time to time from a breakdown of the accumulation process. Crisis is a periodic result of the inherent mechanisms at work in a capitalist economy and not the result of wrong policies or exogenous shocks. Even though the characteristics of the neoliberal institutional structure described above are not disputed, a more thorough analysis of the behaviour of a capitalist economy requires their integration into an analytical scheme which includes the explicit consideration of the profit rate and its constituent elements as well as its evolution over time. Thus, leaving the sphere of circulation and distribution and looking at the deeper structure of the economy, a different picture emerges from the examination of the trajectory of profitability and the capital accumulation process. As Shaikh (2011) notes, despite radically changing institutions, regulations and balance of class forces, structural systemic crises reappear every 30–40 years. Those recurrent accumulation crises are inevitable as long as the system depends on the profit motive. The recurrence of crises has to be traced to a more or less common cause. Accumulation is based on profitability, and the determinants of profitability have to be examined carefully in order to understand its different phases. Thus, a number of Marxist authors, despite their differences, Shaikh (2011), Laibman (2010), Brenner (1998, 2006), Moseley (1991, 1997), Bakir and Campbell (2009), Roberts (2013) base their discussion of the entire post-war period and therefore the neoliberal period, and the explanation of the current crisis, on the detailed examination of the profit rate. In their work, a crucial common element emerges, which is the incomplete recovery of the profit rate during the neoliberal years and the fact that even this partial recovery was caused mainly by the attack on wages and labour costs in general.

This chapter claims that inadequate profitability remains the fundamental cause of crisis regardless of the proximate cause each time and this holds true for the case of the Greek economy as well. Here, we present the main points of an account of the crisis based on the Marxian law of the tendency of the rate of profit to fall (Marx (1894): ch. 15). Estimating the main Marxian variables for the entire post-war period (1958–2011) provides us with a powerful way to trace and discuss the trajectory of the post-war Greek economy based on the trend and fluctuations of the profitability of capital and the capital accumulation process in the second section. However, the main contribution of this chapter is the econometric investigation of the long-run trend of the rate of profit (in both its Marxian and net versions) in the third section in the Greek economy following the method introduced recently by Basu and Manolakos (2012) for the US economy. The fourth section presents our conclusions.

II Empirical results: the law of the falling rate of profit in the post-war Greek economy

As we noted above the most crucial element distinguishing Marxist and other heterodox analyses has to do with the importance of the profit rate[9] in the examination of the structure of the capitalist economy in the Marxist tradition.

Figures 6.1–6.7 depict the story of the post-war Greek economic development in terms of the main Marxian ratios, the Marxian rate of profit ($R=S/K$), the net rate of profit ($r=\Pi/K$), the rate of surplus-value ($s=S/V$) and the value and organic (materialised) composition of capital ($k=K/V$ and $k'=K/Y$), where S=surplus-value, V=variable capital, K=private capital stock, Π=profits or property type income, $U=S-\Pi$=wages of unproductive labour and other costs, Y=net output.

The general Marxian profit rate, *R*, which is the one for which Marx derives the law of the falling rate of profit in Volume III of *Capital*, and the net profit rate, *r*, which depends like *R* on the composition of capital and the rate of surplus-value but also on the ratio of the unproductive labour and unproductive costs in general to productive labour, are depicted in Figure 6.1. The net profit rate fell more than the general Marxian profit rate becoming one-third of the latter at the end of the period from one-half at the beginning of the period because unproductive labour and other expenses in the non-production sectors like circulation costs rose significantly in relation to productive labour as shown in Figure 6.2.

The movement of the net profit rate (*r*) delineates three broad phases of profitability, capital accumulation and growth in the Greek economy before the onset of the current crisis. The first one which lasts from the beginning of the period examined here until about the middle of the decade of the 1970s could be characterised as the 'golden age' of Greek capitalism in similar fashion with what happened in advanced capitalist countries after the end of the Second World War as they embarked on the process of reconstruction of their economies from the war. High profit rates, despite a slightly falling trend, caused high rates of capital accumulation and output growth, significant increases in productivity growth and increases in the real wage for productive workers and workers in general even with a rising rate of surplus-value.

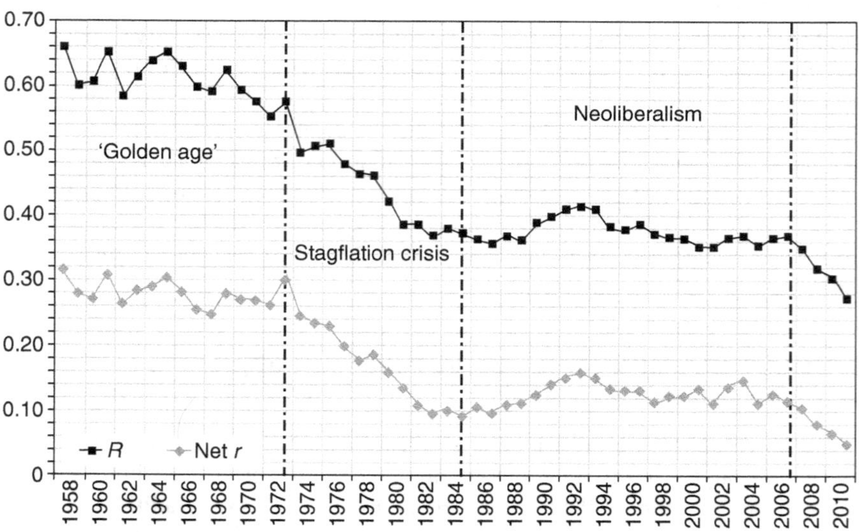

Figure 6.1 The general Marxian (*R*) and the net profit rate (*r*), 1958–2011.

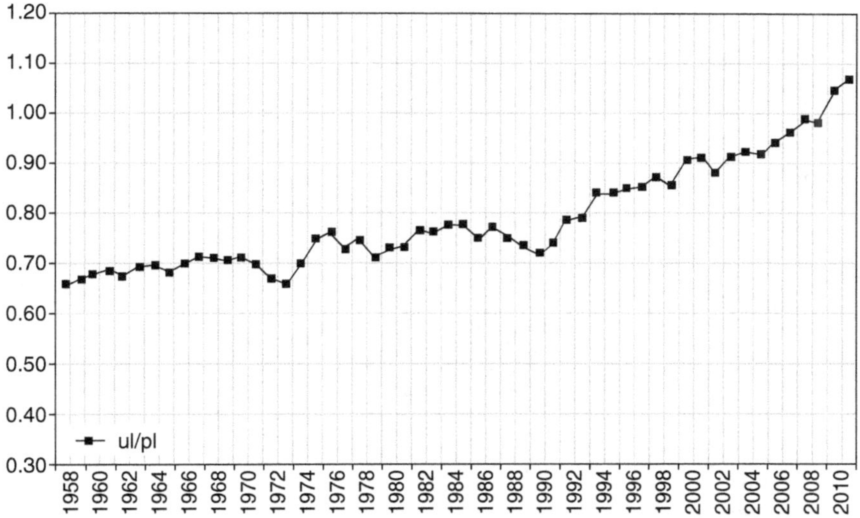

Figure 6.2 Ratio of unproductive labour to productive labour compensation.

The second period is that of the stagflation crisis, starting in Greece around 1973–4, half a decade later than that in advanced capitalist economies, which started in the late 1960s. The significant increase in the organic composition of capital (OCC) during the 'golden age', which is the sufficient condition for the profit rate to fall, combined with the fall in the rate of surplus-value and the profit share as a result of successful labour struggles after the fall of the military dictatorship, produced a sharp fall in profitability, which lasted until 1985, affecting negatively investment, output growth, productivity, real wage growth and employment.

After 1986 and especially after 1991, the third phase, that of neoliberalism, started in the Greek economy again with a time lag of about half to one decade after this policy regime was established in advanced capitalist economies. It is well known that the neoliberal experience meant the dramatic increase in the exploitation of workers in an effort to raise sufficiently the profit rate. However, this recovery in profitability did not and could not happen without a massive devaluation or destruction of the capital stock and a significant decrease of unproductive labour and other similar costs. This event was not politically feasible since it would imply a rise in the unemployment rate at levels similar to those of the Great Depression. Hence, the neoliberal period brought about just a partial recovery of the profit rate, which resulted in a low rate of investment activity, output growth and most importantly slow productivity growth. Even the anaemic output growth of the period, especially after 1995 (when the initial boost of neoliberal arrangements and institutions had lost steam and profitability during the neoliberal period had peaked) was achieved through the indirect

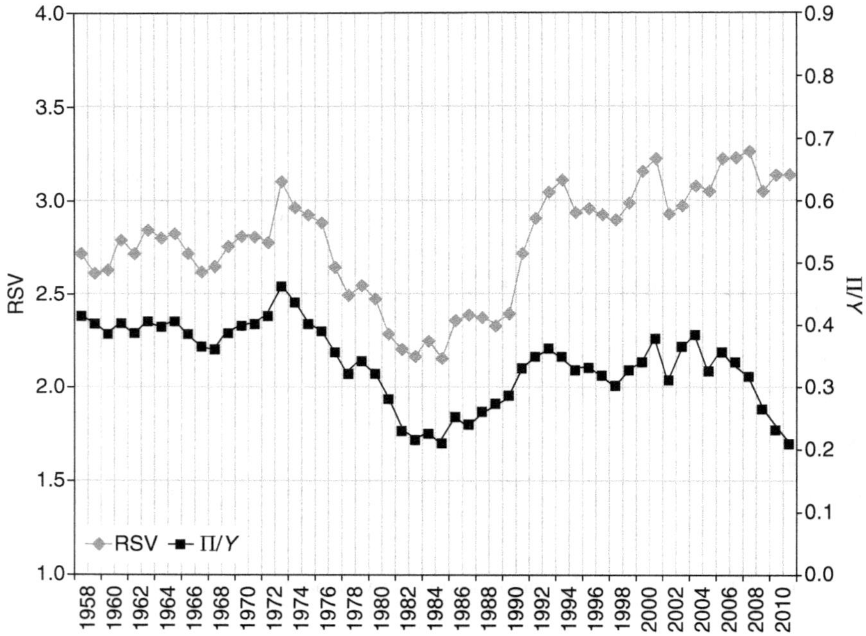

Figure 6.3 The rate of surplus-value (S/V) and the profit share (Π/Y).

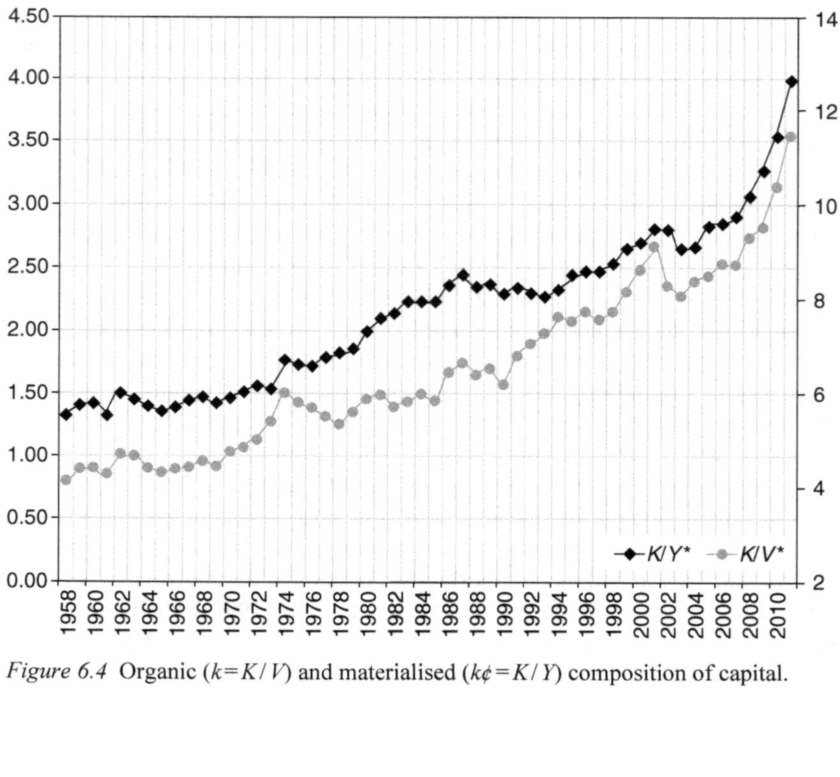

Figure 6.4 Organic ($k=K/V$) and materialised ($k\cent=K/Y$) composition of capital.

impact of the financial bubbles created mostly by the expansive monetary policy of that period. Those bubbles, first in the stock exchange market and then in the real estate sector, created significant 'wealth effects' for the households stimulating consumption demand, the only source of growth during the neoliberal period as low profitability held investment activity down. Figure 6.7 provides one way to look at the 'financialisation' process of the Greek economy during

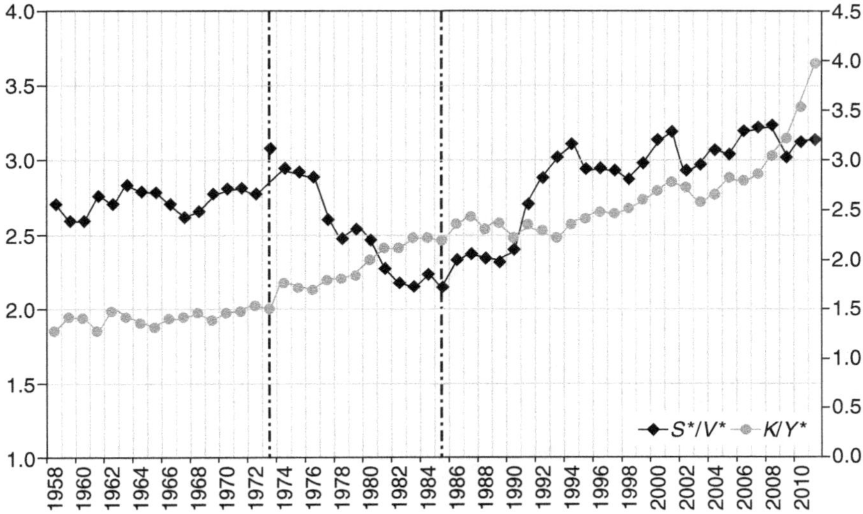

Figure 6.5 The rate of surplus-value (S/V) and the capital–output (K/Y) ratio.

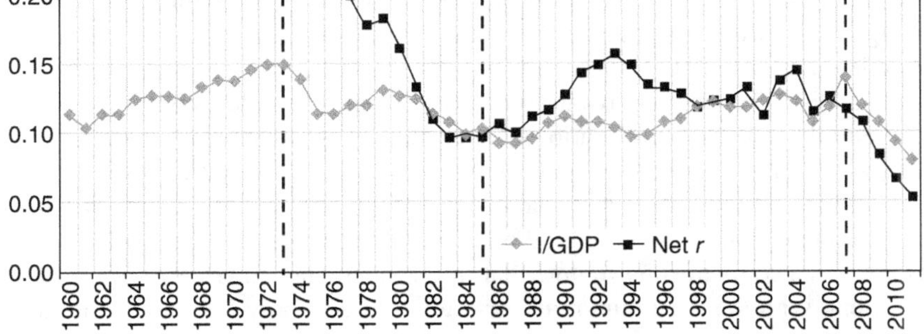

Figure 6.6 The net profit rate and the investment share (I/GDP), 1960–2011.

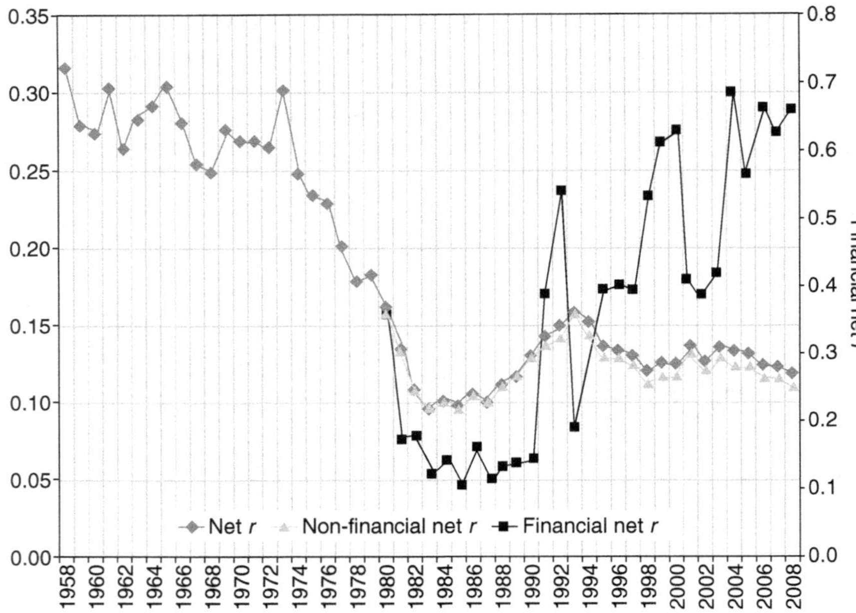

Figure 6.7 The net profit rate, financial and non-financial profit rate, 1958–2008.

the neoliberal period. While in 1985 and in 1990 the profit rate in the non-financial sector was very close to the profit rate of the financial sector, the latter exploded after 1990 remaining at very high levels one year before the beginning of the crisis. The mass of profits of the financial sector was 2 per cent of total profits in 1985 and 1990 and it had increased to 9 per cent of total profits by 2000 staying at this percentage in 2008. This compares to a rise in the share of financial profits in total profits from 10 per cent in 1980, to 40 per cent in 2007 for the US economy.[10] It is generally accepted that the process of financialisation in Greece had not gone as far as in the major advanced capitalist economies. However, when all the bubbles burst the crisis erupted in 2009, this time with a time lag of just two years compared to what had happened in the major capitalist economies. Fundamentally, the crisis resurfaced due to the low profitability of capital, a result of capital overaccumulation since the value composition of capital and the capital–output ratio, K/Y, or materialised composition of capital as Shaikh (1987) and Shaikh and Tonak (1994) call this ratio, were rising throughout the period. This rise could not be offset any more by increases in the rate of surplus-value or by some kind of expansive fiscal or monetary policy.

Here, it is also interesting to note that in recent studies, in Greece, Brazil and Spain along with the very important for the world economy US case,[11] the rate of profit appears to have the same behaviour over the entire post-war period. First, a ‘golden age’ period of high profit rates, strong capital accumulation and output growth, then a crisis period of sharply falling profit rates and, after that, a partial recovery of profitability during the neoliberal era with almost all alternating phases of profitability, determined by the movement of the capital–output ratio or the materialised composition of capital.[12] Thus, it could be argued that both the stagflation crisis of the 1970s and the current crisis are results and expressions of the workings of the law of the falling rate of profit due to the rising organic composition of capital despite a generally rising rate of surplus-value. We try to supplement the empirical support of this argument using statistical evidence for the long-run behaviour of the rate of profit in the next section.

III Is there a tendency for the profit rate to fall in the Greek economy?

Following the recent contribution by Basu and Manolakos (2012) which examines econometrically the existence of a negative trend in the net profit rate in the US economy for the 1948–2007 period, we replicate and extend their approach for the case of the Greek economy.

The law of the falling rate of profit has been interpreted in many different ways, and the exact meaning of the 'law' and the role of 'counteracting tendencies' is still debated in the Marxist literature. According to Shaikh (1983), one way to look at the distinction between laws and tendencies in the context of the Marxian law of the falling profit rate is to regard it as the operation of conflicting but hierarchically equal tendencies where some time one of them prevails (i.e. capitalisation of production) producing a fall in the profit rate and in other instances the opposite tendency (i.e. increases in the rate of exploitation or cheapening of the elements of constant capital) becomes dominant, leaving the profit rate unaffected or even raising it. In other words, according to this view the outcome (a rise or a fall in the profit rate) is conjuncturally determined even during a long enough time span. A different view is that where there is a hierarchy of tendencies and the dominant tendency (i.e. capitalisation of production) always prevails (over a certain long enough period of time) upon the subordinate tendencies, providing the whole process the status of a law.[13] According to this latter view Marx presents the law as a dominant tendency stemming from capitalist competition and technical change which in the long run overcomes all counteracting tendencies. The dominant tendency emerges mainly from the process of continuous technical change, the weapon used by capitalists in conducting their competitive battle in pursuit of the largest possible amount of surplus-value and profit. This tendency results necessarily in a systematic increase of the value and the organic or materialised composition of capital, that is, in an increase of the capital–net output ratio. The latter is the sufficient condition for the rate of profit to exhibit a falling trend sooner or later no matter how fast the rate of surplus-value is rising. In fact, most if not all of the counteracting tendencies that Marx discusses in Volume III of *Capital* have to do with developments which slow down the increase in the composition of capital or increase the rate of exploitation for workers. Thus, we think it is more in the spirit of

Marx's law to test for a negative trend in the rate of profit despite the presence of the countervailing tendencies, instead of controlling for their effect as Basu and Manolakos (2012) do. In this way, Basu and Manolakos test for the weak version of the law of the falling rate of profit in the US economy, and they do so only for the net rate of profit.[14] Below, we test for the existence of a negative trend in both the net and the general Marxian profit rates in the post-war Greek economy. We do so, first, by controlling for the effect of counteracting tendencies as Basu and Manolakos do, and then by simply investigating whether the observed profit rates exhibit a falling trend or not in a statistical sense from the beginning of the post-war period until the onset of the most recent crisis.

a Identifying the time series properties of the profit rate

The Box-Jenkins methodology is a three stage iterative procedure that aims at the identification, estimation and diagnostic checking of a model. In the identification phase, after deciding on the degree of differencing that the series needs in order to be transformed to stationarity, a number of techniques such as the use of autocorrelation and partial autocorrelation functions are employed in order to derive a subclass of parsimonious ARIMA models. The selection of a benchmark model from this short list is made possible through the minimisation of information criteria, such as the Akaike (AIK), Schwarz (SBIC) and the Hanna Quinn (HQIC). Next, during the estimation phase inferences are made on the parameters identified on the previous phase. The final phase consists of a number of diagnostics on the residuals that test the model for a number of problems, such as autocorrelation and heteroscedasticity.

Beginning with the identification phase for the net profit rate (r) we observe that since the Ljung Box Q statistic of the series in levels rejects the null of no autocorrelation up to 20 lags we conclude that the series is not a white noise process. The fact that autocorrelation function (ACF) exhibits a long decay, and that the partial autocorrelation function (PACF) is positive and significant at lag 1, indicates evidence of non-stationarity in the series. Results from the Augmented Dickey–Fuller (ADF) and the Phillips–Perron (PP) unit root tests support the assumption that the net profit rate has a unit root. The existence of a unit root in the net profit rate series indicates that the series has a stochastic time trend.

Turning to the series in first differences, the Ljung Box test indicates that we cannot reject the null and thus that the series is a white noise process. The ADF and PP unit root tests on the first differenced series indicate that the series is stationary. Finally the ACF and the PACF indicate a negative but insignificant autocorrelation and partial autocorrelation in the 1st lag, therefore suggesting that the series possibly has a moving average component. Moreover the 4th and 15th partial autocorrelations are positive and large, although again insignificant, as is the 11th partial autocorrelation that is negative. Summarising, initial inspection of the net profit rate series indicates that a probable model is an ARIMA(0,1,0).

Therefore, since a number of autocorrelations and partial autocorrelations are big enough to give rise to suspicions in order to avoid misspecification we

Table 6.1a ARIMA estimates: AIC

AR/MA	*0.000000*	*1.000000*	*2.000000*	*3.000000*
0.000000	−5.359912	−5.320212	−5.278499	−5.242455
1.000000	−5.316454	−5.302825	−5.262115	−5.346252
2.000000	−5.277254	−5.261816	−5.218658	−5.216770
3.000000	−5.250711	−5.229242	−5.592384	−5.675719

Table 6.1b ARIMA estimates: SBIC

AR/MA	*0.000000*	*1.000000*	*2.000000*	*3.000000*
0.000000	−5.320159	−5.240706	−5.159240	−5.083442
1.000000	−5.236948	−5.183566	−5.103103	−5.147487
2.000000	−5.157995	−5.102804	−5.019893	−4.978251
3.000000	−5.090118	−5.028501	−5.351495	−5.394683

Table 6.1c ARIMA estimates: HQIC

AR/MA	*0.000000*	*1.000000*	*2.000000*	*3.000000*
0.000000	−5.345020	−5.290429	−5.233824	−5.182888
1.000000	−5.286670	−5.258150	−5.202548	−5.271793
2.000000	−5.232579	−5.202249	−5.144199	−5.127419
3.000000	−5.190844	−5.154408	−5.502583	−5.570952

proceed to compare the information criteria on the differenced series when including up to three autoregressive (AR) and three moving average (MA) terms. Results indicate that all three information criteria are minimised when the model in an ARIMA(3,1,3). Looking at roots of the model we find that there is a unit root in the MA part and therefore we have to reduce the MA parts by one. Performing this procedure iteratively we arrive at an ARIMA(0,1,0) validating our initial assumption. Therefore, we conclude that the net profit rate series can be described as a unit root process, thus as a process with a stochastic trend.

Proceeding to the identification of the Marxian profit rate, *R*, we conclude again that the series in levels is not a white noise process as the Ljung Box Q statistic rejects the null of no autocorrelation. Inspecting the ACF and the PACF we find evidence of non-stationarity as indicated by a long decay in the ACF and a significant and positive PACF in lag 1. Testing for a unit root in the series with the ADF and the PP test validates our assumption. Therefore we again conclude that the series is non-stationary, namely, that the series in levels has a stochastic time trend.

Inspecting the series in first differences reveals almost identical results with those of the net profit rate, with the ACF and PACF being negative and insignificant in the first lag and with the PACF being large, but insignificant, at the 4th

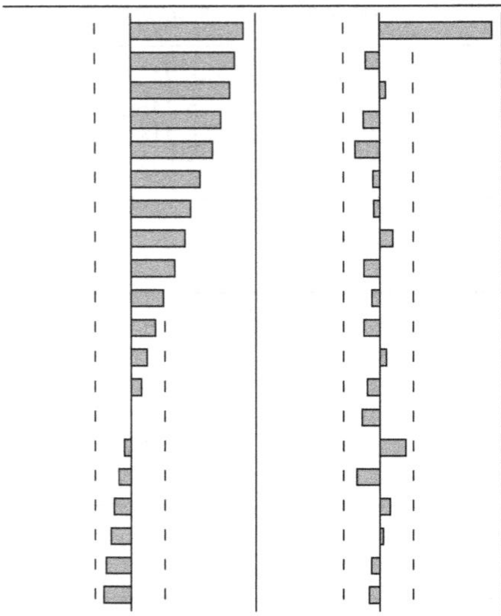

	AC	PAC	Q-stat	Prob.
1	0.942	0.942	46.244	0.000
2	0.877	−0.099	87.152	0.000
3	0.822	0.065	123.89	0.000
4	0.757	−0.138	155.72	0.000
5	0.672	−0.193	181.40	0.000
6	0.588	−0.046	201.49	0.000
7	0.510	−0.020	216.94	0.000
8	0.445	0.104	229.02	0.000
0	0.370	−0.130	237.57	0.000
10	0.292	−0.051	243.05	0.000
11	0.215	−0.111	246.10	0.000
12	0.152	0.042	247.65	0.000
13	0.084	−0.082	248.14	0.000
14	0.006	−0.118	248.14	0.000
15	−0.041	0.232	248.26	0.000
16	−0.089	−0.187	248.87	0.000
17	−0.135	0.083	250.29	0.000
18	−0.167	0.012	252.55	0.000
19	−0.195	−0.062	255.72	0.000
20	−0.227	−0.079	260.16	0.000

Figure 6.8 Sample ACF and PACF for the Greek net profit rate, 1960–2008, level.

and 15th lag (positive) and the 11th lag (negative). Moreover both the ADF and the PP tests indicate that the series in first differences is stationary. Thus, our preferred model seems to be an ARIMA(0,1,0). Using up to three autoregressive and moving average terms and performing the same iterative procedure used for the identification of the net profit rate, utilising the information criteria validates our assumption of an ARIMA(0,1,0).

Summarising, both the Marxian profit rate and the net profit rate were found to be integrated of order one [I(1)], thus, they are processes with a stochastic trend.

b Data

The profit rate data used in this inquiry were presented above and focus on the total private economy, although for the econometric investigation hereon we use data for the period 1960–2008 since this is the time span for which a number of variables used in this investigation are complete and reliable. All data are of annual frequency.

As dependent variables we use both the net and the Marxian profit rates (net r and R respectively) and as independent variables we use the same four variables that Basu and Manolakos use as proxies of the 'counteracting factors' of the fall in the profit rate. Those include a measure of the intensity of exploitation (z_1), measured as the cyclical component of Marxian labour productivity, a measure of the deviation of wages from labour-power (z_2), measured as the cyclical

Table 6.2a ARIMA estimates: AIC

AR/MA	*0.000000*	*1.000000*	*2.000000*	*3.000000*
0.000000	–4.885486	–4.846204	–4.802757	–4.774652
1.000000	–4.865662	–4.836628	–4.796115	–4.759241
2.000000	–4.825636	–4.806076	–4.775042	–5.084060
3.000000	–4.813520	–4.840893	–5.105999	–4.856102

Table 6.2b ARIMA estimates: SBIC

AR/MA	*0.000000*	*1.000000*	*2.000000*	*3.000000*
0.000000	–4.845733	–4.766698	–4.683498	–4.615639
1.000000	–4.786156	–4.717369	–4.637103	–4.560476
2.000000	–4.706377	–4.647064	–4.576276	–4.845542
3.000000	–4.652928	–4.640153	–4.865110	–4.575065

Table 6.2c ARIMA estimates: HQIC

AR/MA	*0.000000*	*1.000000*	*2.000000*	*3.000000*
0.000000	–4.870595	–4.816421	–4.758082	–4.715085
1.000000	–4.835879	–4.791953	–4.736548	–4.684783
2.000000	–4.780961	–4.746509	–4.700583	–4.994710
3.000000	–4.753653	–4.766059	–5.016198	–4.751334

component of real hourly wages, a measure of overpopulation (z_3), proxied by the unemployment rate, and a measure of the relative price of capital (z_4), measured as the ratio of the fixed capital formation deflator to the consumer price index (CPI). Following Basu and Manolakos (2012) cyclical components are derived after applying a Hodric–Prescott filter to the relevant series with a smoothing parameter of 6.2.

Marxian labour productivity is calculated as the ratio of Marxian net value added, deflated by the GDP deflator, to productive labour hours worked. Commonly productivity is understood as being influenced mainly by two components: (a) technological growth, mainly via a growing capital labour ratio, that increases output per worker in the long run, and (b) variations in the intensity of exploitation which emerge independently of technological growth. Assuming that technological growth affects the production process in the long run, whereas changes in workplace conditions have only a temporary effect, by decomposing labour productivity into a trend and a cycle component we aim at isolating the latter. Therefore, by construction, we expect that the cyclical component of labour productivity to be pro-cyclical. Figure 6.10, a scatter plot between the cyclical component of labour productivity and the growth rate of real GDP, confirms our expectation that the measure for the intensity of exploitation is pro-cyclical.

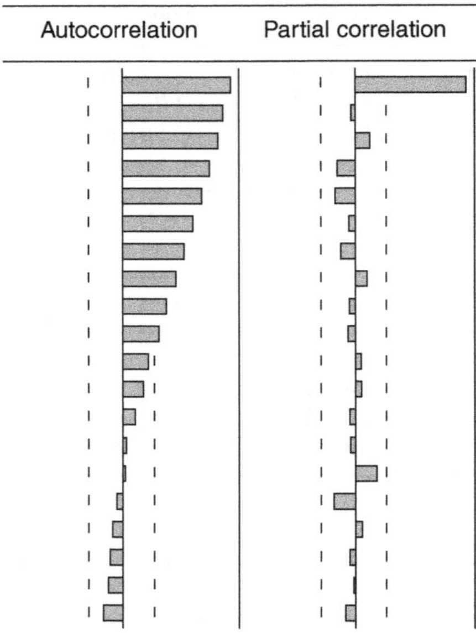

Lag	AC	PAC	Q-stat	Prob.
1	0.944	0.944	46.375	0.000
2	0.886	−0.042	88.131	0.000
3	0.844	0.115	126.87	0.000
4	0.787	−0.178	161.23	0.000
5	0.709	−0.194	189.76	0.000
6	0.632	−0.076	212.96	0.000
7	0.548	−0.145	230.86	0.000
8	0.475	0.093	244.62	0.000
0	0.400	−0.065	254.60	0.000
10	0.314	−0.094	260.93	0.000
11	0.239	0.029	265.70	0.000
12	0.179	0.025	266.85	0.000
13	0.112	−0.053	267.72	0.000
14	0.047	−0.035	268.88	0.000
15	0.009	0.177	267.88	0.000
16	−0.040	−0.206	268.01	0.000
17	−0.086	0.056	268.58	0.000
18	−0.120	−0.054	269.74	0.000
19	−0.153	−0.045	271.71	0.000
20	−0.194	−0.103	274.95	0.000

Figure 6.9 Sample ACF and PACF for the Greek Marxian profit rate, 1960–2008, level.

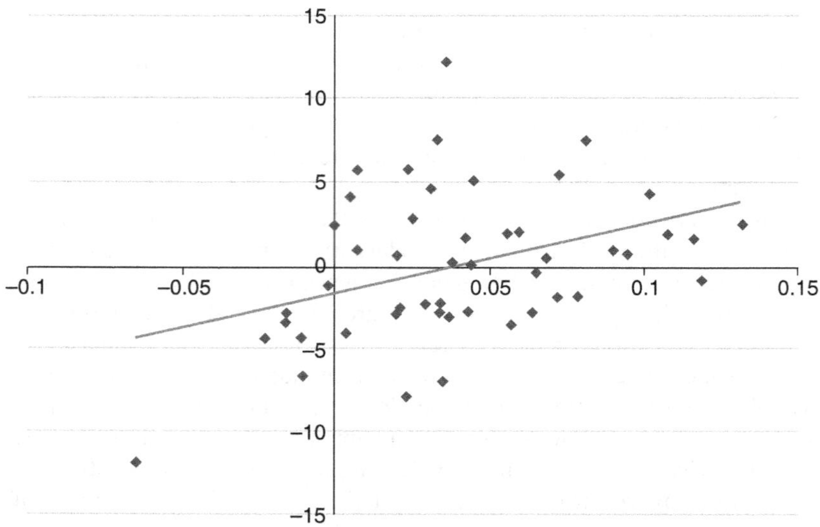

Figure 6.10 Scatter plot of intensity of exploitation and output growth.

Real hourly wage of productive labour is calculated as the compensations of productive labour, deflated by the CPI, to hours worked of productive labour. Assuming that in the long run real wages do not deviate from the value of the labour-power we are able to identify deviations of the real wage rate from its trend with short-term deviations of the value of the labour-power above or below from its 'normal' value. Therefore, again by construction, we expect that the cyclical component of the real wage rate to be pro-cyclical. Figure 6.11, a scatter plot between the cyclical component of real hourly wages of productive labour and the growth rate of real GDP, confirms our expectation that the measure for the deviation of the real wage from the value of labour-power is pro-cyclical.

The unemployment rate is used as a measure of the reserve army of labour that affects the profit rate in two ways: (a) via a decrease in the wage rate, (b) via the formation of new sectors of production with a lower initial OCC. In this context an increase in the unemployment rate (although this being only a proxy for the reserve army of labour), should result in an increase of the profit rate. Figure 6.12, depicting both the unemployment rate and the net profit rate, indicates that this relationship is not perfect as an increase in the unemployment rate is more often than not concurrent with a decrease of the profit rate. Basu and Manolakos (2012) find similar results for the US economy arguing that the effect of this tendency was overwhelmed by changes in the relative price of capital. Moreover, it should be noted that in Greece the falling trend in unemployment until the beginning of the 1970s was a result of the migration of large numbers of workers in advanced capitalist economies, and not the result of the depletion

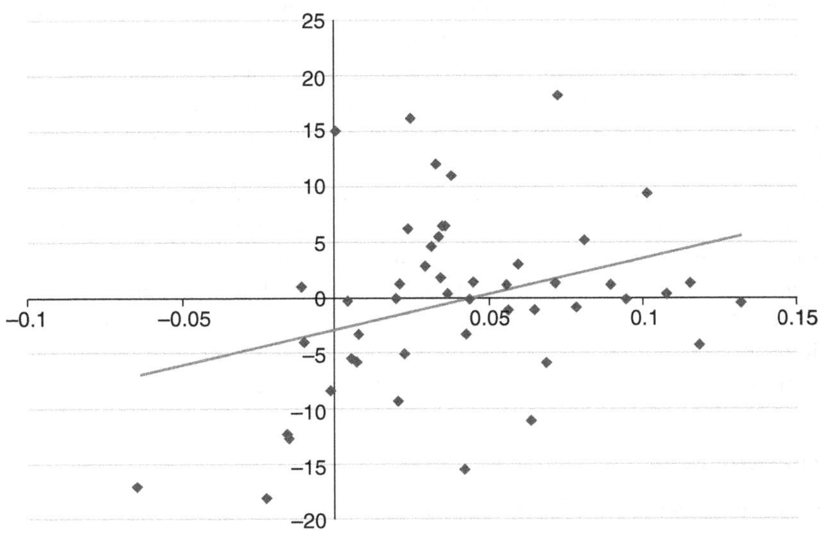

Figure 6.11 Scatter plot of deviation of real wage from the value of labour-power and output growth.

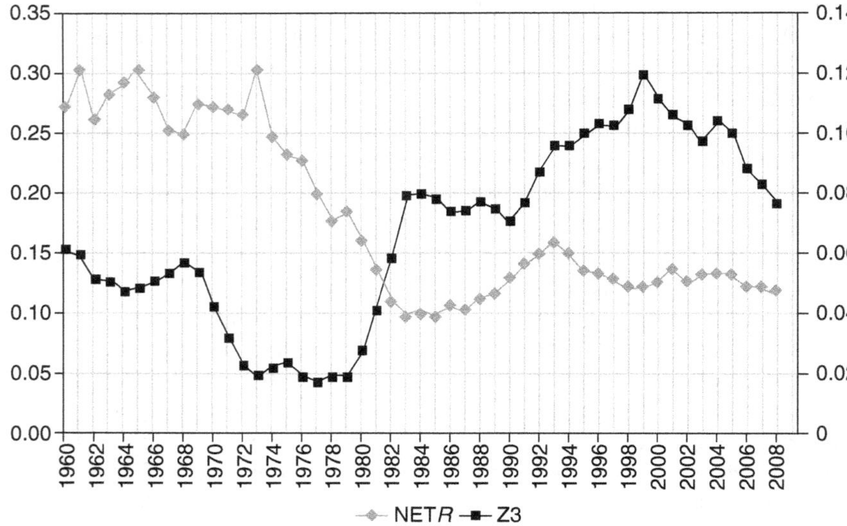

Figure 6.12 Relative overpopulation and the net profit rate.

of the reserve army due to the dynamism of the accumulation process. Therefore, it did not result in an increase in the strength of labour.

Finally, the relative price of constant capital, computed as the ratio of the deflator of gross fixed capital formation to the CPI, is used as a proxy of the cheapening of constant capital. The rationale behind the construction of this measure is that if the price of capital goods does not rise at the same speed as wage goods, due to a faster growth in technology in the capital goods sector, then by construction the value composition of capital, c/v, should fall resulting in an increase in the profit rate. In Figure 6.13, plotting our measure of the relative price of constant capital and the net profit rate, we see that this relationship holds as expected.

Tables 6.3a and 6.3b present the results of unit root test on levels and on first differences using the well-known ADF and PP tests. Results indicate that measures for the intensity of exploitation and the deviation of wages from labour-power are stationary at levels, with all other variables being stationary in first differences. We note that lag selection was based on the Schwarz information criterion with a maximum of ten lags and that estimations included a trend for both profit rate series and for unemployment and the price of capital.

c Econometric methods

Since both the dependent variable and a number of repressors are found not to be stationary performing OLS on the variables in levels could result in spurious results if the variables are not cointegrated. In order to test for cointegration we employ the Johansen and the Engle Granger methodologies.

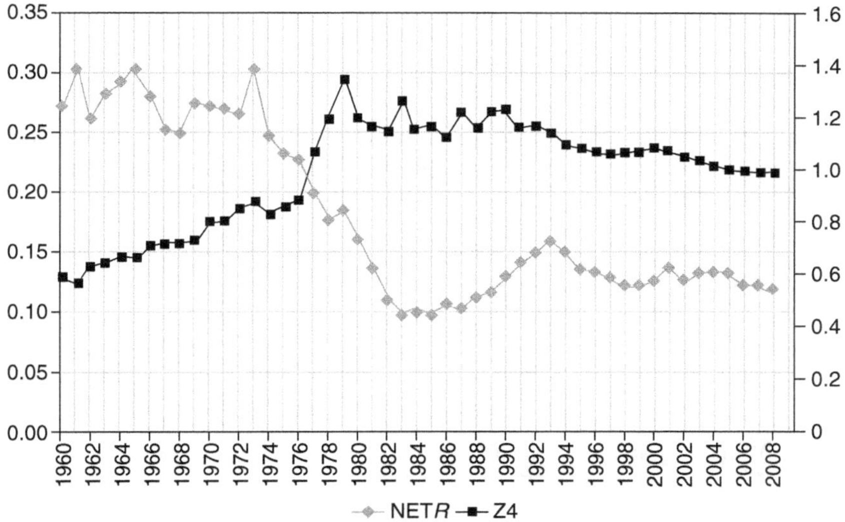

Figure 6.13 Relative price of capital and the net profit rate.

Table 6.3a Unit root tests, levels

Variable	*ADF*		*Phillips–Perron*	
	t-*statistic*	*Probability*	*adj* t-*statistic*	*Probability*
R	–1.445026	0.8344	–1.209393	0.8972
net r	–1.385638	0.8527	–1.390656	0.8512
z_1	–7.220064	0.0000	–14.34693	0.0000
z_2	–6.144564	0.0000	–8.547273	0.0000
z_3	–2.261299	0.4459	–1.873120	0.6528
z_4	–1.080744	0.9217	–0.850010	0.9533

Table 6.3b Unit root tests, first differences

Variable	*ADF*		*Phillips–Perron*	
	t-*statistic*	*Probability*	*adj* t-*statistic*	*Probability*
R	–9.301627	0.0000	–9.188529	0.0000
net r	–7.698093	0.0000	–7.653639	0.0000
z_1	–6.262981	0.0000	–30.25544	0.0001
z_2	–6.708501	0.0000	–15.78841	0.0000
z_3	–3.506230	0.0503	–3.564697	0.0440
z_4	–5.440214	0.0003	–7.857986	0.0000

The Johansen methodology has as its starting point a vector autoregression (VAR) of order p:

$$y_t = \mu + A_1 y_{t-1} + \cdots + A_p y_{t-p} + Bx_t + \varepsilon_t$$

with y_t an $nx1$ vector of I(1) variables, x_t an $mx1$ vector of deterministic variables and ε_t a vector of disturbances. Rearranging the VAR results in an error correction form:

$$\Delta y_t = \Pi y_{t-1} + \sum_{i=1}^{p-1} \Gamma_i \Delta y_{t-1} + Bx_t + \varepsilon_t$$

with

$$\Pi = \sum_{i=1}^{\pi} A_i - 1 \text{ and } \Gamma_i = -\sum_{j=i+1}^{p} A_j$$

By Granger's representation theorem if matrix Π has reduced rank $r<n$, with r the number of cointegrating relationships, then there exist α and β nxr matrices with rank r such that $\Pi=\alpha\beta'$ and $\beta'yt$ is stationary, where α, the adjustment parameters in the vector error correction (VEC) model and each column of β the cointegrating vector. Johansen's method consists of testing through two likelihood ratio tests, the trace and eigenvalue tests, if we can reject the restrictions resulting from a reduced rank of Π.

The Engle–Granger method has two steps. On the first step we estimate the relationship trough simple OLS. On the second step we perform a unit root test on the residuals in order to test for stationarity. It is important to note that conventional critical values do not apply to the particular unit root test and MacKinnon critical values for cointegration tests have to be applied.

d Estimating the model

The hypothesis that we are going to test first, is described by Equation 1:

$$(net)r_t = \alpha + \beta t = \gamma z_{1t} + \delta z_{2t} + \varepsilon z_{3t} + \zeta z_{4t} + \varepsilon_t \quad (1)$$

with (net) r denoting the net profit rate, t a time trend, z_1 a measure of the intensity of exploitation, z_2 a measure of the deviation of wages from labour-power, z_3 a measure of overpopulation and z_4 a measure of the relative price of capital measured as the ratio of the fixed capital formation deflator to the CPI. Subscript t denotes time.

An alternative specification, presented in Equation 2, is to include lags to the dependent and non-stationary independent variables in order to deal with the possibility of spurious results.

$$(net)r_t = \alpha + \beta t = \gamma z_{1t} + \delta z_{2t} + \varepsilon z_{3t} + \zeta z_{4t} + \eta r_{t-1} + \theta z_{3t-1} + \lambda z_{4t-1} + \varepsilon_t \quad (2)$$

Since we are interested not only in the weak case, where the law is validated when controlling for counteracting tendencies, but also in the strong case with counteracting tendencies operating, we modify Equation 1 so as include only a time trend:

$$(net)r_t = \alpha + \beta t$$

Finally, we repeat the same steps for the general Marxian profit rate (R).

e Results

Performing a Johansen test with one lag in levels and two lags on first differences, and assuming the existence of a linear trend, returns that both the trace and eigenvalue tests indicate the existence of a maximum of two cointegrating relationships at the 0.05 level of confidence for the net rate of profit. The results of the trace and eigenvalue tests for the Marxian profit rate under the same assumptions also indicate a maximum of two cointegrating relationships (not reported for brevity).

Results from unit root tests on the residuals from Model 1 (Equation 1) and Model 2 (Equation 2) indicate no cointegration for Equation 1, and cointegration for Equation 2 for both the Marxian and the net rate of profit. Therefore we conclude that there exists a cointegrating relationship between the variables at hand.

Estimating Model 2 by OLS we find that the trend is negative and significant at the 5 per cent for the net profit rate and at the 1 per cent for the Marxian profit rate. The coefficient for the variable that we use as a proxy for the intensity of exploitation (z_1) is found to be positive and significant for both specifications. The coefficient for the variable that we use as a proxy for deviations of wages from the value of labour-power (z_2) is negative and insignificant for both specifications of the profit rate. The coefficients for relative overpopulation (z_3) and the relative cost of capital (z_4) have the expected signs, positive and negative respectively, but are found not to be significant at the 5 per cent with or without a lag.

Eliminating recursively insignificant variables in order to arrive at a more parsimonious model, results to Model 3 that includes a trend, z_1, z_4 and the first lag of the dependent variable in the case of the net profit rate; and z_1, z_3 and the first lags of z_4 and the dependent variable in the case of the Marxian profit rate, all of which have the expected sign. Testing the residuals of Model 3 for stationarity indicates for both specifications are cointegrated.

Having replicated the results of Basu and Manolakos (2012) for the case of Greece and having found broadly similar results, we now turn to estimating the strong case of fitting the net profit rate (r) and the Marxian profit rate (R) only with a linear trend. Results for both specifications indicate that the trend is negative and highly significant, although the very low value of the Durbin–Watson statistic indicates autocorrelation in the residuals. Therefore, we can conclude that

Table 6.4a Estimation results, dependent variable: net profit rate (r)

Dependent variable net r	*Model 1*			*Model 2*			*Model 3*		
	Coefficient	t-*statistic*	p *value*	*Coefficient*	t-*statistic*	p *value*	*Coefficient*	t-*statistic*	p *value*
trend	–0.001	–2.520	0.016	–0.001	–2.155	0.037	–0.001	–1.955	0.057
z_1	0.002	1.925	0.061	0.002	3.902	0.000	0.002	4.313	0.000
z_2	0.000	–0.239	0.812	0.000	–0.733	0.468			
z_3	–0.609	–3.548	0.001	0.014	0.038	0.970			
z_4	–0.216	–9.883	0.000	–0.030	–0.676	0.503	–0.068	–3.512	0.001
z_3 1st lag				0.155	0.403	0.689			
z_4 1st lag				–0.018	–0.425	0.673			
netr 1st lag				0.776	7.382	0.000	0.718	9.325	0.000
Intercept	0.461	23.322	0.000	0.091	1.698	0.098	0.128	3.696	0.001
Adj R^2	0.903			0.958			0.961		
ADF		–3.445			–6.97***			–6.695	
PP		–3.496			–6.96***			–6.707	
LM test (1 lag)		22.475	0.000		0.053	0.819		0.008	0.929
LM test (2 lag)		11.202	0.000		0.055	0.947		0.129	0.879
LM test (3 lag)		7.400	0.001		0.290	0.832		0.238	0.869
Hetero. test		1.434	0.231		0.902	0.525		1.734	0.160

Table 6.4b Estimation results, dependent variable: Marxian profit rate (R)

Dependent variable R	*Model 1*			*Model 2*			*Model 3*		
	Coefficient	t-*statistic*	p *value*	*Coefficient*	t-*statistic*	p *value*	*Coefficient*	t-*statistic*	p *value*
trend	–0.004	–7.083	0.000	–0.003	–7.219	0.000	–0.003	–8.554	0.000
z_1	0.002	2.456	0.018	0.003	4.218	0.000	0.003	5.280	0.000
z_2	0.000	0.727	0.471	0.000	0.509	0.614			
z_3	–0.260	–1.334	0.189	0.728	1.501	0.142	0.545	3.199	0.003
z_4	–0.263	–10.591	0.000	–0.056	–0.967	0.339			
z_3 1st lag				–0.296	–0.583	0.563			
z_4 1st lag				–0.085	–1.562	0.126	–0.118	–3.729	0.001
netr 1st lag				0.636	4.578	0.000	0.688	5.520	0.000
Intercept	0.821	36.597	0.000	0.529	7.483	0.000	0.492	8.330	0.000
Adj R^2	0.943			0.966			0.968		
ADF		–4.318			–5.736***			–5.861	
PP		–4.327			–5.701***			–5.844	
LM test (1 lag)		12.230	0.001		1.010	0.321		0.594	0.445
LM test (2 lag)		6.098	0.005		0.495	0.614		0.293	0.747
LM test (3 lag)		4.326	0.010		0.398	0.755		0.321	0.810
Hetero. test		1.934	0.108		0.656	0.726		0.780	0.570

Note
Critical values for ADF and PP from MacKinnon (2010).

both the Marxian and the net profit rates clearly do have a negative time trend over the entire post-war period despite the presence of the counteracting factors to the operation of the law of the falling profit rate, even though obviously this time trend alone cannot explain the evolution of the dependent variable.

IV Conclusions

In analysing the development of the post-war Greek economy and tracing the roots of its current crisis, the examination of the behaviour of the profit rate and other Marxian variables is of the utmost importance. This study examines these variables. The different phases of the capital accumulation process are distinguished and analysed according to the movement of the profit rate. The 'golden age' of the 1958–74 period of high profitability and strong growth was followed by the stagflation crisis of the 1970s and early 1980s. After 1985 and especially after 1991 the 'neoliberal solution' to the crisis resulted in a modest recovery of profitability, capital accumulation and output growth based exclusively on the huge increase in the rate of exploitation for labour. When the stimulus to aggregate demand provided from personal consumption driven by debt and 'wealth effects', and state deficit spending was removed, the underlying structural crisis in the real economy manifested itself fully from 2009 until today. Thus, the insufficient recovery of profitability during the neoliberal era appears to lie at the core of the economic difficulties currently encountered by the Greek economy. Evidence for that is also provided by the statistical investigation of the trend of the general Marxian and the net profit rates which is negative for both series, both in the presence and the absence of 'counteracting factors'. Thus, the claims of certain Marxists that the present crisis is not a crisis of profitability seem to be unfounded. Low profitability persisted during the neoliberal era and

Table 6.5 Net profit rate regression with time trend

Dependent variable: net profit rate, r	*Coefficient*	*Std error*	t-*statistic*	*Prob.*
C	0.278908	0.011076	25.18197	0.0000
TREND	–0.004140	0.000398	–10.41356	0.0000
adjusted R^2	0.691204			
Durbin–Watson	0.201116			

Table 6.6 Marxian profit rate (R) with time trend

Dependent variable: Marxian profit rate, R	*Coefficient*	*Std error*	*t-statistic*	*Prob.*
C	0.613040	0.013385	45.79934	0.0000
TREND	–0.006536	0.000481	–13.60303	0.0000
adjusted R^2	0.793141			
Durbin–Watson	0.242235			

especially in the years before the onset of the crisis because what was missing from the classical scenario of a definite recovery from a serious crisis was the massive destruction, depreciation and restructuring of capital and/or a technological revolution that would (possibly) raise productivity growth significantly, and lower the OCC. It is evident that this solution could not be politically accepted at that time since it would create social and economic conditions similar to those of the Great Depression. The unprecedented political strengthening of the Left and the social and political upheaval of the last three years, once those drastic measures were gradually introduced, testify for this. It is also evident that presently, capital and the state are attempting to achieve this much needed increase in profitability at all costs even if those include halving the standard of living and ruining the lives of workers and the vast majority of the population. The answer on the part of the dominated classes can only be a challenge to the profit system itself and not the search for some appropriate policy that will benefit both workers and capital.

Notes

1 See Shaikh (1987), Shaikh and Tonak (1994), Moseley (1988, 1991) for the explanation of the crisis on the basis of the classical Marxian approach.
2 Sweezy (1981) and Foster (1987) are typical examples of the underconsumption or lack of effective demand theory of crisis.
3 See Glyn and Sutcliffe (1972), Weisskopf (1979), and Bowles *et al.* (1983, 1986) for representative examples of the wage induced profit squeeze theory of crisis.
4 Harvey (2010) is one exception to this trend, and Laskos and Tsakalotos (2013: 5) accept and adopt his argument at least partly for both the Greek and the world economic crisis.
5 See though, Moseley (1988, 1991), and Shaikh (1978, 1987) for a critique of that argument and different explanations of that crisis.
6 'The neoliberal institutional structure produced large asset bubbles, which provided a longer-lasting resolution of the realization problem' (Kotz (2010): 369).
7 Lapavitsas *et al.* (2010) present a similar argument for the Eurozone and Greece blaming the excessive financialisation of the economy and the neoliberal architecture of the EU for the (mainly financial) crisis, denying any role for the low profitability of capital.
8 Laibman commenting on the arguments put forth by Palley (2009) and Kotz (2009) states 'the obvious problem with this analysis from a Marxist point of view is its unstated implication: the crisis was a crisis of a policy, neoliberalism (despite the use of the word "systemic" by Kotz and others)' (2010: 382).
9 For a detailed account of the method followed in estimating the Marxian categories in the context of the Greek National Accounts and their categories see Maniatis (2005) and Maniatis and Passas (2013).
10 See Maniatis (2012) and Roberts (2013).
11 For a detailed account of the post-war experience of the US economy, paradigmatic of the world capitalist economy, using Marxian categories, see Maniatis (2012). See also Bakir and Campbell (2009, 2010) and Shaikh (2011). The corresponding detailed analysis of the post-war Greek economy is contained in Maniatis and Passas (2013).
12 See Camara (2007) for Spain, and Marquetti *et al.* (2010) for Brazil. The period covered by those studies ends in 2001 and 2003 respectively, so further comparisons regarding the outbreak of the current crisis are not possible.

13 Fine and Harris (1979) and Foley (1986) adhere to the first notion of the law, whereas Shaikh (1983, 1987) and Rosdolsky (1977) are typical examples of the second approach which regards the concrete appearance of the fall in the rate and the mass of profit and the resulting crisis as a necessity.

14 Basu and Manolakos (2012) control for the following 'countertendencies', (a) increasing intensity of exploitation of labour, (b) the relative cheapening of the elements of constant capital, (c) the deviation of the wage rate from the value of labour-power, (d) the existence and increase of a relative surplus population and (e) the cheapening of consumption and capital goods through imports. The second and fifth lower the growth of the composition of capital (and they are grouped together as a single regressor) and the other three increase the rate of surplus-value.

References

Bakir E. and Campbell A. (2009), 'The Bush business cycle profit rate: support in a theoretical debate and implications for the future', *Review of Radical Political Economics* 41(3).

Bakir E. and Campbell A. (2010), 'Neoliberalism, the rate of profit and the rate of accumulation', *Science and Society* 74(3).

Basu D. and Manolakos P. (2012), 'Is there a tendency for the rate of profit to fall? Econometric evidence for the US economy, 1948–2007', *Review of Radical Political Economics* 45(1).

Bowles S., Gordon D. and Weisskopf, T. (1983), *Beyond the Wasteland: Democratic Alternatives to Economic Decline*, New York: Doubleday.

Bowles S., Gordon D. and Weisskopf T. (1986), 'Power and profits: the social structure of accumulation and the profitability of the post-war US economy', *Review of Radical Political Economics* 18(1&2).

Brenner R. (1998), 'The economics of global turbulence: a special report of the world economy, 1950–98', *New Left Review* 229.

Brenner R. (2006), *The Economics of Global Turbulence*, London: Verso.

Camara S. (2007), 'The dynamics of the profit rate in Spain', *Review of Radical Political Economics* 39(4).

Crotty J. (2000), 'Structural contradictions of the global neoliberal regime', *Review of Radical Political Economics* 32(3).

Dumenil G. and Levy D. (2010), *The Crisis of Neoliberalism*, Cambridge, MA: Harvard University Press.

Fine B. and Harris L. (1979), *Rereading Capital*, London: Routledge.

Foley D. (1986), *Understanding Capital: Marx's Economic Theory*, Cambridge, MA: Harvard University Press.

Foster J.B. (1987), 'What is stagnation?' in Cherry R., D'Onofrio C., Kurdas C., Michl T., Moseley F. and Naples M. (eds), *The Imperiled Economy*, New York: Union for Radical Political Economics.

Glyn A. and Sutcliffe B. (1972), *Capitalism in Crisis: British Capitalism, Workers and the Profit Squeeze*, Middlesex: Penguin Press.

Harvey D. (2010), *The Enigma of Capital*, London: Profile Books.

Kotz D. (2003), 'Neoliberalism and the SSA theory of long-run capital accumulation', *Review of Radical Political Economics* 35(3).

Kotz D. (2008), 'Contradictions of economic growth in the neoliberal era: accumulation and crisis in the contemporary U.S. economy', *Review of Radical Political Economics* 40(2).

Kotz D. (2009), 'The financial and economic crisis of 2008: a systemic crisis of neoliberal capitalism', *Review of Radical Political Economics* 41(3).

Kotz D. (2010), 'The final conflict: what can cause a system-threatening crisis of capitalism?' *Science and Society* 74(3).

Laibman D. (2010), 'Capitalism, crisis, renewal: some conceptual excavations', *Science and Society* 74(3).

Lapavitsas C., Kaltenbrunner A., Lindo D., Michell J., Painceira J.P., Pires E., Powell J., Stenfors A. and Teles N. (2010), 'Eurozone in crisis: beggar thyself and thy neighbour', *Research on Money and Finance*, Occasional Report.

Laskos C. and Tsakalotos E. (2013), *Crucible of Resistance: Greece, the Eurozone, and the World Economic Crisis*, London: Pluto Press.

MacKinnon J. (2010), 'Critical values for cointegration tests', Queen's Economics Department Working Paper No. 1227.

Maniatis T. (1996), 'Testing Marx: a note', *Capital and Class* 59(Summer).

Maniatis T. (2005), 'Marxian macroeconomic categories in the Greek economy', *Review of Radical Political Economics* 37(4).

Maniatis T. (2012), 'Marxist theories of crisis and the current economic crisis', *Forum for Social Economics* 41(1).

Maniatis T. and Passas C. (2013), 'Profitability, capital accumulation and crisis in the Greek economy, 1958–2009: a Marxist analysis', *Review of Political Economy* 25(4).

Marquetti A., Maldondo Filho E. and Lautert V. (2010), 'The profit rate in Brazil', *Review of Radical Political Economics* 42(4).

Marx K. (1894/1981), *Capital: A Critique of Political Economy, Vol. III*, New York: Penguin.

Moseley F. (1988), 'The rate of surplus-value, the organic composition and the general rate of profit in the US economy, 1947–1967: a critique and update of Wolff's estimates', *American Economic Review* 78(1).

Moseley F. (1991), *The Falling Rate of Profit in the Post-war United States Economy*, New York: St. Martin's Press.

Moseley F. (1997), 'The rate of profit and economic stagnation in the US economy', *Historical Materialism* 1(1).

Palley T. (2009), 'America's exhausted paradigm: macroeconomic causes of the financial crisis and Great Recession', New American Contract Policy Paper, www.newamerica.net/publications/policy.

Roberts M. (2013), 'From global slump to long depression', *International Socialism* 140(October).

Rosdolsky R. (1977), *The Making of Marx's Capital*, London: Pluto Press.

Shaikh A. (1978), 'An introduction to the history of crisis theories', in *U.S. Capitalism in Crisis*, New York: URPE.

Shaikh A. (1983), 'Economic crises', in T. Bottomore *et al.* (ed.) *A Dictionary of Marxist Thought*, Cambridge: Harvard University Press.

Shaikh A. (1987), 'The falling rate of profit and the economic crisis in the US', in Cherry R., D'Onofrio C., Kurdas C., Michl T., Moseley F. and Naples M. (eds), *The Imperiled Economy*, New York: URPE.

Shaikh A. (2011), 'The first Great Depression of the 21st century', in Panitch L., Albo G. and Chibbert V. (eds), *The Crisis this Time: Socialist Register 2011* 47.

Shaikh A. and Tonak E.A. (1994), *Measuring the Wealth of Nations: The Political Economy of National Accounts*, Cambridge: Cambridge University Press.

Sweezy P. (1981), *Four Lectures on Marxism*, New York: Monthly Review Press.

Weisskopf T. (1979), 'Marxian crisis theory and the rate of profit in the postwar U.S. economy', *Cambridge Journal of Economics* 3(4).

7 Profitability and crisis in the Greek economy (1960–2012)

An investigation

George Economakis, George Androulakis and Maria Markaki

I Introduction

In the conjuncture of global economic crisis, the Greek economy emerged as a 'weak link' of the Eurozone. Since 2010, external deficit coverage of the Greek economy is based on lending from the support mechanism of troika (EC, IMF and ECB), in accordance to the Memoranda embedded in the Greek legislation, from 2010–12.

This chapter focuses on three questions, attempting to understand the reasons behind these developments:

- The possible interdependence between low international competitiveness of the Greek economy and debt crisis.
- The factors that affect the profitability of the Greek economy for a broader time period (1960–2012).
- The factors affecting profitability in the current crisis of the Greek economy (2007–12).

II Public debt and international competitiveness

Is the Greek crisis a mere public debt crisis?

The global economic crisis turned part of private debt into public debt, which led to a crisis of insolvency, due to the soaring of interest rates. Thus, the global crisis at this stage appears as a public debt crisis, which for the first time after the Second World War affected the advanced capitalist social formations to a great extent (Milios (2011)).

The gross public debt in the advanced economies continued to grow as a percentage of GDP, exceeding for the first time 100 per cent in 2011. More precisely: in 2011 it was 105.5 per cent of GDP, in 2012 110.7 per cent and it will reach 113.6 per cent in 2013. In the Eurozone, the gross public debt increased from 88.1 per cent of GDP in 2011 to 92.9 per cent in 2012, and it will reach 94.5 per cent in 2013 (Bank of Greece (2013a): 32, table III.1).

The Greek public debt is much higher than the Eurozone public debt. The consolidated debt of the general government, as a percentage of GDP, increased from 110.0 per cent of GDP in 2005 to 170.6 per cent in 2011 (Bank of Greece (2013b): 41, table 22).

Is this high public debt the main cause of the current Greek crisis and bankruptcy?

If it were so other economies would have been bankrupt before Greece, e.g. the Japanese, whose gross public debt as a percentage of GDP was higher than 200 per cent in 2011–12 and is expected to reach 224.3 per cent in 2013 (Bank of Greece (2013a): 32, table III.1).

In Japan's example we can, however, point out other important macroeconomic variables which make the public debt only a part of the economic problem and not the actual problem. In the Japanese economy, household net saving rates, as a percentage of household disposal income, were positive, during the period 2000–11, and there were around 2.2 per cent for the years 2009–11 (OECD Stat Extracts). As a result, national saving decisively contributes to the domestic financing of public debt. At the same time, the current account balance as a percentage of GDP is also positive: 2.1 per cent in 2011, 1.1 per cent in 2012 and it will reach 1.2 per cent in 2013 (Bank of Greece (2013a): 32, table III.1). Consequently, the Japanese economy generates net claims on the rest of the world – despite the very high public debt.

During the period 2000–11, in the Greek economy, unlike the Japanese, the high public debt was accompanied by negative household net saving rates, as a percentage of household disposable income. In recent years, the rates diminished further: from –2.9 per cent in 2009 to –12.5 per cent in 2011 (OECD Stat Extracts). According to Fotopoulos (2010: 51), the low level of savings in the Greek economy is due to the 'nature' of economy, as an economy of services, which, in conjunction with the massive influx of remittances from abroad (shipping, immigration, etc.), created a highly consumerist society. In this decade, the Greek economy's consumerist character intensified further, something that excludes every idea of financing the public debt from domestic sources. Moreover, as Oikonomou (2010: 30, 28) points out, since domestic net saving was not enough to carry a minimum level of new investments, the Greek economy was dependent on foreign capitals to an extent that was unique within the Eurozone.

In addition, the current account balance is steadily negative and deteriorating from the mid-1990s until 2008 (see Figure 7.1), when the single EU market was introduced and the drachma was revaluated in real terms (in order to join the European single currency). These developments, even before Greece's entry into the Eurozone, removed its ability to use exchange rate policy as a means of addressing the competition of foreign goods (Economakis (2011)).

CAD's reduction after 2008 is mainly due to the drastic reduction of the trade deficit because of the depression and the consequent reduction of import payments. CAD's further improvement after 2012 is moreover due to the amelioration of income balance because of the decrease in net interest payments on the public debt – by virtue of private sector involvement (PSI) implementation – and to the time shift in interest payments on the support mechanism's loans, as a result of interest rates readjustment. To a lesser extent, deficit reduction reflects

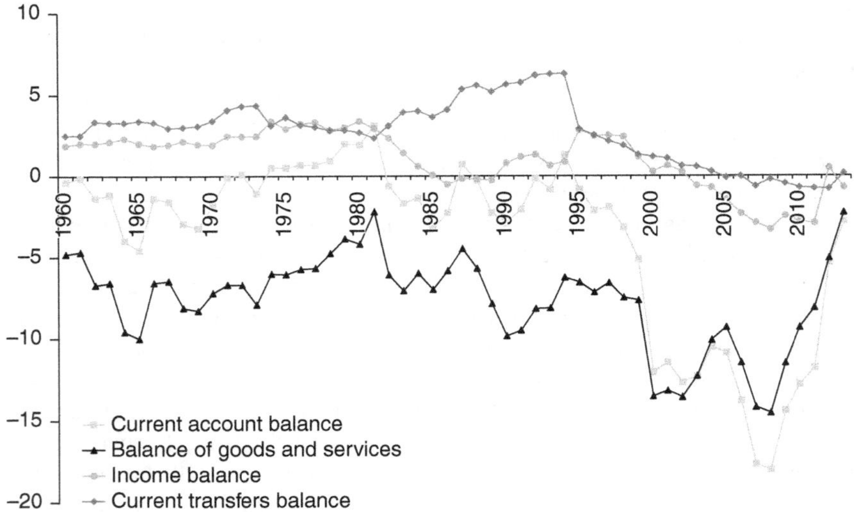

Figure 7.1 Current account balance and sub-balances of the Greek economy as a percentage of GDP, 1960–2013.

a recovery in exports of goods, owning to the improvement in cost competitiveness (i.e. labour costs reduction) (see Bank of Greece (2013a): 107, 113).

However, despite these developments, the Greek economy continues to build up net liabilities internationally, contrary to the whole Eurozone, which exhibits current account surplus: 0.5 per cent of GDP in 2011, estimated 1.4 per cent in 2012 and expected 1.9 per cent in 2013 (Bank of Greece (2013a): 32, table III.1).

It must be noted that the negative national saving and the high public debt negatively affect the current account balance (TDH).[1] In recent years and until 2012, the deterioration of income balance, shown in Figure 7.1, mainly reflects higher interest payments of the Greek state (Bank of Greece (2012): 86–7). However, the determinant factor of the serious CAD is the low international competitiveness of the Greek economy, as recorded by the balance of goods and services.[2]

As seen in Figure 7.1, the balance of goods and services is constantly negative for the entire period 1960–2013, reflecting the Greek economy's chronic competitiveness problem.[3] From the same figure it can be observed that after 1981 (country's entry to the then EEC), and especially from the mid-1990s to 2008, the balance of goods and services deteriorated further. Consequently, the reduction of over-indebtedness and ultimately bankruptcy of the Greek economy in public debt is a misleading simplification.

However, why did the Greek economy emerge as the chief 'weak link' during the global economic crisis?

To answer this question we need to look at key aspects of the Greek economic development in recent years, especially after the country's entry into the Eurozone.

Prior to this, a closer look at the problem of over-borrowing of the Greek economy should be made.

The over-borrowing from international capital markets

The gross external debt (of private and public sector) is powered by CAD. The Greek economy exhibits a serious deterioration of the gross external debt. The gross external debt from 138.25 per cent of the GDP in 2007 reached 177.41 per cent in 2011 and it is estimated at 224.29 per cent in 2012 (Bank of Greece (2013b): 38, table 19). Moreover, Greece's negative net international investment position, which reflects the country's foreign liabilities, also deteriorates; as a percentage of GDP, in 2010 it amounted to –98.4 per cent, while, according to estimates, in 2012 it will reach –112.8 per cent (Bank of Greece (2013b): 37, table 18).[4]

The coverage of CAD should be financed with equal net capital inflows. The combined CAD and capital account deficit corresponds to the external financing requirements of the economy. According to the Bank of Greece (2012: 91), in the Greek case usually only a small part of CAD is financed by net unilateral capital transfers, which mainly include EU transfers. Thus, CAD's bulk is financed by financial flows that are recorded in the financial account balance. The latter, together with the capital transfers balance, should always be equal to CAD.

The financial account includes: foreign direct investment (FDI), portfolio investment, 'other' investment (which includes loans and deposits) and changes in reserve assets.

FDI is low and has a minimal share in CAD financing. In 2000–5, this share was 0.4 per cent, while in 2006–8 0.2 per cent (Bank of Greece (2012): 93).[5] In 2009–12, the already low FDI almost sub-tripled (Bank of Greece (2013a): 120). According to the Bank of Greece (2012: 93), low FDI reflects a serious problem of the Greek economy. CAD is not financed 'with healthy, long-term funds' that do not create debt. On the other hand, the production base of the Greek economy is 'deprived of the advantages of technology and know-how transfer that usually accompany FDI'.

Thus, in 2000–8, the financing of CAD relied on international capital market funding, mainly through the issuance of bonds and Treasury bills – that create debt (Bank of Greece (2012): 96, Lapavitsas *et al.* (2010): 9, 11, 13).

From 2009, the debt crisis emerged in Greece as the country was excluded from international capital markets and the spreads on Greek government bonds were high. As a result, the portfolio investment did not contribute to CAD's financing. The latter depends mainly on the support mechanism of troika ('other' investment) (Bank of Greece (2012): 94, 96).

Therefore, the Greek economy depends on the support mechanism of troika as the over-indebtedness from international capital markets could not be continued. In this sense Memoranda do not concern only public debt but mainly the competitiveness of the Greek economy.

But how is this process of bankruptcy related to the development of the Greek economy, especially after its entry into the Eurozone?

The development with Euro

After Greece's entry in the Eurozone and before the global economic crisis, the Greek economy experienced high growth rate, as expressed by GDP's average growth rate. More precisely, after its membership in the Eurozone (2001–2) the average GDP growth rate was 3.8 per cent, while from 2003–7 economic growth accelerated to 4.3 per cent (see Oikonomou (2010): 7).

However, this period of 'over-growth' was also a period of high CAD, which created needs for augmenting external borrowing.

More precisely: the economic growth during the 2000s emanated mainly from the sectors of non-tradable goods and services (Oikonomou (2010): 7). As seen from Table 7.1, the ratio of tradable to non-tradable goods and services is higher in the EU27 against Greece for the period 2000–10, which has a ratio less than one.

Thus, after Greece's entry into the Eurozone, the Greek economy based its development on the growth of productive sectors not exposed to the international competition – comparatively more than the EU-27 as a whole. Therefore, the type of development of the Greek economy during the 2000s neither presupposed nor led to the improvement of its international competitive position.

As a result, the rising incomes in the sectors of non-tradable commodities augmented the demand of tradable from aboard (Oikonomou (2010): 45–6, 58, Gibson (2010): 33ff.). Yet, imports are mainly characterised by higher income elasticity of demand against domestically produced and exported commodities (Bank of Greece (2003): 32, Bank of Greece (2009): 121, Gibson (2010): 344). This 'reflects ... the inability of domestic supply to meet *domestic and foreign demand in terms of both composition and growth*' (Bank of Greece (2009): 121)

Table 7.1 Ratio of tradable* to non-tradable** goods and services (gross value added, constant prices 2005)

	2000	*2001*	*2002*	*2003*	*2004*	*2005*	*2006*	*2007*	*2008*	*2009*	*2010*
EU27	1.072	1.058	1.041	1.031	1.028	1.019	1.026	1.039	1.019	0.977	0.992
Greece	0.866	0.797	0.777	0.716	0.695	0.693	0.666	0.648	0.661	0.689	0.601

Source: Authors' calculations using Eurostat's data

Notes

* Agriculture, Forestry and Fishing, Mining and Quarrying, Manufacturing, Accommodation and Food Services, Financial and Insurance Activities and Other Service Activities.

** Energy, Constructions, Storage-Transportation-Telecommunications, Trade Services, Public Sector, Other Services.

The classification is based on NACE Rev. 1.1; the distinction between tradable and non-tradable goods and services is based mainly on Gibson (2010).

– which is an expression of the 'low competitiveness' of the Greek economy[6] (see also Oikonomou (2010): 46). Simultaneously, the high income elasticity of demand for imported (industrial in general) goods is combined with low price elasticity of demand for these goods.

Therefore, the economic growth was accompanied by increasing import payments (see also Bank of Greece (2000): 209), especially in the absence of any kind of (trade or exchange rate) protective policy within the frame of EU-EMU. GDP was increased, inasmuch as the increase in demand for tradable commodities from aboard was outweighed by the increase in domestic demand for non-tradable. Consequently, the very model of Greek capitalism, within the frame of EU-EMU, led to an economic growth that was accompanied by high external deficits.[7]

The significant reduction in the cost of borrowing in the 2000s formed the basis for this type of development (see also Pelagidis (2010)). This reduction was the result of the single monetary policy, which was less tight for Greece than it was for most countries of the Eurozone, due to differential inflation which entails lower real interest rates (Oikonomou (2010): 8). Thus, the short-term real interest rates in the 1990s were for Greece at an average of 5.4 per cent, while after 2000 came close to 0 per cent – becoming for long periods even negative. These conditions led to the over-expansion of (private and public) domestic lending, further enhancing expansion of domestic demand (Milios (2011)).

Economic growth with high CAD reached its limit in 2007 (see Oikonomou (2010): 8), when the onset of global economic crisis blocked this type of development. In the conjuncture of global economic crisis, as the financial sphere entered a process of reassessment of credit risks, the transfer of 'savings' from the European 'centre' to the European 'periphery' stopped (see Milios (2011)) and the Greek economy emerged as EMU's chief 'weak link'. The following reduction of domestic and foreign demand marked the beginning of the deep depression that continues until today.

III Profit rate and underconsumption in the Marxian theory of economic crises

The key points of Marx's theory of economic crises, on the basis of which we will proceed to our investigation of the factors affecting the profitability of the Greek economy, are the following.[8]

The organic composition of capital and the profit rate

Developing his theory of 'The Law of the Tendencial Fall in the Rate of Profit', Marx (1991: 317ff.) attempted to show that technological innovation – introduced into production by the individual capitalist in the context of economic competition in order to increase labour productivity – could cause a TRPF.

Marxian analysis is based on the concepts of TCC (the quantity in material terms of means of production per unit of living labour) and VCC or OCC (the ratio of constant to variable capital, in value terms) (Marx (1991): 241ff., Milios *et al.* (2002): 145). Given that TCC increases with accumulation and technological innovation, Marx maintained that if all other factors remain constant, a fall in the profit rate may emerge if VCC increases due to a more rapid increase in TCC than the labour productivity it creates (Marx (1991): 317ff.).

Considering that the rate of profit is a dependent variable (*p*) we may write:

$$p = \frac{s}{C+v} = \frac{s/v}{C/v + 1}, \tag{1}$$

where C=constant capital, s/v=rate of exploitation (rate of surplus-value) and C/v=VCC or OCC.

If TCC increases more rapidly than the labour productivity, C/v rises (Stamatis (1997): 65ff.). In all cases where this increase is more rapid than the increase in s/v (an increase following technological progress, as the latter, by increasing labour productivity, lowers the price of the – constant or slightly variable – real wage) the profit rate falls (Milios *et al.* (2002): 146).

Marx's analysis does not exclude the possibility of the containment or reversal of the TRPF. The latter is active to the degree that OCC rises and 'all other factors remain constant' (Milios *et al.* (2002): 146–7, Marx (1991): 170–81).

The overaccumulation of capital

In his previous analysis Marx has considered the numerator of the fraction of equation (1) as constant (given rate of surplus-value), investigating the effect of a rise in OCC on the dependent variable (profit rate). In the third section of the 15th chapter of Volume III of *Capital*, 'Surplus Capital alongside Surplus Population' (Marx (1991): 359ff.), Marx, using the 'ceteris paribus' method, studies the influence of s/v on p by considering C/v as a constant quantity. Here we find his theoretical notion of the 'overaccumulation of capital'. Marx argues that surplus-value rate changes are due to the lack of additional workers (very low unemployment rate) and subsequent (real) wage increases.

Nevertheless, the surplus-value rate depends also on other factors, which Marx 'omitted' using his method of abstraction (Milios *et al.* (2002): 195).

The 'realisation' problem

Crises are characterised by a 'plethora of capital', which 'means ... overproduction of means of production... that can function as capital'. The function of capital presupposes the ensuring of a profit rate which corresponds to 'the "healthy" and "normal" development of the capitalist production process' (Marx (1991): 359, 364). This profit rate is the '*usual profit rate*' (Marx (1969): 494). 'Once the rate of profit goes below the usual range, a curtailment of operations on the part of capitalist will set in' (Sweezy (1970): 142). Thus, the realisation problem (underconsumption) is merely a consequence of the profitability problem and a 'form of appearance' of crisis: the curtailment of operations on the part of the capitalist class, once the rate of profit goes below the usual rate, appears 'in the form of unsold (consumption and investment) commodities' (Milios *et al.* (2002): 159, 177, 188). Nevertheless, the subsequent underconsumption reacting negatively upon the degree of capital utilisation (underemployment of capital) leads to the intensification of profit rate fall, since declining degree of capital utilisation means decreasing profit rate (Stamatis (1986): 9).

However, Marx's work is rather ambiguous on the issue of underconsumption. For example, in Volume III of *Capital* there are extracts that favour an underconsumptionist interpretation of economic crises, considering underconsumption as an independent, or exclusive causal agent of capitalist crises. In these cases Marx ascribes the economic crises to the 'antagonistic conditions of distribution, which reduce the consumption of the vast majority of society to a minimum level', in other words to 'the poverty and restricted consumption of the masses' (Marx (1991): 352–3, 615).

The economic crisis as a condition of 'self-preservation' of capital

According to Marx, 'the relations corresponding to a "healthy" movement of capitalist production' will be restored, through the destruction and devaluation of constant capital and the creation of 'an artificial surplus population', which the economic crisis generates (Marx (1991): 362–4). Thus, the crisis acts as a mechanism for 'self-preservation' of capital, although 'these regularly recurring catastrophes lead to their repetition on a higher scale, and finally to its violent overthrow' (Marx (1981): 749–50).

IV Profitability and international competitiveness of the Greek economy: an empirical study

We will investigate the factors affecting the profitability of the Greek economy on the basis of the Marxian theory of crisis, for the period 1960/1965–2012.[9]

Net capital stock return

Considering that the core of the Marxian theory of economic crises concerns the falling profit rate, *net capital stock return* is used as an indicator which approximates the Marxian profit rate, and could be the subject of empirical study and measurement (see among other works Duménil and Lévy (2002, 2004)).

Net capital stock return (r) is expressed by the following equation:

$$r = \frac{Y - L}{K}, \tag{2}$$

where Y=net product (or income), L=labour compensation and K=net capital stock.

Equation (2) is a modified version of the Marxian equation (1).

Dividing the terms of the fraction (2) with Y, relation (3a) or relation (3b) is derived. Then, dividing the numerator and denominator of (3a) with N, where N is the magnitude of employment (hired labour plus self-employment) relation (4) is derived:

$$r = \frac{1 - \frac{L}{Y}}{\frac{K}{Y}}, \tag{3a}$$

or

$$r = \frac{\frac{\Pi}{Y}}{\frac{K}{Y}}, \tag{3b}$$

and

$$r = \frac{1 - \frac{\frac{L}{N}}{\frac{Y}{N}}}{\frac{\frac{K}{N}}{\frac{Y}{N}}} \tag{4}$$

where,

Π = profits,

$$1 - \frac{L}{Y} = 1 - \frac{\frac{L}{N}}{\frac{Y}{N}} = \frac{\Pi}{Y} = \text{profit share of income (or profit share in net product)},$$

which is related to the Marxian rate of surplus-value (see Laibman (2010): 384),

L/Y = labour share of income (or labour share in net product),

$$\frac{K}{Y} = \frac{\frac{K}{N}}{\frac{Y}{N}} = \text{ratio of net capital stock to net product},$$

i.e., the amount of net capital stock required to produce one unit of product, that resembles to the Marxian OCC (see Laibman (2010): 384), Y/N=labour productivity, L/N=average labour compensation (average wage), K/N=intensity of net capital stock, or the net capital stock per employee, which resembles the Marxian TCC.

Assumptions and restrictions of the analysis

The investigation of the profitability of the Greek economy concerns the total economy, and not only the business-capitalist sector.[10]

Therefore, Y refers to the entire economy.

Respectively, L is the sum of the total compensations of employees (of private and public sectors) and of inferred compensations of self-employed, since for the latter there are no available data. For the estimation of the compensations of self-employed the number of self-employed is multiplied by the average wage of labour. It is assumed namely that the rewards of self-employed tend to be equal to the equivalent of the average labour compensation (for the theoretical foundation of this position see Economakis *et al.* (2010): 476). It must be noted that L includes the remunerations of top managers of private capitalist sector of the economy, part of which are not wages but profits (see Economakis *et al.* (2010): 476). So, the (capitalist) profits are underestimated.

Since Y refers to the entire economy, that is to the capitalist and non-capitalist modes of production (see Economakis (2005)), the difference $Y-L=\Pi$ does not specifically concern the (capitalist) profit. It rather corresponds to a concept of surplus. Therefore, r is in reality a percentage of surplus and not of profit – according to the Marxist terminology. Although Π is wider of (capitalist) profits, we refer to Π as profits for simplification.

K, respectively, refers to the entire economy.

The value of the public services is equal to the operating costs of the state apparatus, i.e. profits are not included. Thus, the estimation of r underestimates (capitalist) profits, given that it includes the compensations of employees in public sector and the non-business capital. However, we suppose that the general trends of profitability variations are depicted.

One particular issue concerns the question of 'productive' and 'unproductive' labour, in business sector. In this study it is supported that from the standpoint of the capitalist production process, 'productive labour' is the labour paid from variable capital. Correspondingly, 'production' is any process in which labour-power is exchanged for capital (Economakis *et al.* (2010)).[11] Regarding the non-capitalist producers, there is no question of 'productive' or 'unproductive' labour, since 'their production does not fall under the capitalist mode of production' (Marx (1978): 407).

The source of quantitative variables of analysis is AMECO. The monetary magnitudes are in Mrd EURO at constant 2005 prices. Y (net domestic product is given at market prices. N is given in thousands of workers. Net domestic potential product (Y^*) is calculated from the corresponding gross size by subtracting for each year the depreciation of capital. Prices for 2011 are estimates and for 2012 projections.

Before proceeding to the quantitative investigation, the basic periodisation of the period 1960–2012 is examined.

Net capital stock return during the period 1960–2012: a basic periodisation

Figures 7.2, 7.3 and 7.4 depict respectively r, K/Y and L/Y from 1960–2012. Figure 7.5 shows the relation between Y/N and L/N, for the same period.

As seen from Figure 7.2, four basic sub-periods can be distinguished during the period 1960–2012: two upward and two downward.[12]

- *1960–73*. During the global capitalist crisis of the mid 1960s to early 1970s, 1973 is considered a benchmark in the Greek economy, when the post-war 'golden age' of Greek capitalism ended in conditions of rising class struggle and disintegration of the military dictatorship (see Mavroudeas (2011): 401–2). During this sub-period, r was in its highest level for the whole period (1960–2012), peaking in 1973. Correspondingly, in 1973 L/Y displayed the lowest level for the entire period and K/Y one of the lowest. A special feature of the period was the increasing divergence between Y/N and L/N at the expense of the latter. Although wages follow labour productivity over the considered period, this divergence was maintained in all cases – despite fluctuations.

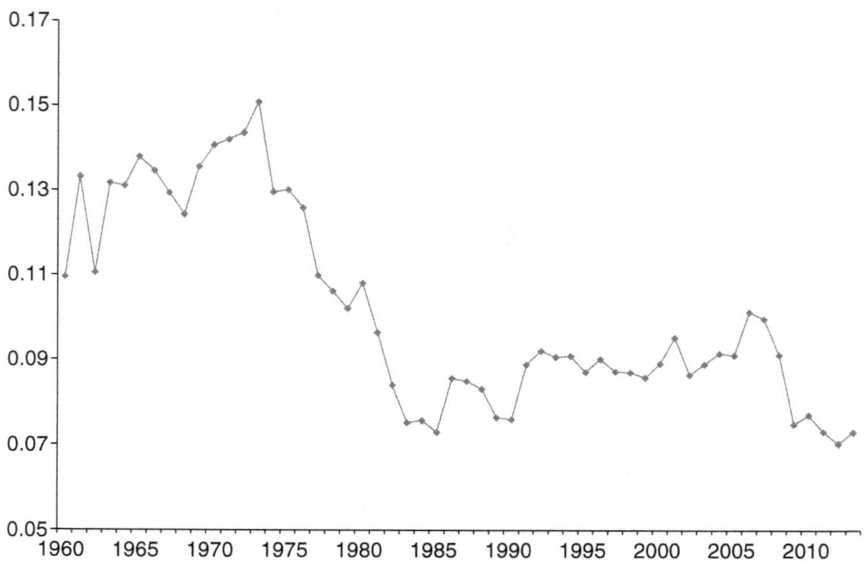

Figure 7.2 Net capital stock return, 1960–2012.

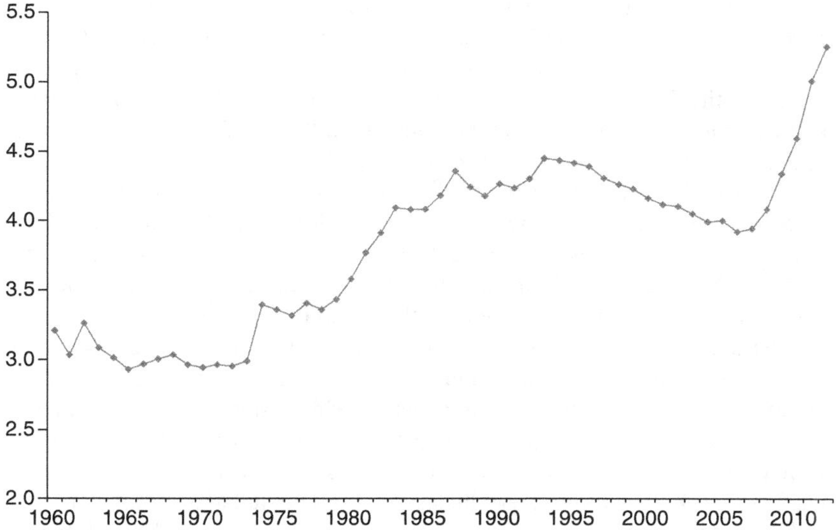

Figure 7.3 Ratio of net capital stock to net product, 1960–2012.

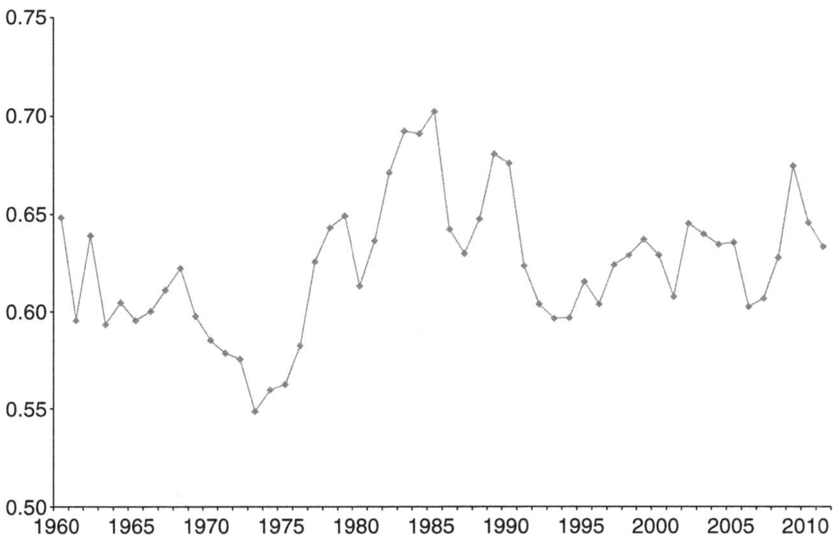

Figure 7.4 Labour share in net product, 1960–2012.

- *1974–85*. The decline in profitability of this period ended in 1985, when the social-democratic government of Panhellenic Socialist Movement (PASOK) turned to restrictive policies and launched the neoliberal era in Greece (Maniatis and Passas (2013), Mavroudeas (2011): 402–3). During this period of the falling r, both K/Y and L/Y were increased – with minor variations. From equation (4) it can be understood that Y/N did not increase so much as to offset the increases in K/N and L/N.
- *1986–2006*. The weak recovery of profitability led to profitability levels well below those of the 'golden age' of Greek capitalism. K/Y, after the initial fluctuations, fell slightly towards the end of this sub-period. The non-significant decrease, however, of K/Y indicates that there was not sufficient destruction of capital during the crisis, so as to ensure the restart of capitalist accumulation on smaller and healthier bases (Mavroudeas (2011): 402). This explains why the recovery (increasing of r) was limited (Maniatis and Passas (2013)).[13] L/Y appeared slightly downward in its general trend, despite minor fluctuations. The downward trend was more apparent after 1990 when neoliberal policies were explicitly adopted (Mavroudeas (2011): 403). These policies widened the gap between Y/N and L/N. Nevertheless, L/Y did not fall to the level of 1973.
- *2007–12*. In the new incipient period of economic crisis, which exhibited in 2012 the lowest level of r for the entire period, we will focus below. We note at present the dramatic rise in K/Y and the small increase in L/Y. L/Y increased initially – as L/N continued to rise while Y/N declined – falling after 2009. In 2012, however, it was still higher than 2007.

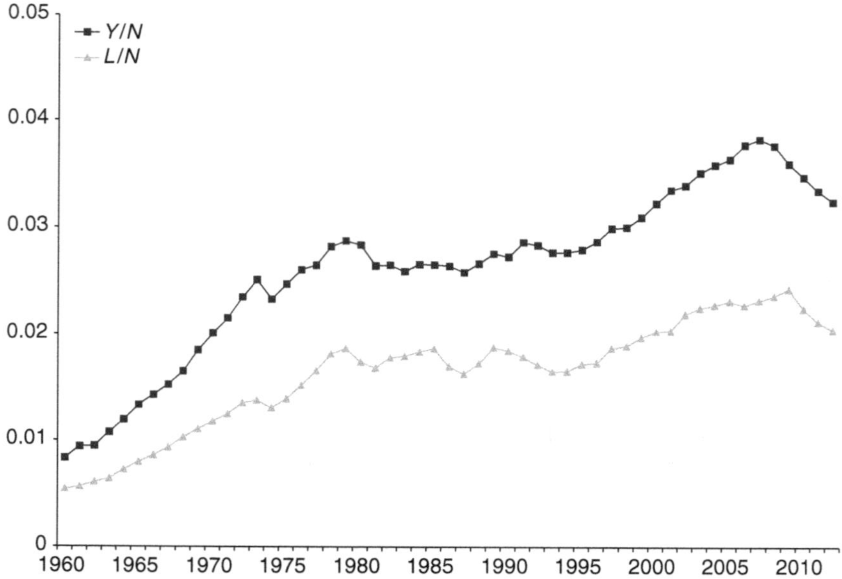

Figure 7.5 Productivity of labour and average labour compensation, 1960–2012.

V Further quantitative analysis

The variables

We will consider r as the dependent variable, and on the basis of Marx's theory of economic crises we will develop mathematical models in order to explore the factors that mainly affect it, for the period 1960/1965–2012.

First, relation (3b), which incorporates the key variables of Marx's analysis of the falling profit rate, is examined:

- The variable Π/Y refers to the theory of overaccumulation of capital,[14] since, for given Y/N, it expresses the impact of variations of L/N on profitability; here on r.
- The variable K/Y refers to the theory of rising OCC, since, for given Y/N, it expresses the impact of variations in K/N on profitability; here on r.

Beyond the variables of (3b), the impact of two additional variables on r will be determined. These are:

- The variable Y/Y^*, that is the 'capacity utilisation ratio'. This variable could show the potential impact of insufficient demand (underconsumption) on profitability (Cámara Izquierdo (2010): 19ff.); here on r. It must be noted that the underconsumptionist component Y/Y^* does not express only the Marxian concept of underconsumption as 'poverty and restricted consumption of the masses'. The insufficient demand – expressed as deviation of Y from Y^* – could originate either from the side of capitalists or wage-earners (and self-employed, in our analysis), and vice versa. Thus, for example, for given Y^* a rising Y, and consequently a rising capacity utilisation ratio of an economy, could be accompanied by a reduction of L (and thus an augmentation of Π, higher than the reduction of L), since $Y=\Pi+L$.
- The variable X/M, that is the export/import coverage index (where, X=exports of goods and services and M=imports of goods and services), which expresses the balance of goods and services in terms of ratio of its components. This variable could show the possible impact of Greece's low international competitiveness on r.[15]

Mathematical models and result analysis

a The variables of Marxian analysis

According to relation (3b), r is a function of Π/Y and K/Y. Therefore relation (3b) is written:

$$r = f\left(\frac{\Pi}{Y}, \frac{K}{Y}\right) = \frac{\frac{\Pi}{Y}}{\frac{K}{Y}}. \qquad (3b')$$

It is obvious that for the signs of partial derivatives of r holds that

$$\frac{\partial r}{\partial\left(\frac{\Pi}{Y}\right)} > 0, \frac{\partial r}{\partial\left(\frac{K}{Y}\right)} < 0 \tag{3c}$$

and hence net capital stock return is an increasing function of profit share in net product a decreasing, correspondingly, function of ratio of net capital stock to net product.

From relations (3b′) and (3c) it is inferred that Y/Y^* may cause only indirect impact on r.

Therefore, by analogy to equation (3b′), it can be considered that there are functions g_1, g_2 linking the variable Y/Y^* with the variables Π/Y and K/Y – even if not expressed analytically. That is:

$$\frac{\Pi}{Y} = g_1\left(\frac{Y}{Y^*}\right) \tag{3d}$$

$$\frac{K}{Y} = g_2\left(\frac{Y}{Y^*}\right) \tag{3e}$$

Consequently, for the estimation of the possible total (positive or negative), impact of Y/Y^* on r, the sign of partial derivative

$$\frac{\partial r}{\partial\left(\frac{Y}{Y^*}\right)}$$

should be estimated which, according to the chain rule, is given by the following relation:

$$\frac{\partial r}{\partial\left(\frac{Y}{Y^*}\right)} = \frac{\partial r}{\partial\left(\frac{\Pi}{Y}\right)} \frac{\partial\left(\frac{\Pi}{Y}\right)}{\partial\left(\frac{Y}{Y^*}\right)} + \frac{\partial r}{\partial\left(\frac{K}{Y}\right)} \frac{\partial\left(\frac{K}{Y}\right)}{\partial\left(\frac{Y}{Y^*}\right)}. \tag{5}$$

Since the partial derivatives are on average related to long-term variations in the respective magnitudes, for the estimation of their signs the linear approximation of functions has been chosen.

Each partial derivative on the right side of (5) is approximated well by the (β) coefficient of the respective linear relation.[16]

The graph of functions' flows (f, g_1, g_2) is depicted in Figure 7.6.

More precisely, ρ is the correlation coefficient of the variables connected by each flow and β is the corresponding linear regression coefficient.

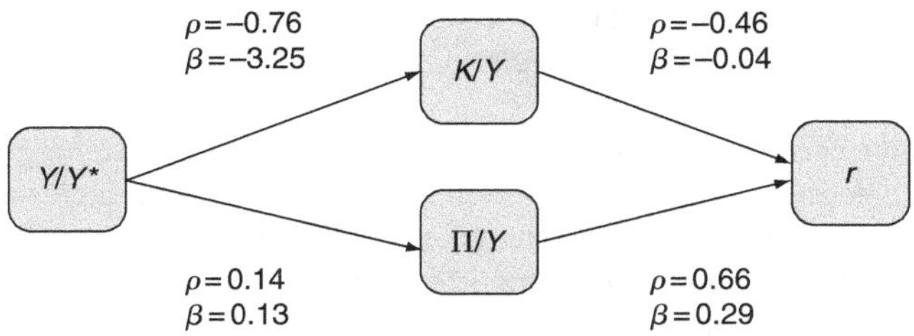

Figure 7.6 Graph of functions' flows.

On the basis of relation (3b′) it is evident that the variable Π / Y (and not the variable K / Y) exerted the highest (direct) impact on r from 1960–2012.

To examine the impact of variable Y / Y^* on r, the product of β coefficients should be taken, according to relation (5). This product also gives the estimation for the signs of partial derivatives – i.e. the relation of Y / Y^* to r.

The impact of Y / Y^* to r is positive and is equal to:

$$(0.29 \times 0.13) + (-0.04 \times -3.25) = 0.0377 + 0.13 = 0.1677 \text{ (relation 5).}$$

Therefore, it is also connoted that the impact of Y / Y^* on r, from 1965–2012, was stronger than the impact of K / Y (higher coefficient β), but less significant than the impact of Π / Y (lower coefficient β), from 1960–2012.

Given the above, it is also inferred that the Marxian theory of overaccumulation of capital reveals the main cause of changes in profitability in Greek capitalism, in the examined period.

According to linear functions, the relation between Y / Y^* and K / Y is negative, and this is consistent with the theory since, *ceteris paribus*, underconsumption leading to capital's underemployment increases the ratio K / Y.

The relation between Y / Y^* and Π / Y is (weakly) positive, i.e. for given L, an increasing capacity utilisation ratio in the Greek economy due to rising Y is related to an increasing profit share in net product, as the relation

$$\frac{\Pi}{Y} = 1 - \frac{L}{Y}$$

indicates.

b The probable impact of international competitiveness

On the basis of previous analysis it can be inferred that the probable impact of X / M on profitability (i.e. on r) is also indirect and it could be expressed through the impact of X / M on Π / Y and K / Y.

Since a clear causal relation between the variable X / M and the variables that directly affect r is not indicated by the theory, X/M is not embedded in a mathematical model. However, the correlations between X/M and the variables Π/Y and K/Y will be investigated.[17] These correlations for the period 1960–2012 are depicted in Figure 7.7.

The weak positive correlation between X/M and K/Y indicates that, for given Y/N, a relative increase of exports was accompanied by a relative increase in K/N. A possible explanation is that the relative increase of export receipts is related to the production of tradable commodities of higher income elasticity of demand, which are produced under higher TCC (Economakis *et al.* (2011)).

The weak (but less than before) positive correlation between X/M and Π/Y could be explained by the positive impact of a positive balance of goods and services on Y, and through it on Π/Y – for given L. Correspondingly, it can be explained by the weak negative correlation between X/M and L/Y (ρ=–0.26). This negative correlation implies that, for given Y/N, the export performance of the Greek economy is probably dependent on the low labour compensations (as the Bank of Greece supports – see above), but only weakly.

Consequently, a contradictory trend emerges: on the one hand X/M is correlated (weakly) positively with K/Y, and thus it probably has a weak negative impact on r; on the other hand X/M is correlated (weakly) positively with Π/Y, and thus it probably has a weak positive impact on r. The final (indirect) correlation of X/M and r is (weakly) positive (ρ=0.09), but it is essentially insignificant. Nevertheless, from the positive sign of this correlation can be implied that the export performance of the Greek economy in the examined period was not primarily linked to the production of high K/Y but of low L/Y products. This indicates that the low international competitiveness of the Greek economy is related to exports of low labour costs.[18] From this point of view 'Kaldor's paradox' is rather confirmed.

In any case it should be noted that the pressure of international competition is not confirmed as crucial for the profitability of the Greek economy. This finding, at least in the 2000s, should be seen in conjunction with the fact that for the entire period after Greece's entry into the Eurozone, Greek economic development was based – comparatively more than the EU-27 as a whole – on the growth of productive sectors not exposed to international competition (see above). Consequently, a strong portion of domestic entrepreneurial strata (capitalist and/or middle class)

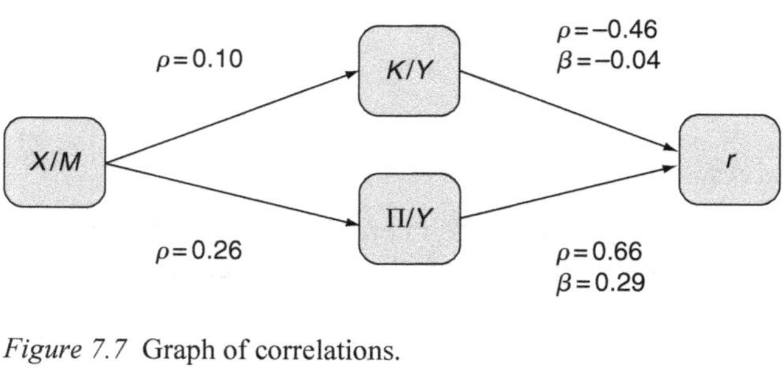

Figure 7.7 Graph of correlations.

based their profitability on the existing type of incorporation of Greek capitalism into the international level (EU-EMU), i.e. on a type of capitalist development based on international heavy borrowing. These strata are not affected by the worsening international competitive position of the Greek economy.

VI A brief note on the nature of the current crisis of the Greek economy

In Table 7.2 the changes observed in r and the variables Y/N, L/N, K/N, Y/Y^* and K, N, in the period 2007–2012 are depicted.

On the basis of relation (4) and from the data of Table 7.2 it can be inferred that r decreased under the impact of L/N, which decreased less than the Y/N, so that L/Y increased slightly and, on the other hand, of K/N, which increased while Y/N dropped. The decrease of the latter is due to the considerable reduction of Y (–23.35 per cent), which exceeded the reduction of N (–9.61 per cent). Therefore, the dramatic increase of K/Y in this sub-period, pointed out above, was due to the rising K/N in conditions of Y/N decrease.

Moreover, Y/Y^* displayed a very important reduction, which implies a considerable reduction of capacity utilisation ratio. The latter highlights the causes behind K/N increase. More precisely, K/N rise was not due mainly to K increase (it increases only 2.24 per cent) but N reduction. Consequently, in the given technological level, K/N rise implies capital's underemployment, which was due to the reduction of Y/Y^*.

The underconsumption, however, is only the form of appearance – in the conjuncture of global economic crisis – of Greek capitalism's deeper problems, i.e. of the type of its development, mainly in the 2000s. The economic growth with high CAD reached its limit when the onset of the global economic crisis blocked this type of development, since the transfer of 'savings' from the European 'centre' to the European 'periphery' stopped. The ensuing implementation of the Memoranda's austerity measures blocked capitalist reproduction displaying underconsumption crisis.

VII Epilogue

According to Marx, the economic crisis acts as a mechanism of 'self-preservation' of capital, which restores the 'healthy' movement of capitalist production, through the destruction and devaluation of constant capital and the creation of an 'artificial surplus population'.

Table 7.2 Percentage changes, 2007–12

r	Y	Y/N	L/N	K/N	Y/Y^*	K	N
–29.48	–23.35	–15.20	–11.94	13.11	–16.17	2.24	–9.61

Source: Authors' calculations using AMECO's data.

However, the current crisis of the Greek economy – besides the instability that entails for capital domination – does not seem to act as a mechanism for its productive reorganisation and restoration of profitability, given the absence of any kind of (trade or exchange rate) protective policy – i.e. within the frame of EU-EMU. On the contrary, a dead end of capitalist strategy emerges.

The austerity policy and the resultant depression lead to a rapid decrease in profitability, because of the activation of the underconsumptionist component of crisis. As a result, the current crisis requires Keynesian type measures to boost demand and thus reduce loss of income for wage earners. At the same time, Keynesian type measures will exacerbate the CAD problem – considering Greece's low international competitiveness.

Given that Greece is dependent on troika's support mechanism, any strategy of the domestic bourgeoisie and its political staff addressing the current crisis requires the political approval of lenders (troika). Such a 'political solution' seems to be the common aim both for the governmental supporters of the Memoranda and the social-democratic opposition of the Coalition of the Radical Left (SYRIZA).

Specifically, SYRIZA suggests a Keynesian type economic proposal which disputes neither the international economic relations of the country (EU-EMU) nor the type of Greek capitalist development. Obviously, the implementation of this proposal depends on the political acceptance by the troika of a regime of continuing over-borrowing. However, the social-democratic proposal has strong social support from the working strata and domestic entrepreneurial strata (capitalist and/or middle class) that base their profitability on the existing type of capitalist development within the EU-EMU frame.

From the view point of a communist strategy the question is how the current crisis of Greek capitalism will be the starting point for disputing not only Greek capitalism's specific model but also the very capitalist exploitative relation. Greece's exit from EU-EMU is a transitional target in this direction provided that it is accompanied by an overall challenge of capitals' economic and political power.

Notes

1 The sum of differences savings minus investments and public revenues minus public expenditures is identically equal to the current account balance. Usually, in macroeconomic theory this identity is transformed to a theoretical explanation of the factors affecting current account balance.

More precisely, if

$$(S-I)+(T-G)=CA$$

(where, S: savings, I: investments, T: taxes, G: public expenditures and CA: current account balance) then, a $FD(T-G<0)$ could cause a CAD – under the precondition that the difference between savings and investments ($S-I$) is zero or negative or positive but less than FD. There is a tendency at this point that concerns the polemic against public spending in particular. Thus the impact of the competitiveness of an economy (as is reflected in the balance of goods and services) on the formation of the other variables of identity is ignored.

More precisely, if

$$GNP = DD + CA$$

(where, *GNP*: gross national product and *DD*: domestic demand) and

$$CA = NX + NFI + CT$$

(where, *NX*: balance of goods and services, *NFI*: income balance and *CT*: current transfers balance), then a rising positive *NX*, given the other sub-balances of *CA*, augmenting *CA* also augments *GNP*. Assuming that savings is a function of disposable income, then, *ceteris paribus*, the increase of *GNP* increasing disposable income will increase savings, and so the difference $(S-I)$. Also, assuming that taxes depend on income levels, then, *ceteris paribus*, the increase of *GNP* will increase *T* and consequently the difference $(T-G)$.

2 According to Lapavitsas *et al.* (2010: 16), the CAD of 'peripheral' EU countries (Greece, Portugal and Spain) had mainly to do with their low competitiveness relative to the 'core' and not with their public sector, which did not create systematic financial deficits, although it has been repeatedly described by the official rhetoric as prodigal and ineffective.

3 The current transfers balance has shown a declining trend over time. According to AMECO's data, depicted in Figure 7.1, it becomes negative from 2005 to 2012, subsequently surcharging the current account balance in recent years.

4 For the methodology of calculation of the 'Gross External Debt' and 'International Investment Position' see Bank of Greece (2010: 134–5). According to this methodology, gross external debt liabilities do not include '(i) foreign direct investment relating to equity capital and reinvested earnings and, (ii) portfolio investment in equity' (Bank of Greece (2010): 135).

5 The Bank of Greece (2012: 91) divides the period from the beginning of the 2000s until the outbreak of the debt crisis into two sub-periods: 2000–5 and 2006–8. The first sub-period is characterised by a smooth and relatively stable evolution of CAD. During the second sub-period CAD deteriorated strongly and continuously.

6 This is a chronic structural weakness of the Greek economy, which however deteriorates after Greece's entry in the EU.

7 The official position, as is expressed by the Bank of Greece (2010: 16–18), supports that the high CAD, the growth of the external debt and the deterioration of Greece's negative net international investment position is a result of the 'losses in competitiveness' of the Greek economy. These are mainly related to the rigidities in the labour market that led to wage increase and losses in price competitiveness. However, the 'international competitiveness' of a national economy is not a matter of 'price' or 'cost' competitiveness. It is mainly dependent on 'non-price' factors such as technological opportunities, technical infrastructure and production capacities, which constitute the productive structure and the related 'externalities' (see Ilzkovitz *et al.* (Internet): 2, Nurbel (2007): 65). Furthermore, Kaldor's post-war findings indicate that the countries that had the greatest increase in their market share also had the highest decline in price competitiveness (i.e. the highest increase in unit labour costs) (Felipe and Kumar (2011): 3–4). This is known as 'Kaldor's paradox'. Moreover, the Greek economy was an economy of low wages within the EU-15 frame – even before Memoranda. During the period 2000–10, the Greek average annual wages (in 2010 USD PPPs and 2010 constant prices) remained the lowest in the EU-15, with the exception of Portugal (OECD Stat Extracts).

8 For a detailed analysis on the Marxian theory of economic crises and of Marxist controversies on the Marxian theory of economic crises, see Milios *et al.* (2002), Economakis *et al.* (2010).

9 Since 1960 there are available data for all the variables of our analysis, except the potential product where available data exists from 1965.

10 It should be noted that a relevant application of fixed capital return in the Greek economy for the period 1964–2004 indicated that the diachronic trends of performance of the overall economy did not differ significantly from those of the business sector (Ioakeimoglou and Milios (2005): 38).

11 The Marxist bibliography reflects a theoretical contradiction in Marx's work in this subject. In the *Grundrisse* (Marx (1981)) as in Volume I of *Capital* (Marx (1990)), Marx clearly considers the capital in all sectors of the economy as equally productive. Nevertheless, in Volume III of *Capital* (Marx (1991)), Marx regards the capital in the commodity circulation process as unproductive. Many Marxist theoreticians embrace the latter viewpoint (see among others Shaikh and Tonak (1994)).

12 Interestingly, the periodisation of Maniatis and Passas (2013), although resulting from a different Marxist methodology, is similar to ours – except the last crisis, whose beginning, unlike us, is defined after 2007.

13 According to Marx, the crisis carries the risk of capitalism's overthrow. In the Greek case, from the political changeover (fall of dictatorship) until 1985, the awareness of this risk was expressed mainly by the Keynesian policies of state regulation and income redistribution applied by the governments, which aimed at the relaxation of post-dictatorship political radicalism and its incorporation into the system. However, these policies failed to cope with the economic crisis, since they applied successful post-war directions in a totally different conjuncture. These policies had confronted the structural crisis of 1929–30, but they did this after the two World Wars which caused a drastic depreciation of overaccumulated capital (Mavroudeas (2011): 402).

14 We note that in the relevant Marxist discussion this factor is mainly connected with the so-called 'profit squeeze theory'. In this theoretical direction are included, among others, the works of Weisskopf (1979) and Wolff (1986), despite their differences (see Economakis *et al.* (2010)).

15 The possible impact of competitiveness on capital profitability has been introduced in Marxist discussions by Brenner (1998). His explanation of the decline of the profit rate in the US manufacturing sector through international competition (US, Germany and Japan) in the 1970s and 1980s resulted, according to Shaikh (1999: 136) in the 'Smithian error' – 'that a fall in one sector's rate of profit can drag down the general rate of profit'.

16 In all variables detrend techniques and techniques for the elimination of autocorrelation were applied before their introduction in the models.

17 In all variables detrend techniques and techniques for the elimination of autocorrelation were applied before their correlation.

18 The Greek economy, and its export structure, is dominated by sectors mainly associated with the primary production and its manufacture, which produce commodities of low income elasticity of demand. These sectors are of low technology and low and medium-low skilled labour (Economakis *et al.* (2011)). The latter is related to lower labour compensations.

References

AMECO: http://ec.europa.eu/economy_finance/ameco/user/serie/SelectSerie.cfm.

Bank of Greece (2000), *Annual Report 1999*, Athens.

Bank of Greece (2003), *Annual Report 2002*, Athens.

Bank of Greece (2009), *Annual Report 2008*, Athens.

Bank of Greece (2010), *Annual Report 2009*, Athens.

Bank of Greece (2012), *Annual Report 2011*, Athens.

Bank of Greece (2013a), *Annual Report 2012*, Athens [in Greek].
Bank of Greece (2013b), *Summary of Annual Report 2012*, Athens.
Brenner R. (1998), 'The economics of global turbulence', *New Left Review* 229.
Cámara Izquierdo S. (2010), 'Short and long-term dynamics of the U.S. profit rate in the context of the current crisis', Paper presented at the Congrès Marx International VI 'Crises, Révoltes, Utopies', Université de Paris-Ouest-Nanterre-La Défense, France, 22–25 September.
Duménil G. and Lévy D. (2002), 'The profit rate: where and how much did it fall? Did it recover? (USA 1948–2000)', *Review of Radical Political Economics* 34(4).
Duménil G. and Lévy D. (2004), 'The real and financial components of profitability (USA 1952–2000)', *Review of Radical Political Economics* 36(1).
Economakis G. (2005), 'Definition of the capitalist mode of production: a re-examination (with application to non-capitalist modes of production', *History of Economics Review* 42.
Economakis G. (2011), 'Greek economic crisis and EU: the crisis of the extraverted model of development of Greek capitalism', *Outopia* 96 [in Greek].
Economakis G., Anastasiadis A. and Markaki M. (2010), 'US economic performance from 1929 to 2008 in terms of the Marxian theory of crises, with some notes on recent financial crisis', *Critique* 38(3).
Economakis G., Markaki M. Anastasiadis A. and Papalexiou G. (2011), 'Competitiveness of the Greek economy: a sectoral investigation', in Scientific Association of Political Economy (ed.), *Economic Crisis and Greece*, Athens: Gutenberg [in Greek].
Eurostat: http://epp.eurostat.ec.europa.eu/portal/page/portal/statistics/search_database.
Felipe J. and Kumar U. (2011), 'Unit labor costs in the Eurozone: the competitiveness debate again', Levy Economics Institute of Bard College, Working Paper 651.
Fotopoulos T. (2010), *Greece as a Protectorate of the Transnational Elite: The Need for Immediate Exit from the EU and for a Self-dependent Economy*, Athens: Gordios [in Greek].
Gibson H. (2010), 'Sectoral growth of the Greek economy for the period 1995–2003', In Oikonomou G., Sabethai I. and Simigiannis G. (eds), *Current Account Balance of Greece: Causes of Unbalances and Proposals of Policy*, Athens: Bank of Greece [in Greek].
Ilzkovitz F., Dierx A., Galgau O. and Leib K. (Internet), 'Trade performance and structural competitiveness. Developments in the Euro area: are member states equipped to meet the globalization challenges of the 21st century?' Available at: http://research.stlouisfed.org/conferences/integration/Galgau-paper.pdf.
Ioakeimoglou E. and Milios J. (2005), 'Capital accumulation and profitability in Greece (1964–2004)' *Theseis* 91 [in Greek].
Laibman D. (2010), 'Capitalism, crisis, renewal: some conceptual excavations', *Science and Society* 74(3).
Lapavitsas C., Kaltenbrunner A., Lambrinidis G., Lindo D., Meadway J., Michell J., Painceira J.P., Pires E., Powell J., Stenfors A. and Teles N. (2010), 'The Eurozone between austerity and default', RMF occasional report.
Maniatis T. and Passas C. (2013), 'Profitability, capital accumulation and crisis in the Greek economy 1958–2009: a Marxist analysis', *Review of Political Economics* 25(4).
Marx K. (1969), *Theories of Surplus Value* Part II, London: Lawrence & Wishart.
Marx K. (1978), *Theories of Surplus Value* Part I, London: Lawrence & Wishart.
Marx K. (1981), *Grundrisse*, London: Penguin Books.
Marx K. (1990), *Capital*, Vol. I, London: Penguin Books.
Marx K. (1991), *Capital*, Vol. III, London: Penguin Books.

Mavroudeas S. (2011), 'Greece and European Union: capitalist crisis and inter-imperialist contradictions', in Scientific Association of Political Economy (ed.), *Economic Crisis and Greece*, Athens: Gutenberg [in Greek].

Milios J. (2011), 'The Greek crisis as a version of the global economic crisis and EMU crisis', Paper presented at the International Conference 'Public debt and austerity policies in Europe: the response of the European left', organised by: European Left Party, Coalition of the Left and N. Poulantzas Institute [in Greek].

Milios J., Dimoulis D. and Economakis G. (2002), *Karl Marx and the Classics: An Essay on Value, Crises and the Capitalist Mode of Production*, Aldershot, Burlington, VA, Singapore and Sidney: Ashgate.

Nurbel A. (2007), 'The global competitiveness of the nation: a conceptual discussion', *Journal of Business and Economics Research* 5(10).

OECD Stat Extracts: http://stats.oecd.org/.

Oikonomou G. (2010), 'Current account: conclusions of analysis and policy recommendations', in Oikonomou G., Isaac S. and Georgios S. (eds), *Current Account Balance of Greece: Causes of Unbalances and Proposals of Policy*, Athens: Bank of Greece [in Greek].

Pelagidis T. (2010), 'The Greek paradox of falling competitiveness and weak institutions in a high GDP growth rate context (1995–2008)', GreeSE Paper No. 38 (August) Hellenic Observatory Papers on Greece and Southeast Europe – LSE.

Shaikh A. (1999), 'Explaining the global economic crisis', *Historical Materialism* 5.

Shaikh A. and Tonak A. (1994), *Measuring the Wealth of Nations*, Cambridge: Cambridge University Press.

Stamatis G. (1986), 'The crisis and the illusions for its overcoming', *Theseis* 15 [in Greek].

Stamatis G. (1997), *Introduction to Political Economy*, Athens: Hellinika Grammata [in Greek].

Sweezy P. (1970), *The Theory of Capitalist Development: Principles of Marxian Political Economy*, New York and London: Modern Reader Paperbacks.

Weisskopf T. (1979), 'Marxian crisis theory and the rate of profit in the postwar U.S. economy', *Cambridge Journal of Economics* 3.

Wolff E. (1986), 'The productivity slowdown and the fall in the US rate of profit, 1947–76', *Review of Radical Political Economics* 18(1&2).

8 The Greek crisis

A dual crisis of overaccumulation and imperialist exploitation

Stavros Mavroudeas and Dimitris Paitaridis

I Introduction

In Mainstream accounts Greek capitalism's crisis that led to the imposition of the troika (EU–IMF–ECB) Economic Adjustment Programmes is a twin deficits crisis (fiscal and current account deficits) that is not related to the 2007–8 global crisis. Moreover, its causes are attributed to policy errors and/or 'shallow' structural problems concerning competitiveness (see Chapter 1 of this volume). Similarly, Heterodox and Radical explanations take the one or the other side of the fiscal–current account deficits duo as a cause of the Greek crisis (see Introduction). In contrast, this chapter offers a Marxist structural explanation of the Greek crisis. It situates its deeper causes not on circulation relations (finance) but on production relations. Without resorting to crude reductionism and leaving space for degrees of freedom, financial problems are considered as consequences of deeper situated productive problems.

In this vein, the Greek crisis is (a) closely related to the 2007–8 global capitalist crisis and (b) geared in the antinomies of the productive structure of Greek capitalism. Moreover, its causes are a fusion of internal and external processes. Thus, it is characterised as a *dual crisis of overaccumulation and imperialist exploitation*. The overaccumulation component constitutes the internal cause and stems from the tendential fall of the profit rate (TRPF) that led to the 1973 crisis, was aggravated by the simultaneous fall of the military dictatorship, was not resolved decisively by the subsequent neo-conservative restructuring policies and resurfaced with the 2007–8 crisis. The external cause is Greek capitalism's downgrading within the international division of labour, the failure of its imperialist ambitions and its imperialist dominance and exploitation by the euro-core countries. Their combination resulted in the current crisis of Greek capitalism. The twin deficits are a corollary but not a cause of it.

The chapter is structured as follows. In order to fully comprehend the current Greek crisis a long-run perspective should be adopted and Greek capitalism has to be situated within the international division of labour. Thus the historical course and particularly the post-war evolution of Greek capitalism are presented in the second section. The main argument is that Greek capitalism is a second-generation, middle-range capitalism with limited imperialist abilities. Then the roots of the current Greek crisis are traced back to the 1973 crisis and the limited success of the subsequent capitalist restructuring waves. The 1973 global capitalist crisis ended the post-war 'Golden era' of robust capitalist accumulation and ushered a prolonged period of weak economic performance (accurately branded as 'silent depression'). For Greek capitalism it was doubly onerous as it was accompanied with the fall of the military dictatorship that led to the collapse of capital's repression mechanisms that suppressed labour demands and bolstered capitalist profits.

The third section analyses the internal dimension of the Greek crisis. Our empirical analysis confirms that this is an *à-la*-Marx crisis of falling profitability. That is, it was caused by the TRPF – due to the increase of the OCC – that resurfaced at the beginning of the twenty-first century. Thus, contrary to the mainstream twin deficits and the radical financialisation explanations, it is shown that the causes of the crisis lay in the 'deep' productive structure of Greek capitalism and were subsequently expressed in the rest of the total circuit of capital (circulation and distribution).

The fourth section examines the external dimension of the crisis. It is shown that Greece's accession to the European integration process led to a deteriorating competitiveness. This loss of competitiveness had both policy and structural causes. By ceding the control of the monetary and fiscal instruments of economic policy to Brussels, Greek capitalism lost critical means for supporting its competitiveness. This was aggravated further by the fact that it had to compete with more developed capitalisms (i.e. with higher capital–labour ratio). When more developed capitals compete unhindered with less developed ones the former are able to reap off extra-profits from the latter. Therefore, this combination has resulted in relations of imperialist exploitation (i.e. unequal exchange) that exist within the EU and which divide it between euro-core and euro-periphery economies.

Finally the last section concludes by analysing how and under what concrete circumstances the Greek crisis erupted. It is argued that the 2007–8 crisis in the leading capitalist economies triggered Greek capitalism's own profitability and overaccumulation problems. This ended the period of 'artificial growth' and ushered Greek capitalism into deep crisis.

II The turbulent course of Greek capitalism

Greek capitalism is a second-generation capitalism because it followed capitalism's pioneers (Western Europe and Japan) with a significant time lag.[1] On the other hand Greek diaspora capital was quite developed both in the West and in the Ottoman Empire. This engrafted Greek capitalism with angst to catch-up with its neighbouring West. Because also of the internationalised character of the Greek diaspora capital and the limited geographical area of the first independent Greek state, Greek capitalism had from its very beginning an inherent tendency to expand its 'vital space'. This equipped it with strong imperialist tendencies which, however, were inherently unstable and weak because of the lack of a strong national arm. These took the form of periodic forays to other areas with middle-brow and short-term results followed by retrenchments in its national basis.

Greek capitalism was consolidated during 1830–70 and the first signs of an anaemic growth appeared. Agriculture, commerce and shipping were the main economic sectors whilst industrialisation was very limited. Active economic policies were absent and the economy was export oriented (mainly certain exportable agricultural products) due to the lack of a sufficiently developed internal market. Capitalist relations were further bolstered and developed during 1870–80 with the creation of necessary infrastructure and the introduction of protectionist and monopolist elements. The war effort and the territorial expansion (1880–1920) that followed facilitated a robust growth that was reinforced by the state interventionist and protectionist policies of the following period (1920–40). The Second World War, the Axis occupation and the near collapse of the economy and the civil war that followed disrupted violently capitalist reproduction. After an initial period of stabilisation and reconstruction of capitalist relations Greek capitalism was restructured along state-monopolist lines (1944–58). This restructuring set the ground for the subsequent 'golden era' (1958–73), characterised by high rates of accumulation and profitability and extended industrialisation. In a nutshell, after the Second World War and the civil war and thanks to its post-war restructuring and also the defeat of the Left, Greek capitalism narrowed its gap and its time lag with the more advanced European countries, exhibited a marked increase in its competitiveness and ascended within the international division of labour. State economic interventionism played a crucial role in the 'golden era' as during almost all Greek capitalism's history.[2] However, the Greek post-war 'golden era' differed substantially from the Western one in that it did not include a developed welfare state and was based on the suppression of workers' rights and pay. Moreover, it had a significant imperialist component as Greek capitals expanded remarkably their activities particularly in the Mediterranean area and the Middle East.

Similarly with the more developed Western capitalisms the 1973 global crisis put an end to Greek capitalism's 'golden era'. As in the West (Shaikh and Tonak (1994)) the 1973 crisis in Greece was an overaccumulation crisis caused by a falling profit rate due to the increase of the organic composition of capital (OCC). The overaccumulation crisis was simmering in Greek capitalism since its 'golden age' as the increase of the rate of surplus-value started slowing down whereas OCC was rising rapidly (see following section). This caused a TRPF that was subsequently expressed in a curtailment of investment and ushered the system in a long period of anaemic performance. This meant that, in the given historical conjecture, capitalist accumulation had surpassed its social and technical limits and a great amount of capitals could not be invested profitably. Moreover, the 1973 crisis was a structural crisis and not a simply cyclical one: it marked the end of an era and necessitated a radical reconfiguration of the internal structure of the capitalist system.

However, the 1973 crisis had also a crucial national specificity that differentiated Greek capitalism's subsequent path from that of the West (see Mavroudeas

(2013)): it coincided with the fall of the military dictatorship and the reappearance of the labour movement as a critical factor. In order to defuse popular radicalism, Greek capital was obliged to resort to progressive Keynesian policies of income redistribution in favour of the working class. Hence, Greek capitalism's *sui generis* de-coupling from the West continued albeit in a new version. Whereas during the post-war period the West adopted progressive Keynesian policies of income redistribution Greek capitalism followed conservative Keynesian policies with limited concessions to the working classes. When, facing the 1973 crisis, the West espoused neo-conservatism Greek capitalism was obliged to resort to progressive Keynesian policies. This placed additional burdens on capital's profitability and accumulation.

Thus the post-dictatorship governments employed policies trying to combine (a) growth (which was slowing down due to global economic crisis) and (b) managed pro-labour income redistribution but in a manner not dramatically detrimental to capitalist profitability. So, the redistribution policies not only improved labour's position but at the same time helped to defuse the post-dictatorship popular radicalism and accommodate it in an elaborate patronage system.

At the same time Greek capital made the strategic choice to participate in the European integration process and Greece became an EEC full member in 1981. The reasons behind this choice were threefold: (a) to secure the system from popular radicalism, (b) to push through capitalist restructuring with the help of the then EEC and (c) to upgrade Greek capitalism from middle-range imperialism to a partner in one of the major global imperialist blocs. This contemporary 'Big Idea' of Greek capitalism was fraught with risks from its very beginning (see section IV below). Especially, it led to a declining competitiveness that caused a deteriorating CAD.

However, these progressive Keynesian policies failed to address the economic crisis and to bolster the profit rate (see next section) because they applied the successful post-war recipes in totally different socio-economic conditions. Post-war growth-boosting Keynesian policies were successful because the war had devalorised the previously overaccumulated capitals. This was not the case with the 1973 crisis as capitals remained critically overaccumulated in the aftermath of the crisis.

Therefore, as soon as the post-dictatorship popular radicalism was checked, Greek capital abandoned progressive Keynesian policies and turned to capitalist restructuring policies which cover the whole 1985–2007 period. Thus, it followed the Western example but with a noticeable time lag.

First, conservative Keynesian restructuring policies (anti-cyclical demand-led growth policies but without pro-labour income redistribution) were employed. At the same time Greece's accession in the EEC removed trade protectionism and dealt a severe blow to Greek capital's competitiveness against the more developed EEC economies. The conservative Keynesian policies had limited results as they failed to suppress adequately wages and devalorise overaccumulated capitals.

They were succeeded by the already dominant in the West neo-liberal restructuring policies (formally introduced in 1990). As Greek capitalist restructuring was already lagging significantly, Greek neo-liberal policies almost bypassed monetarism (closed economy neo-liberalism) and espoused directly open economy neo-liberalism. EEC and EU directives played a crucial role in this. The neo-liberal agenda (opening of the economy, privatisations, curtailment of the welfare system, tax reforms benefiting the wealthy, deregulation of labour market and the financial system, etc.) guided all the subsequent governments. Neo-liberal restructuring policies bolstered more forcefully than their conservative Keynesian predecessors labour exploitation which was expressed in the increase of the rate of surplus-value. Of particular significance was the marked increase of the actual work-time from the mid-1990s and onwards (Mavroudeas (2013)), which reinvigorated the extraction of absolute surplus-value, after a considerable dormancy period.

Concurrently, the Eastern Bloc's disintegration opened a new area of opportunities for Greek capital, particularly in the Balkans. Taking advantage of its geographical proximity and EU membership, it penetrated these countries reaping imperialist extra-profits. Moreover, the massive migration to Greece from these – and later from others as well – countries facilitated the depression of wages (especially in certain sectors, e.g. construction) and the expansion of flexible working relations.

Greece's 2001 accession in the EMU complicated the situation further. Greek capitalism attempted to decisively upgrade its position within the international division of labour by participating in the upper tier of European integration. But this strategic choice was risky since the severe constraints on national monetary, industrial and commercial policies weakened further Greek competitiveness vis-à-vis the euro-core countries which were characterised by productive superiority. In the beginning, these problems were ameliorated by securing – thanks to the euro – cheap credit that promoted an artificial growth. This was boosted further by the organisation of 2004 Olympic Games in Athens whose exorbitant and over-priced works bolstered Greek (and Western) capitals' profitability but at the same time worsened FD.[3] Essentially, whenever capital accumulation faltered the Greek state stepped in and, directly or indirectly, subsidised it. The ballooning FD was manageable because of the cheap foreign loans and the relatively high growth rates of the Greek economy.

On top of that Greek capitalism, during that period, followed the international trend of aggressively employing credit and fictitious capital expansion (the so-called 'financialisation'). Cheap credit was boosted by euro's low interest rates. The stock market became a major source of enterprise finance, whereas traditionally its role and size were minimal. Private consumption was artificially ballooned via cheap personal credit offered by the banks which increased private debt. It should be noted, however, that Greek capital's leverage operations and the private debt were significantly smaller than those of its Western counterparts (see Chapter 5 of this volume).

All these unsustainable and conjectural factors led to an 'artificial boom' period with better than the rest of the EU growth rates. This 'artificial boom' period had another hidden handicap: there was a steep increase of unproductive activities (particularly around finance and trade) which eroded internally profitability's foundations (see next section).

To sum up, the period 1985–2007 was marked by capitalist restructuring waves which strived to reverse the falling profit rate trend and the overaccumulation of capital. Their policies revitalised the counteracting forces to the TRPF by (a) increasing the rate of surplus-value, (b) reducing the value of labour-power, (c) reducing the value of constant capital, (d) reducing turnover time, (e) increasing foreign trade and (f) reaping imperialist extra-profits from abroad. These restructurings were only partially successful. There was a recovery of the profit rate but this never reached the level achieved in the beginning of its fall. Moreover, capital was insufficiently devalorised as Greek capitalism shied away from the deep and painful devalorisation required. Thus the fundamental problems remained and the 'financialisation' tricks and the 'artificial growth' only postponed and at the same time augmented them.

The 2007–8 crisis ended abruptly this euphoria. The 'artificial boom' collapsed and the lurking profitability crisis resurfaced. The 'financialisation' deus ex machina postponed the crisis but, at the same time, amplified further the problem of overaccumulation. As soon as productive capital's profitability – under the auspices of which surplus-value (and thus total profit) is generated – started faltering then the crisis tendancies re-emerged in all their glory. 'Financialisation' gave only a temporary respite to the crisis of profitability but at a very high cost. It increased significantly the portion of surplus-value extracted by productive capital but accruing to money capital. This aggravated further the falling profitability of productive capital and set the whole house on fire. Additionally, imperialist extra-profits collapsed as the Balkan economies entered recession[4] and competition with other stronger imperialisms was aggravated. Also, the global financial collapse ended cheap credit. Thus, Greek capitalism abruptly fell in crisis.

III The internal cause: a profitability crisis

For Marxist analysis capitalism is an economic system inherently prone to crises. The latter are neither an exceptional result of erroneous actions nor an abnormal phenomenon. On the contrary, they are part of capitalism's normal modus operandi. Capitalism's functioning is characterised by mid-term boom–bust cycles that exhibit – over a longer time span – more violent fluctuations. The latter constitute economic crises, i.e. violent and abrupt disruptions of the accumulation process. The crisis mechanism – and also its milder cycles – is related to capitalism's fundamental motive: profit. For Marx the continuous quest for increased profits falls prey, from time to time, to itself. By accumulating profits at an increasing rhythm it stumbles upon objective (social and technical) barriers that make further accumulation unprofitable. Thus overaccumulation occurs: more capital has been accumulated than that that can be reinvested profitably.

The fundamental mechanism that leads the system into crisis is Marx's famous TRPF law. This mechanism is geared in the sphere of production and then transmitted to the rest of the circuit of capital (circulation and distribution). However, while TRPF constitutes the essential mechanism of the crisis, the latter can be expressed through various forms depending on historically specific elements. The solution of the crisis can come only through a destruction process: overaccumulated capitals have to be devalorised. Simultaneously, the counteracting forces to the TRPF have to be invigorated. In this way the system returns to a leaner and sounder basis, the profit rate recovers and capitalist reproduction process restarts.

In order to test the falling profitability hypothesis for the post-war Greek economy National Accounts data have to be reformulated in a manner reflecting the Marxian categories and particularly the distinction between productive and unproductive labour.[5] The classification between productive and unproductive activities is presented in the Appendix to this chapter. The method employed is the one proposed by Shaikh and Tonak (1994). For the purposes of our analysis we used data from various databases such as the EU KLEMS,[6] the Hellenic Statistical Authority (EL.STAT.), the Annual Macro-Economic database (AMECO) and also from other studies (e.g. Skountzos and Mattheos (1980)). Maniatis and Passas (2013) and in Chapter 6 of this volume offer a similar analysis. Our research differs in two aspects. First, the consumption of fixed capital of the unproductive trade and royalties sectors and the intermediate inputs of royalties sector are included in the Marxian value added. Second, the agricultural sector is included in our estimations.

The rationale of the first inclusion is that the value of these sectors flows from the sphere of production. However, the second inclusion requires a more detailed justification.

Often Marxist empirical studies of the Greek economy refrain from including the agricultural sector in their calculations since the latter is characterised mainly by family farming. Capitalist activities are mainly found upstream of farming (seeds, chemicals, machinery, etc.) and downstream of farming (food processing, distribution, retail). This exclusion is misleading for a number of reasons. We argue that Greek agriculture is (a) from its very beginning, indirectly subordinated to capital accumulation and (b) undergoing a serious contemporary transformation towards direct subordination to capital accumulation.

Indirect subordination to capitalism is effected mainly through *relations of circulation*. In a nutshell, as small farmers acquire their inputs from and produce their output for capitalist markets they actually relinquish control of their production and reproduction process to capital. There are two main channels of this subordination: (a) dependence upon capitalist finance for credit and (b) contract farming.

Vergopoulos (1975) has accurately argued that family farming does not constitute a separate mode of petty commodity production but it is functionally linked to capitalist accumulation. Greek industrial capital preferred family farming (as opposed to a capitalist land-owning one) since this provided it with cheaper inputs. Thus, apart from a brief period of peculiar cooperation (during the Trikoupi administration) industrial capital sided with peasants against big land-ownership. This culminated in the policies of land redistribution at the beginning of the twentieth century that weathered away big land-ownership and established the small family farm character of Greek agriculture. This process is far from an 'anomaly' in capitalism. Mann and Dickinson (1978) have shown that the persistence of small farming is derived from special obstacles that capital faces in agriculture and which impede it from following the path of industry. A major obstacle is that production time lapses behind labour-time in agriculture (as natural processes are involved in the maturation of its produce), leading to lower productivity and profit rate. Capital avoids being tied up during these periods and prefers to 'subcontract' these processes to small farmers. This does not make small farmers independent petty commodity producers. On the contrary, most of their inputs come from and most of their outputs are destined for the capitalist markets. In this way small farmers do not actually control the nature and tempo of their production process and cannot sell their produce in an open market: they become a mere capitalist operative irrespectively of retaining ownership of some of the means of production. Vergopoulos (1975) shows that this process indeed took place in Greek agriculture.

The notorious dependence upon credit from the banking sector (especially the privatised in 2013 Agriculture Bank of Greece) indirectly subordinates agriculture to capitalism by transferring a part of its surplus product to capital in the form of interest. According to the last available annual economic survey of the Agriculture Bank of Greece (2011) the loans provided to the agricultural sector were €2,073,973,000 for the year 2010 and €1,761,638,000 for 2011.

The expansion of contract farming enforced further this process (Moissidis (1986, 1988)) as small farmers effectively lose their control on the means of production and become similar to piece-rate wage workers ('propertied labourers' according to Davis (1980)).

Direct subordination of agriculture to capitalism takes place through *relations of production*. This implies that wage agricultural labour is increasing. This is a rather complicated issue. Setting aside whether family labour conceals within it covert forms of wage labour, data show a weak increase in wage labour and employers (see Figure 8.1). However, these data do not measure (a) seasonal and casual wage labour and (b) undeclared labour both of which have a significant presence. In particular the latter plays nowadays a crucial role in the capitalist penetration of Greek agriculture.

Before the 1990s casual and seasonal labour was particularly important in Greek agriculture. Family farming required from time to time – particularly during harvest periods – significant labour input. Students, casual workers and Romanies offered its main pools. However, from the 1980s Greece was transformed from a traditionally migrant-exporting country to a migrant-importing one. It began with small immigration waves from Eastern and Central Europe, Soviet Union, Africa and Asia (Kasimis *et al.* (2003)). These were followed in the 1990s with big immigration waves; particularly after the collapse of the Eastern Bloc (with an influx of migrants from the neighbouring Balkan countries) and the Schengen Agreement (which for a number of reasons made Greece

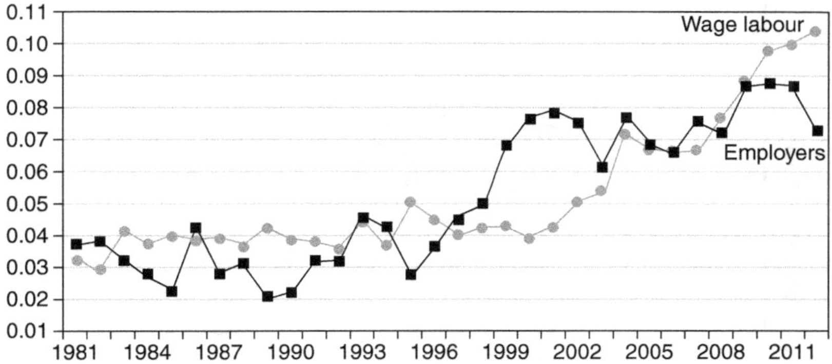

Figure 8.1 Wage labour and employers as a percentage of total employment in agriculture (source: Hellenic Statistical Authority (EL.STAT.)).

a 'concentration camp' for immigrants trying to get to Western Europe but not permitted to). According to the 2001 Population Census, immigrants correspond to approximately 7 per cent of the population and 9 per cent of the labour force. It is estimated that 17.5 per cent of them are employed in the agricultural sector representing 11.6 per cent of agricultural employment (Cholezas and Tsakloglou (2008): 10). This migrants' influx transformed radically Greek agriculture. Cheap immigrant labour was extensively employed in farming (for both economic and prestige reasons) and, at the same time female family labour was reduced. The net effect is an increase of wage labour in agriculture. At this point there is a significant hurdle with the data as the majority is illegal immigrants and official data underestimate seriously their presence.

This increase in wage labour in agriculture is related also to the increase in land concentration. Greek agriculture is characterised by small lots and significant land fragmentation. However, several studies (e.g. Moisidis (1986), Tsoulfidis (2009)) show that there is a small tendency towards land concentration and centralisation. This is reinforced by land leasing which increases the cultivating areas of the bigger farmers. By extending Tsoulfidis' (2009) data for the period 1950–2003 till 2007 (from the *Concise Statistical Yearbook 2009* (2010)) we verify this tendency as there is an increase of the bigger than 100 stremmas lots.

Last, there is a marked increase of agro-industries during the recent decades. These cover mainly other activities than farming and they employ wage labour. According to the *Statistical Yearbook* agro-industry joint stock companies vary from 2.55 per cent for 2002 to 2.31 per cent for 2006 of the total companies.

For the abovementioned reasons we include in our estimations of capital accumulation and profitability the agriculture sector of the Greek economy.

The Marxian Value Added (*MVA*) is defined as the sum of (a) the net value added in the production sectors (NVA_{Prd}), (b) the total gross output in the trade

Table 8.1 Number of agricultural and livestock holdings, by size-classes of their utilised agricultural area (area in stremmas = 1,000 m^2)

Year	*1–9* *%*	*10–49* *%*	*50–99* *%*	*100–199* *%*	*200+* *%*	*Total*
1950	2,308,498 6.40%	15,627,746 43.34%	7,967,315 22.10%	3,658,871 10.15%	6,492,425 18.01%	36,054,855 100%
1961	1,319,882 3.59%	16,583,395 45.15%	11,432,086 31.12%	4,981,308 13.56%	2,416,085 6.58%	36,732,756 100%
1971	1,134,820 3.16%	14,950,600 41.69%	10,926,000 30.47%	5,529,880 15.43%	3,321,640 9.26%	35,862,940 100%
1977	1,073,150 2.41%	22,824,270 51.29%	9,951,090 22.36%	6,174,030 13.87%	4,477,160 10.06%	44,499,700 100%
1981	1,205,524 3.40%	13,420,524 37.85%	10,041,824 28.32%	6,089,860 17.18%	4,697,200 13.25%	35,454,932 100%
1987	1,117,547 3.25%	11,353,703 33.03%	9,252,499 26.92%	6,658,137 19.37%	5,986,941 17.42%	34,368,827 100%
1991	1,046,566 2.84%	10,495,484 28.53%	8,578,825 23.32%	7,710,873 20.96%	8,954,895 24.34	36,786,643 100%
1997	961,553 2.59%	10,384,722 28.00%	8,574,208 23.12%	7,806,836 21.05%	9,361,760 25.54%	37,089,079 100%
2003	1,109,093.7 2.80%	9,519,630.1 23.99%	7,516,398.8 18.94%	7,298,906.6 18.40%	14,233,714 35.87%	39,677,743 100%
2007	1,190,657.2 2.92%	9,602,161.5 23.56%	7,720,858.8 18.94%	7,544,772.2 18.51%	14,703,807.9 36.07%	40,762,257.6 100%

sectors (GO_{Trd}), (c) the total gross output in the royalties sector (GO_{Ry}) and (d) the net indirect business taxes (*NIBT*) which is estimated as the difference between business taxes and subsidies. We exclude from *MVA*'s estimation, the *Public Administration and Defence* sector and the *Private Households with Employed Persons* sector as well, because the wages paid to these sectors are financed by taxes and personal incomes which have already been considered in the value added of the rest of the sectors. We also exclude the rent paid by home-owners because it is a totally imputed measure and does not contribute to the new value produced.[7]

$$MVA = NVA_{Prd} + GO_{Trd} + GO_{Ry} + NIBT = S + V \tag{1}$$

As we can see in relation (1), Marxian value added also consists of two parts. The first one is the surplus-value (*S*) that comprises the net profits of the productive sector, the gross output of the two unproductive sectors (free of imputed rents) and the net indirect taxes paid to the government. The second one is the variable capital (*V*) which is total wages paid to the productive workers.[8] Dividing total surplus-value by the variable capital, we derive the rate of surplus-value (*RSV*) which denotes the rate of exploitation of the productive workers. The *RSV* can be also expressed as the ratio between productivity and the real wage of productive workers. From Figure 8.2 we can see[9] that the 1958–73 'golden age' of Greek capitalism is characterised by high productivity and vigorous accumulation. After 1973, the growth of productivity slows down whilst during the 1980s it remains stagnant. In the beginning of the 1990s productivity rises again till the middle of 2000s when it starts to decline bearing similarities with that of the mid-1970s (i.e. signifying the onset of another crisis).

Real wage (the other component of surplus-value) for the whole period follows productivity but it never gets higher. The increasing lagging of real

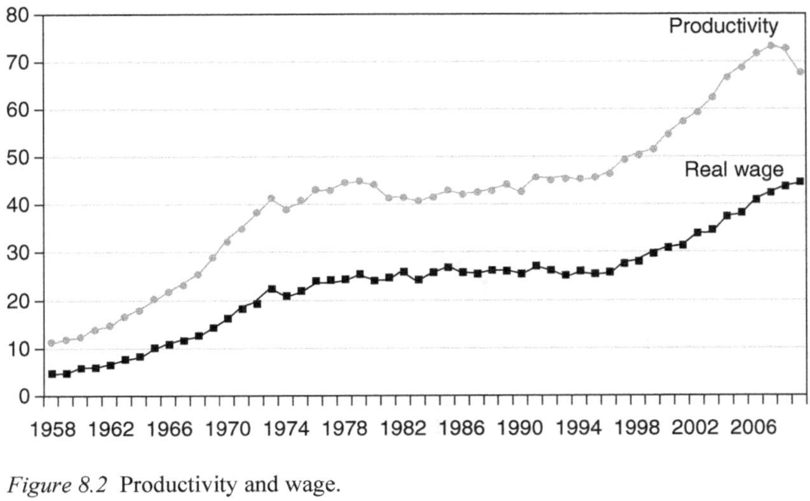

Figure 8.2 Productivity and wage.

wages behind productivity increases during the 1990s was the result of the weakening of the labour movement, 'deindustrialisation', growth of unproductive activities and the implementation of neo-liberal policies. The combination of a vigorous growth of productivity and an anaemic growth of real wage resulted in an unprecedented increase of the rate of surplus-value during the period 1958–2009. But, this increase wasn't without fluctuations. Particularly, during the period 1958–73 the rate of surplus-value exhibits a moderate decline. From the beginning of 1970s till the early 1980s, the decline accelerates and then it is totally reversed to reach its highest peak in the middle of the 2000s. Finally, in the last years of our analysis, the rate of surplus-value sharply drops indicating capitalists' inability to extract more surplus-value due to decreasing productivity.

Figure 8.4 depicts the evolution of the *VCC* which is captured by the ratio of fixed capital stock (*C*)[10] to variable capital (*V*). It exhibits a steady increase for

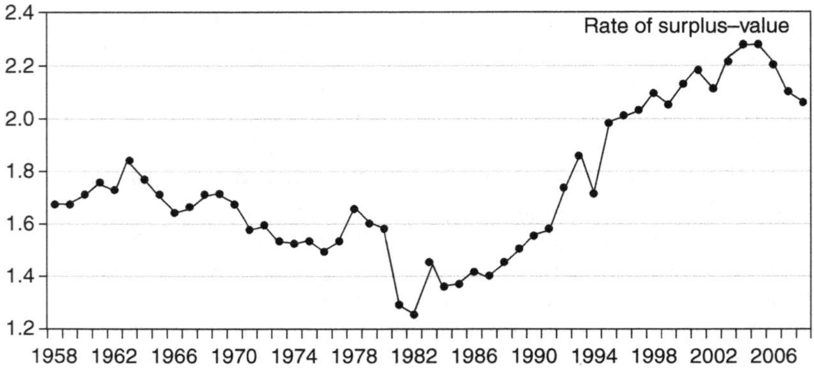

Figure 8.3 The rate of surplus-value.

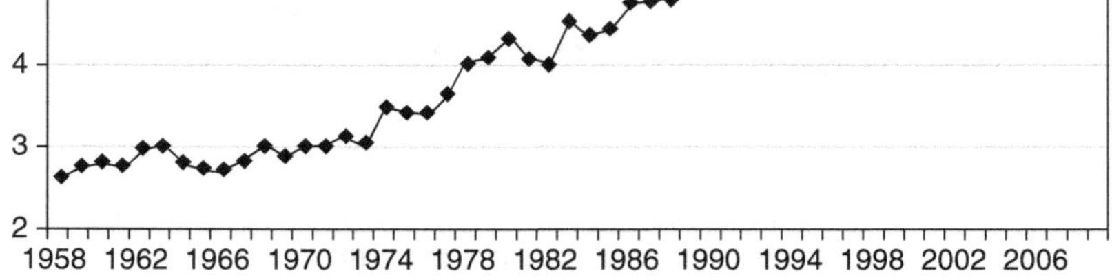

Figure 8.4 The VCC.

almost the whole period. However at the beginning of the 2000s it stagnates; which can possibly be attributed to the 'deindustrialisation' of the Greek economy and significant relocation of Greek manufacturing enterprises to the Balkans and Eastern Europe. The slowdown of the *VCC* was the main reason for the decline of productivity and consequently of the rate of surplus-value.

The *VCC* shows the degree of mechanisation and the state of technology in an economy, while the rate of surplus-value shows the distribution of income and at the same time the part of production that is directed to unproductive activities. Dividing the rate of surplus-value by the *VCC* we derive the general profit rate which amounts to the ratio between surplus-value and fixed capital (S/C). The evolution of the general profit rate is portrayed in Figure 8.5 and from its trajectory we can distinguish three phases before the onset of the current crisis. The first one is the period 1958–73 where the general profit rate is at a high level though with a small decline. The second one is the period of crisis (1973–85) when the general profit rate falls dramatically. This steep fall is attributed to the combination of a falling rate of surplus-value and an increase in the *VCC*. The third period is that of capitalist restructurings (1985–2009) when the general profit rate displays a slight recovery and then remains stagnant. This is attributed to the ongoing increase in the *VCC* which counterbalanced the proportional increase in surplus-value. The fact that the *VCC* was never devaluated (in contrast with the US; see Paitaridis and Tsoulfidis (2012)) contributed to an anaemic recovery of the general profit rate. This picture discloses the chronic structural problems of the Greek economy which never succeeded in having an adequate recovery of its general profit rate, foreshadowing an upcoming deep crisis. Finally, during the last years of our analysis the general profit rate starts to decline and the Greek economy enters into a new phase of crisis.

Figure 8.6 portrays the net profit rate which is the ratio of net profits to gross fixed capital. The net profit rate determines the profitability of enterprises and,

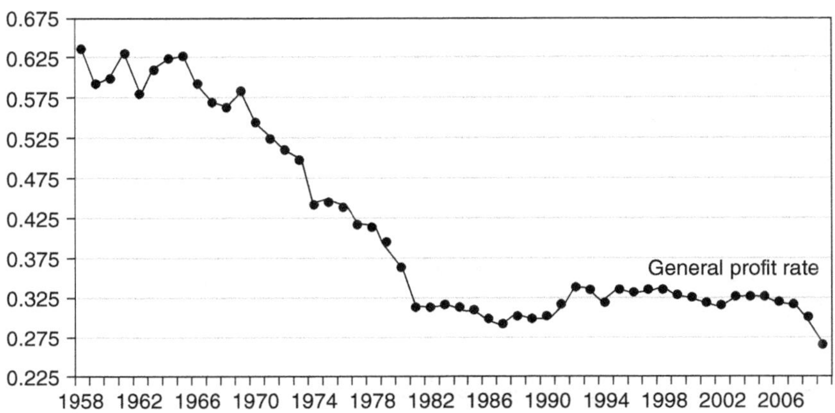

Figure 8.5 The general profit rate.

consequently, investments and growth. Similarly with the trajectory of the general profit rate we can distinguish three phases:

1 The 'golden age' exhibits a high level of the net profit rate.
2 During the crisis the net profit rate declines sharply.
3 During the capitalist restructurings period the net profit rate recovers but anaemically.

Similarly with Laibman (2010), Shaikh (2010) and Maniatis and Passas (2013), we estimate a 'counterfactual' profit rate. This is the profit rate that would exist if real unit wage cost had remained at its 1985 level (instead of falling significantly). It can be seen that the whole anaemic recovery of the profit rate comes exactly from this reduction of the real wage. In other words, without this real wage reduction the falling profitability trend would have continued.

Though, according to Paitaridis and Tsoulfidis (2012) the net profit rate in and itself is not enough to determine the investment behaviour of capitalists since a huge (low) stock of capital could give higher (lower) profits. Furthermore, investment behaviour is determined not only by the (falling) net profit rate but from various factors among which expectations. In Marx, expectations are not subjective, as in the Keynesian analysis, but rather derived by the movement of the general profit rate which signifies the health of the system. Indeed, we can see from Figure 8.7 and Table 8.2 that, despite the low net profit rate, net investment measured at 2005 prices reveals a positive growth during the mid-1990s reaching its highest peak at 2005.[11] At the same time an analogous growth is exhibited by the net profits measured at 2005 prices. Eventually, net investment falls and it is associated with the stagnation on the mass of profits. Concluding, a fall in the net profit rate is not enough to cause crisis but it must be combined with a falling general profit rate.

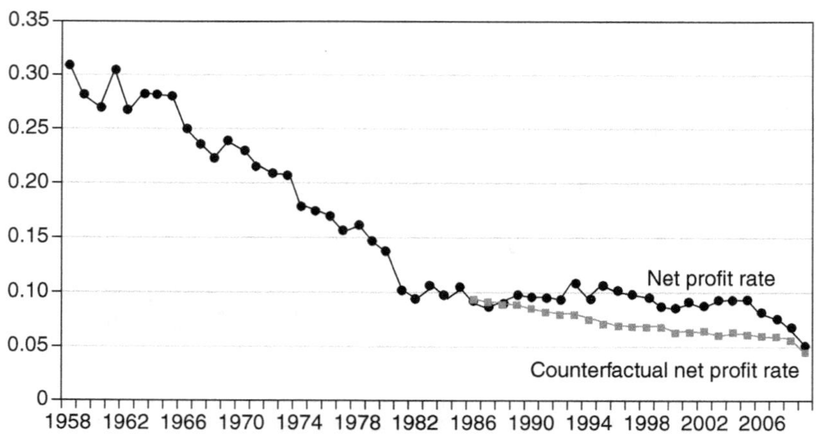

Figure 8.6 Net profit rate.

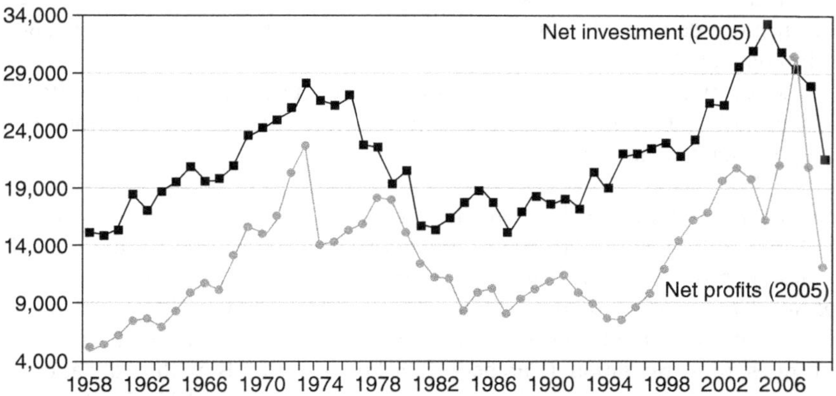

Figure 8.7 Net profits and net investment at 2005 prices (source: AMECO, 2014).

Concluding, the results are consistent with the Marxian thesis that the outbreak of the crisis is a result of a long and lasting fall of the general profit rate which in turn shapes the net profit rate and thus investment behaviour. The fact that the general profit rate never really recovered from the previous crisis through the normal process of capital devalorisation, soon led to a state of overaccumulation which is characterised by the lack[12] of alternative profitable opportunities. This situation was temporarily surpassed by the expansion of credit which offered a way out to the overaccumulated capitals and at the same time preserved economic growth. Once this solution reached its barriers the fundamental mechanism behind the current crisis (the structural weakness of the real economy) reappeared in all its glory.

IV The 'external' cause: euro-centre imperialist exploitation

The 'internal' cause of Greek capitalism's crisis was aggravated by the 'external' imperialist economic exploitation from the more developed euro-core countries. This took place through two conduits:

Table 8.2 Average annual growth rates (%)

	Golden age (1958–73)	*Crisis (1973–85)*	*Restructuring (1985–2009)*
Productivity	8.50	0.29	1.90
Real unit wage	9.76	1.13	1.13
Rate of surplus-value	–0.60	–0.90	1.36
VCC	1.01	3.07	1.98
General profit rate	–1.61	–3.97	–0.63
Net profit rate	–2.61	–5.71	–2.88
Net profits (2005)	4.10	–3.33	0.55
Net investments (2005)	9.78	–6.93	0.84

a A structural channel. Greek capitals compete within the Common Market with more developed capitals. This results in a 'broad' unequal exchange (Emmanuel (1972)) that benefits the latter.

b A policy channel. By directly or indirectly ceding the control of monetary, fiscal and trade policy to the EU, Greek capitalism lost critical means for supporting its competitiveness.

The structural channel results from the significant differences between Greek capitalism's and its euro-core peers' productive structures. The equalisation of the rates of profit (and thus the process of price formation) redistributes the *surplus-value* produced *among capitalists*, either from capitalists with lower OCC to those with higher OCC or from capitalists with higher to those with lower rates of exploitation (Carchedi (2001)). This holds within a national economy and within a multi-national common market like the EU. Greek capitalism has a lower OCC and a higher rate of exploitation.[13] Consequently, euro-core capitals reap extra-profits through the value transfers from their euro-periphery competitors. This 'broad' unequal exchange is reflected in the Terms of Trade (ToT) between them and in a worsening trade balance for the latter. This channel is additional reinforced by the dominance of euro-core oligopolies in the Common Market that reap also monopolist extra-profits.

The policy channel is the product of the policy dominance of euro-core capitalisms within EU's commanding heights. Therefore, crucial policy choices follow the prerogatives of these capitalisms even to the detriment of those of the euro-periphery. Typically, ECB's monetary policy adjusts to the necessities of euro-core economies (e.g. euro's exchange rate).

Figure 8.8 plots Greece's trade performance by estimating the intra EU-15 ToT.[14] Additionally, this is compared to the performance of Sweden and Austria. We opted for these countries for the following reasons:

a Sweden is an EU euro-core economy but not a member of the EMU.

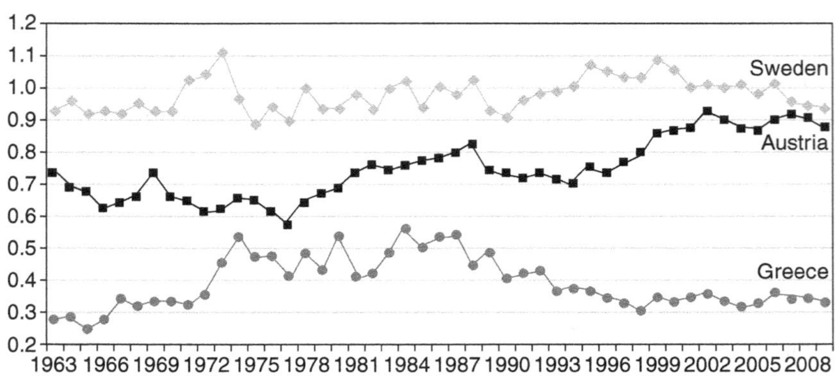

Figure 8.8 Intra EU-15 terms of trade (source: AMECO, 2014).

b Austria is an EU euro-core economy that participates in the EMU.
c Greece, Sweden and Austria have approximately the same population.

Greece's ToT fall short against those of Sweden and Austria. However from 1963 till 1981, when Greece became an EEC full member, its ToT exhibited an annual growth of 2.1 per cent and managed to converge with the other two countries, and especially with Austria. From 1981 to 2002 (when EMU was inaugurated) the ToT declined annually by 0.06 per cent denoting loss of competitiveness in relation to the rest of the EU-15 countries.[15] Finally, from 2002 to 2009, ToT remained stable which meant that the accession in the eurozone did not affect significantly the already impaired Greek competitiveness. So for Greece, the exposition to the Common Market and then the gradual loss of monetary and fiscal instruments resulted in a serious ToT decline. Turning now to the other two countries, Sweden exhibited an annual increase of 0.5 per cent till 1995, when it became an EU full member. From 1995 to 2009 its ToT exhibited an annual decline by 0.1 per cent whilst the decision not to participate in the EMU did not actually change the trend. Finally, Austria exhibited a ToT increase till its entrance in the EU in 1995, by 0.1 per cent per year. From 1995 to 2009 the Austrian economy exhibited an annual increase of 1.1 per cent, whilst the decision of entering in the EMU did not change the trend either.

From the examination of the ToT the following conclusions can be drawn. Both Greece and Sweden suffered a deterioration of their ToT after their accession in the Common Market but to differed extents as the former is a less developed economy. Moreover, Greece's trade relations were and became even more geared to the Common Market whereas Sweden preserved a high extra-EU-15 ratio. This deterioration was preserved, although not affected significantly, by the EMU. On the contrary, Austria – a euro-core and EMU economy – benefited clearly from European integration. In a nutshell, euro-core EMU members gained from the European integration process against both euro-periphery EMU members and euro-core non-EMU members. This suggests that the European integration process has a layered hierarchy that benefits those at its commanding heights.

Given the strategic importance of Greek capitalism's choice to participate in the European integration process, how can this deteriorating competitiveness be explained? Greek capitalism's participation was fraught with aspirations but also dangers from its very beginning. Greek capital aspired to (a) upgrading from a middle-range imperialism to a 'partner' in a first-class imperialist club and (b) the enhanced ability first to secure the system (in the immediate post-dictatorship period) and then to push forward capitalist restructurings. The risks were (a) the downgrading within the ranks of this imperialist club and (b) the loss of autonomous policy instruments in the face of grave contingencies. In a broader sense, participation in European integration constituted Greek capitalism's contemporary 'Big Idea'[16] of becoming a significant regional imperialist power (see Mavroudeas (2013)).

All these advantages and disadvantages were ultimately related to Greece's productive structure. Before its participation in the EEC Greek capitalism had a rather coherent productive structure (with strong backward and forward inter-sectoral linkages between its sectors) which was competitive both against the European economies and other economies in the Mediterranean region particularly. This productive structure was heavily protected and supported through direct and indirect means. The economy's opening through the Common Market dismantled this protective shell. Greek capital failed to restructure adequately in order to remain competitive in the new environment. It mainly strived to reduce wages (and thus increase cost competitiveness) but failed to restructure successfully its productive structure (and thus structural competitiveness). Greek capital (technologically traditional, small size and used to short-term investment) could not withstand the competition from larger and more technologically advanced euro-core capitals and led to an abrupt increase of trade deficit. Interestingly, this deterioration was not confined to the intra-EU trade relationships but it was generalised for the extra-EU as well.[17] This was accompanied by a decline in those manufacturing sectors that were more exposed to international competition (Petrakos and Zikos (1996)). Additionally, as trade relations with the EU took on a largely inter-industry character, it pressurised Greek capital-intensive industries and led to a return to labour-intensive industrial specialisation of Greek capitalism's earlier stages of its development. This reinforced the Greek export sector's notorious dependence upon imports and weighted crucially upon the trade balance. Moreover, in the face of intensified euro-core competition, Greek capital barricaded itself in sectors producing non-internationally tradable goods and/or covertly protected through crony relations with the political elite. The net result was a weakening of Greece's productive structure. This does not imply a widespread deindustrialisation but rather a retreat to weaker industrial specialisation and a loss of the internal coherence of its productive structure. Inter-sectoral linkages became weaker as even vibrant industries were more related to euro-core activities than to native ones.

There were some feeble attempts to reverse this trend that did not produce significant results. The EU offered funds – in the form of national and regional cohesion aid – which in monetary terms were insignificant compared to the cumulative trade deficits with the EU (Petrakos and Zikos (1996)). They actually acted as a masquerade for the continuing deterioration of Greece–EU trade and the increasing role of euro-core capitals within the Greek economy.

Nowadays, it is evident that Greek capital lost its 'Big Idea' bet. Greece's trade balance with the EU worsened rapidly since its entrance in The Common Market and deteriorated further with its accession in the EMU. This problem is acknowledged even by mainstream supporters of the participation in European integration. For example, Papazoglou (2009: 40) accepts that 'Greece's participation in the Single Market did not cause significant structural changes that would contribute to strengthening, both in terms of price and quality, the competitiveness of Greek products in international markets'. Similarly, Malliaropoulos (2010) admits that Greece's competitiveness deteriorated significantly since

EMU. Estimates of this deterioration in terms of relative unit labour costs, for the period 2000–9, vary between 9 per cent (IMF) and 27 per cent (Bank of Greece). Based on relative prices, competitiveness deteriorated since 2000 by between 18 per cent (ECB, Bank of Greece) and 21 per cent (IMF).

The only area where Greek capitalism's contemporary 'Big Idea' brought results was in the 1990s when the Eastern Bloc collapsed. Greek capitals, strengthened by their EU membership, expanded aggressively in mainly the Balkan economies and reaped imperialist extra-profits in the same manner as their euro-core peers reaped from them. This Balkan 'Eldorado' lasted till the eruption of the 2007–8 global crisis. The latter hit hard the Balkan economies and intensified intra-imperialist antagonisms within them. The result was a serious setback in Greek capital's ability to reap extra-profits from them.

In a nutshell, Greek capitalism's accession in European integration traumatised its productive structure, burdened it with value transfers to its euro-core peers (because of 'broad' unequal exchange) and only partially compensated with imperialist extra-profits from mainly the Balkan region. Thus, Greek capitalism became more structurally fragile. This fragility was brought to the fore when the 2007–8 crisis erupted.

V The eruption of the Greek crisis

Thus, by 2007 Greek capitalism was at a razor's end. It had a partial profit rate recovery, capital devalorisation was insufficient, imperialist profits compensated unequal exchange with the euro-core, fictitious capital operations have postponed the problems and instigated a 'bogus growth' period. At the same time Greek capitalism's 'deep' structural problems were aggravated.

The eruption of the 2007–8 global crisis blew this house of cards apart. As the insufficient capital devalorisation hit back and the profitability problems resurfaced in the leading capitalist economies the crisis spread worldwide. In Greek terms this meant that the native capitalist problems of overaccumulation and insufficient profitability resurfaced together with a series of structural problems whose effects were delayed. Similarly with the West productivity growth started faltering and together with this the extraction of surplus-value. The 'flight ahead' via fictitious capital expansion and public FD was suddenly discovered to be unsustainable and thus 'artificial growth' abruptly ceased. The fundamental reason behind this halt is the fact that capitalist growth based on fictitious capital and public borrowing is ultimately a 'wager to expected surplus-value'. If this expected surplus-value is not realised (at least sufficiently) in the foreseeable future then the bet is uncovered and losses have to be paid. Moreover, the whole process is halted as it is proved unviable; even if it was successful in the past. In this way the economic fundamentals (and first of all productive and social relations) reassert themselves and revoke back to reality the exuberant flight of capitalist accumulation.

For Greek capitalism this meant that the 'artificial growth' period has ended. There were some feeble attempts in the beginning to extend it or at least ease the fall by increasing public support to the private sector but its only result was FD's further increase:[18] the private sector used this support to save its skin (i.e. 'fix' enterprise balance sheets and protect private incomes) instead of investing it. At the same time the faltering of Balkan economies and the aggravation of intra-imperialist antagonisms in them curtailed Greek capital's 'subsidisation' by imperialist profits. Then the deep seated problems of capitalist accumulation in Greece appeared in the misleading form of the twin deficits. The faltering of capitalist accumulation led to the inability to sustain FD and a run-away FD to GDP ratio. The long-term structural loss of competitiveness resulted to a worsening CAD that was additionally burdened by the increasing foreign debt. In both cases the 'deep' structural problems of capitalist accumulation caused both deficits instead of the misleading Columbus' egg dilemma of the mainstream TDH.

Appendix

The classification of sectors into productive and unproductive

TABLE A

Productive activities	*Unproductive activities*	
	Trade sectors	*Royalties sectors*
1. Agriculture, hunting, forestry and fishing	13. Sale, maintenance and repair of motor vehicles	16. Financial intermediation
2. Mining and quarrying	14. Wholesale trade and commission trade	17. Real estate activities
3. Manufacturing	15. Retail trade	18. Renting of machinery and equipment
4. Electricity, gas and water supply		19. Other business activities
5. Construction		
6. Hotels and restaurants		
7. Transport, storage and communication		
8. Computer and related activities		
9. Research and development		
10. Education		
11. Health and social work		
12. Other community, social and personal services		

Notes

1 For a detailed account see Mavroudeas (2013).
2 As a second-generation capitalism Greece is typical of Gershenkron's (1962) 'late development': a strong developmental state actively supports and guides capital accumulation. This is the fundamental reason behind the persistent and notorious Greek fiscal deficits.
3 In 2004 the FD/GDP ratio exhibited its first serious deterioration by increasing from 5.77 to 7.49 per cent; an almost 30 per cent increase (AMECO).
4 Apart from their own internal problems, the Balkan economies worsened because of their integration with the EU. As 60 per cent of their trade is with the EU the crisis hit severely their exports. It also curtailed immigrant remittances from EU to them.
5 For a detailed analysis of this distinction see also Gough (1972) and Savran and Tonak (1999). In a nutshell, for Marx (1976: 644) 'the only worker who is productive is one who produces surplus-value for the capitalist, or in other words contributes towards the self-valorisation of capital'. Respectively, the labour-power employed in the circulation of commodities, money and titles is considered as unproductive. The output of these activities is simply a portion of the surplus-value created by productive labour and extracted from it.
6 EU KLEMS stands for EU level analysis of capital (K), labour (L), energy (E), materials (M) and service (S) inputs.
7 The imputed rent constitutes a significant part of total GDP. Indicatively, for 1958 it was estimated as 9.94 per cent of total Gross Value Added whilst for 2009 it was 9.69 per cent. The estimation of imputed measures reflects Neoclassical utilitarianism which argues that whatever is useful it finally contributes to production.
8 Productive workers are defined as those employed at the productive sectors except for managers, lawyers, clerks and sellers since these kinds of workers are employed at the circulation of products rather production.
9 The growth rates of the rate of productivity as well as the other variables for selective time periods are displayed in Table 8.2. For the estimation of the average annual rate of growth of a variable X, we use the ratio $\ln(Xt+1/Xt)/\Delta t$, where 'ln' is the natural logarithm and 'Δt' is the time distance between $t+1$ and t.
10 The data on fixed capital refer to the nonresidential private gross fixed capital and are derived from Skountzos and Mattheos (1992) and unpublished series of the ELSTAT. The only exception is the last year of our analysis where we made extrapolation with data from AMECO.
11 However, investment as a share of GDP did not reach its previous peak in 1973.
12 Shaikh (1992) explicitly recognises the systematic relationship between the net profit rate (r), the mass of real net profits (π), and the manifestation of crisis.
13 The European integration process has reinforced by pressing its less developed members to boost absolute surplus-value. As they lag technologically and are unable to compete with their developed peers on the basis of relative surplus-value, their only solution is the extension of working time (Carchedi (1999)).
14 ToT are estimated as the ratio between exports of goods (fob) to imports of goods (cif).
15 Spain follows the same trajectory with an annual rise of 4 per cent for the period 1963–85 (the year when Spain became a full EEC member) followed by a significant decline of 1.0 per cent per year for the period 1985–2009.
16 'Big Idea' is an infamous Greek term referring to Greek capital's aim, at the end of the nineteenth century, to replace the collapsing Ottoman Empire which led to a national disaster.
17 Although the extra-EU ToT were unfavourable for Greek capital, they improved considerably during the 1960–81 period by a 3.06 per cent average. During 1981–2002, extra-EU ToT declined by 3.21 per cent, losing all their previous gains. Finally,

for the period 2002–9 the extra-EU ToT continued declining by 2.32 per cent per year (AMECO, 2014). *In toto*, it seems that Greek capitalism's trade performance vis-à-vis the rest of the world did not benefit by its participation in the European integration.

18 The FD/GDP, after a decrease during 2005–7, started climbing again rapidly: from 6.76 per cent to 9.93 per cent (2007–8) and from 9.93 per cent to 15.63 (2008–9) (AMECO, 2014).

References

Agriculture Bank of Greece (2011), 'Annual economic survey', Athens.

AMECO (2014), http://ec.europa.eu/economy_finance/ameco/user/serie/SelectSerie.cfm

Carchedi G. (1999), 'The Euro and Europe's labor', in Bellofiore R. (ed.), *Global Money, Capital Restructuring and the Changing Patterns of Labor*, London: Edward Elgar.

Carchedi G. (2001), *For Another Europe: A Class Analysis of European Economic Integration*, London: Verso.

Cholezas I. and Tsakloglou P. (2008), 'The economic impact of immigration in Greece: taking stock of the existing evidence', *IZA DP* 3754.

Davis J.E. (1980), 'Capitalist agricultural development and the exploitation of the propertied laborer', in Buttel F. and Newby H. (eds), *The Rural Sociology of the Advanced Societies: Critical Perspectives*, Montclair: Allanheld, Osum.

Emmanuel A. (1972), *Unequal Exchange: A Study of the Imperialism of Trade*, New York and London: Monthly Review Press.

Gerschenkron A. (1962), *Economic Backwardness in Historical Perspective*, Cambridge, MA: Harvard University Press.

Gough I. (1972), 'Marx's theory of productive and unproductive labour', *New Left Review* 12.

Hellenic Statistical Authority (2010), *Concise Statistical Yearbook 2009*, Piraeus: Hellenic Statistical Authority.

Kasimis C., Papadopoulos G.A. and Zacopoulou E. (2003), 'Migrants in rural Greece', *Sociologia Ruralis* 43(2).

Laibman D. (2010), 'Capitalism, crisis, renewal: some conceptual excavations', *Science and Society* 74(3).

Malliaropoulos D. (2010), 'How much did competitiveness of the Greek economy decline since EMU entry?', *Economy and Markets* 5(4), Eurobank.

Maniatis T. and Passas C. (2013), 'Profitability, capital accumulation and crisis in the Greek economy 1958–2009: a Marxist analysis', *Review of Political Economics* 25(4).

Mann S. and Dickinson J. (1978), 'Obstacles to the development of a capitalist agriculture', *Journal of Peasant Studies* 5(4).

Marx, K. (1976), *Capital*, Vol. I, London: Penguin.

Mavroudeas S. (2013), 'Development and crisis: the turbulent course of Greek capitalism', *International Critical Thought* 3(3).

Moissidis A. (1986), *Rural Society in Contemporary Greece: Productive and Social Structure in Greek Agriculture 1950–1980*, Athens: Foundation for Mediterranean Studies [in Greek].

Moissidis A. (1988), *Contract Farming in Greece: A Contemporary Form of Embedment of the Agricultural Sector into Capitalism*, Athens: Agriculture Bank of Greece [in Greek].

Paitaridis D. and Tsoulfidis L. (2012), 'The growth of unproductive activities and the phase change in the US economy', *Review of Radical Political Economy* 44(2).

Papazoglou C. (2009), 'Is indeed poor Greece's export performance?', *Economic Bulletin* 32, Bank of Greece [in Greek].

Petrakos G. and Zikos S. (1996), 'European integration and industrial structure in Greece: prospects and possibilities for convergence', in Paraskevopoulos C.C., Grinspun R. and Georgakopoulos T. (eds), *Economic Integration and Public Policy in the European Union*, London: Edward Elgar.

Savran S. and Tonak A. (1999), 'Productive and unproductive labour: an attempt at clarification and classification', *Capital and Class* 23(2).

Shaikh A. (1992), 'The falling rate of profit as the cause of long waves: theory and empirical evidence', in Kleinkenecht A., Mandel E. and Wallerstein I. (eds), *New Findings in Long-wave Research*, New York: St. Martin's Press.

Shaikh A. (2010), 'The First Great Depression of the 21st Century', *Socialist Register* 47.

Shaikh A. and Tonak A. (1994), *Measuring the Wealth of Nations: The Political Economy of National Accounts*, New York: Cambridge University Press.

Skountzos T. and Mattheos M. (1980), *Input: Output Tables of the Greek Economy, 1958–1977*, Athens: Centre of Planning and Economic Research.

Skountzos T. and Mattheos M. (1992), *Net Fixed Capital Stock, Depreciation of Fixed Capital Stock, Gross Fixed Capital Formation, 1950–1990*, Athens: Centre of Planning and Economic Research.

Tsoulfidis L. (2009), *Economic History of Greece*, Thessaloniki: University of Macedonia Press.

Vergopoulos K. (1975), *The Agrarian Problem in Greece: The Issue of the Social Incorporation of Agriculture*, Athens: Exantas [in Greek].

Part III

Crisis, poverty and the labour market

9 Economic crisis, poverty and deprivation in Greece

The impact of neoliberal remedies

Christos Papatheodorou

I Introduction

The current economic crisis has revived the debate on the nature and causes of economic fluctuations. The main question that drives this debate is whether an economic crisis is the result of certain imbalances in particular sectors of the economy or whether it is endemic in capitalist economies, reflecting their systemic and structural problems. Obviously, the answer to this question is not value free and is rooted to certain theoretical hypotheses about economy and society. This is probably the ultimate battlefield for the major theoretical paradigms concerning the organisation and administration of modern economies, with profound policy implications, affecting any proposed remedies for dealing with the economic crisis and its consequences, economic and social.

Despite this theoretical debate on the nature and causes of the economic crisis, no one doubts its impact on poverty and on the deterioration of the level of livings of the most vulnerable population groups. This is most evident in the case of Greece, where the consequences of the economic crisis are more severe. Still, instead of disputing the dominant paradigm for organising and administrating the modern capitalist economies, the recent economic crisis has served as an alibi for further strengthening the neoliberal policies for fiscal discipline, reduction of public spending and labour market deregulation (Papatheodorou *et al.* (2012)). This is odd bearing in mind that neoliberal policies gained ground after the economic crisis of the mid-1970s, when government ability to stabilise economy through interventions was questioned. In 2008 and 2009 more voices were heard contesting that the neoliberal policies have proven incapable to administrate modern economies. But this reaction proved ephemeral. The claims for the renaissance of Keynesian perspectives regarding the need for state involvement in the economy, only served to legitimise the generous state support of the financial institutions at that time. The 2007–8 economic crisis did not dispute the dominance of neoliberal perspectives.

Utilising available data and empirical evidence, this chapter discusses the impact of the current economic crisis on poverty and social deprivation in Greece in a comparative analysis with other EU countries. Drawn from Political Economy, it tests the main arguments and the resulting policies of the dominant neoliberal rhetoric concerning the organisation and administration of the economy and of the crisis. It focuses on their impact on social inequality, poverty and deprivation, as well as on the weakening of the social protection system.

The rest of the chapter is structured as follows: the next section discusses the perspectives on economic crisis and poverty that dominated public discourse and served to legitimise the neoliberal remedies. The validity of these perspectives is tested in Section III by utilising theoretical and empirical evidence. Section IV examines the impact of economic crisis and of the neoliberal remedies on poverty and deprivation. The final section summarises findings and puts together some concluding remarks.

II The dominant perspectives on inequality and poverty

In order to strengthen neoliberal perspectives, the economic crisis was presented not as a global issue but rather as a problem of individual countries reflecting their own imbalances and weaknesses. Public discourse at a national and international level presented the Greek crisis as an isolated incident, not connected with the global economic crisis. Greeks were perceived as accountable for this crisis, and as having had enjoyed high consumption and standard of livings well beyond their means during the pre-crisis period. They were also accused of working less hard than other Europeans, and for being supported by a generous social protection system. Under the mainstream hypothesis of moral hazard, Greeks had to be penalised. With the large support of the media and despite the lack of any empirical plausibility, these views were widely reproduced and dominated public debate and official rhetoric in Greece and abroad, contributing in legitimising austerity and stabilisation measures that were implemented as the remedy to reduce the huge public debt, and to cure economic crisis.

How convincing are these arguments? Can they efficiently address the issue of the existing inequality and poverty in Greece and the impact of the economic crisis and austerity measures? In dominant discourse, income inequality and poverty are perceived as associated mainly with certain personal characteristics and attributes. It is broadly claimed that people's income is mainly earned through their participation in the labour market. Thus earnings are seen as playing a principal role in explaining income differences among individuals and households. Within this dominant discourse, earnings are considered as reflecting people's productivity which depends on the different skills they possess. Genetic characteristics determine potential talents and abilities (skills) that could be further cultivated through education and training (see Taubman (1978)). Given the genetic characteristics, individual income is perceived as largely depending on personal choices through a utility maximisation process. Thus certain personal characteristics are acknowledged as the main determinants of each person's particular place in the distribution of income, leaving some room for stochastic effects. Other sources of household income, such as capital and other forms of property income, have not gained the same significance in explaining income inequality. Furthermore these income sources were significantly underestimated in relevant statistics (Atkinson and Bourguignon (2000), Papatheodorou (2004)).

These opinions have dominated public and academic dialogue preventing any analysis of inequality and poverty within the framework of class analysis, as Political Economy and particular Marxist Political Economy have traditionally done. Or, using the mainstream terminology, they discouraged analysis of the impact of functional income distribution on the distribution of personal income and poverty. Of course, mainstream economics have acknowledged the impact of macroeconomic factors on inequality and poverty. Within the Neoclassical framework, this impact is largely restricted to that of economic growth and unemployment rate. Concerning the impact of growth, Kuznets' (1955) argument of the inverted U-shaped relation between income inequality and economic growth has dominated the relevant debate.[1] In the process of economic growth, income inequality initially increases but after reaching a certain point, it decreases. It is thus generally believed that in developed countries economic growth can reduce income dispersion and poverty. In the same vein, 'trickle-down theory' further legitimises neoliberal policies arguing that all population would gain from economic growth. Thus, government support to the entrepreneurs or to the wealthy population (i.e. benefits and tax cuts) would positively affect the whole economy and, consequently, it would benefit the poor.

As far as the unemployment rate is concerned, it is broadly perceived as having a crucial negative impact on inequality and poverty. Paid employment is widely acknowledged as the key remedy to escape poverty. Thus it is claimed that reducing unemployment would be the most effective measure to alleviate poverty. These views were further strengthened since the late 1980s, when the concept of social exclusion was introduced and remained dominant for almost two decades in the EU social policy agenda. In EU policy discourse, the concept of social exclusion is primarily defined as the exclusion from the labour market (e.g. Levitas (1996, 2000), Dafermos and Papatheodorou (2012)). Thus improving employability and removing barriers to labour market participation became the social policy priority. Under the neoliberal argument, unemployment is not involuntary and thus there is reason to oppose any interventions or regulations imposed on the labour market such as the minimum wage, collective agreements and unionisation. Considering unemployment mainly as structural, the proposed policies to enhance employment at the national and at the EU level are those of the labour market deregulation, of promoting higher flexibility in labour contracts and of improving employability.

Within this framework, hostility against social benefits was cultivated, arguing that these benefits act as a disincentive to work. In general, social protection and the corresponding social spending in Greece were regarded as a major contributor to the huge public debt and thus to the economic crisis. Social protection was accused of being particularly generous, compared to the country's economic growth, promoting the high standard of living that the Greeks had supposedly enjoyed. These viewpoints helped legitimise cuts in social expenditures as the main ingredient of austerity policies.

We ought to emphasise that there is no specific and broadly accepted theory of personal income distribution within the Neoclassical paradigm. Departing from the mainstream hypotheses, there is a branch of views that focuses on different aspects and characteristics, such as the impact of education and training, intelligence, stochastic factors and so on (see Atkinson and Bourguignon (2000)). Different theories focus on the effect that certain personal characteristics have on individual income.[2] Core in this analysis is the assumption that people could transform their potential talents that are genetically determined, to abilities through education, training or experience. People, acting rationally and having a good (if not a perfect) knowledge of all the alternatives, current and future, choose the proper mix of education, experience, training, effort that could maximise the current value of their total utility during their life-spam. The gains that determine people's utility are monetary and non-monetary. One particular perspective though has largely dominated the relevant academic and public discourse. This is the Human Capital theory and the corresponding 'earning functions'. According to this, low incomes and consequently poverty are mainly associated with the low productivity from certain parts of the population due to inadequate education and training (Mincer (1958), Becker (1993)). The dominance of this view is apparent in the proposed measures to alleviate poverty and deprivation nationally and internationally. During the period before the current economic crisis, removing barriers for people in education and training gained priority in the poverty alleviation measures in most EU countries.

III Testing the validity of the dominant discourse. What does the evidence show?

Before we proceed to analyse the impact of the economic crisis and austerity policies on inequality and poverty, it is crucial to test the validity of the aforementioned perspectives in explaining poverty and legitimising neoliberal remedies. Are these views documented by empirical evidence? A close look into certain features of poverty and inequality in Greece and the EU during the pre-crisis period can prove very apocalyptic and particularly helpful in assessing the impact.

In examining poverty, the definition proposed by Eurostat, and broadly used in relevant studies, is also here used.[3] Poverty threshold is set at 60 per cent of each country's median equivalised disposable income. The disposable household income is defined as the total income of all household members plus the income received at the household level, minus the income taxes and social security contributions. Unit of analysis is the individual. The modified OECD equivalence scale is used in order to make comparable individuals living at households of different size and composition.[4]

The comparative analysis is restricted to the oldest EU-15 member states. There are two main reasons for this. First, these are the countries where comparable data and estimates on income, poverty and living conditions are available since the mid-1990s. Second, it is a more suitable group of countries for assessing the impact of social protection on poverty and inequality. Broadly acknowledged is the crucial role of social protection and of relevant spending on poverty and inequality, and in explaining the differences on these figures between countries and populations (see Atkinson (1998), Papatheodorou and Dafermos (2010), Dafermos and Papatheodorou (2013)). There has been a large and long lasting academic debate on the social protection systems that the EU-15 countries have developed, which allows us to group them into distinctive welfare regimes. Many of the new EU member states are economies in transition and the same is true for their social protection system. Adopting the classification proposed by Papatheodorou and Petmesidou (2004, 2005) in the analysis of inequality and poverty, the EU-15 countries were grouped into four social protection systems or welfare regimes (see also Dafermos and Papatheodorou (2012, 2013)). These are the social-democratic (Denmark, Sweden, Finland, Netherlands), the conservative-corporatist (Austria, Belgium, Germany, France), the liberal (United Kingdom, Ireland), the Southern European (Italy, Spain, Greece, Portugal). This classification is based on Esping-Andersen's (1990) welfare regime typology and the followed debate concerning the social protection system that has developed in the Southern European countries (see Leibfried (1992), Ferrera (1996)).

As portrayed in Figure 9.1, since the mid-1990s, where comparable data on an annual basis are available, and before the onset of the economic crisis, the relative poverty risk in Greece has remained practically unchanged at 20 to 22 per cent. Small fluctuations over time do not indicate any clear trend. During the pre-crisis period the country's relative risk of poverty was considerably higher than the corresponding average figure for EU-15 and for EU-27 (15–17 per cent).

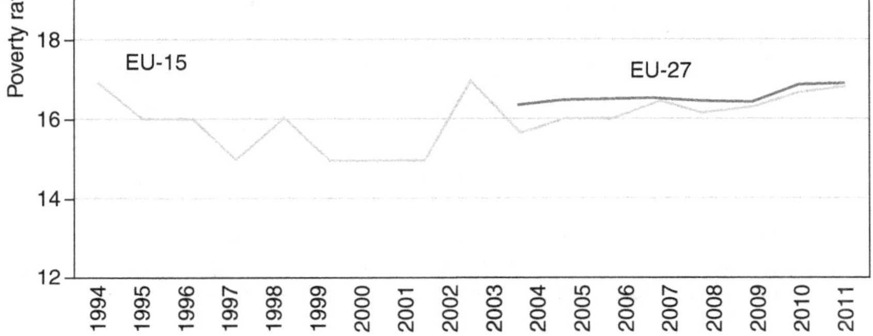

Figure 9.1 Poverty rates (%) in Greece and the EU, 1994–2011 (1995–2012 surveys) (source: estimates based on Eurostat's data: http://epp.eurostat.ec.europa.eu).

Overall, as Figure 9.2 shows, the average poverty rate in Greece for the period 1995–2012 (that refer to 1994–2011 incomes) was the highest among all EU-15 countries. On average, during that period, 20.7 per cent of Greeks were below the poverty line. The observed differences in poverty rates between the EU-15 countries seem to correspond to the social protection system that these countries have developed. The lowest poverty rates were found in Scandinavian countries which have developed a social-democratic welfare regime. Their social protection system is characterised by generous and universal benefits that aim to promote equality, financed by heavy taxation. Low poverty rates were also found in countries that are clustered in conservative-corporatist regimes, also characterised by fairly generous social provisions, linked to people's employment status. The highest poverty rates are found in the Southern European countries and in those that have developed a liberal social protection system (UK and Ireland). The liberal regime is characterised by less generous means-testing provision and the prominent role of the market in the distribution of resources.

The above estimates are based on poverty lines defined at a national level. In other words, different poverty thresholds are applied to EU countries that correspond to the level and the distribution of household income in each one of them.

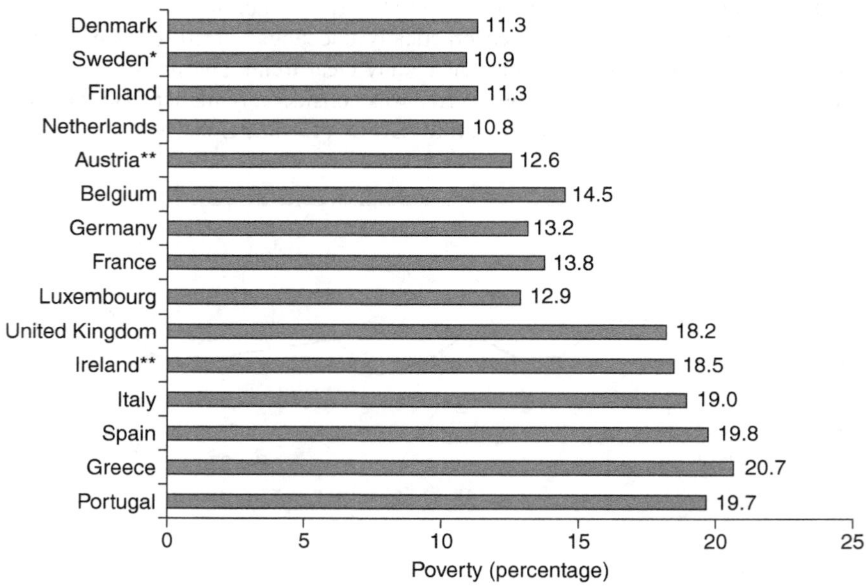

Figure 9.2 Poverty rates in the EU-15, 1994–2011 (1995–2012 surveys), average values (poverty threshold is set to 60% of the national median equivalised disposable income) (source: estimates based on Eurostat's data: http://epp.eurostat.ec.europa.eu).

Notes
* (1997–2011).
** (1994–2010).

As other studies have shown, estimates based on a common to all EU countries poverty line could help uncover the true dimensions of the differences in the standard of livings between the Greeks and the rest of the Europeans (Papatheodorou and Dafermos (2010)). Figure 9.3 provides comparable estimates on poverty rates in the EU, based on Greek poverty threshold and adjusting for differences in purchasing power between countries. These estimates reveal that differences in poverty between EU countries are considerably larger than those based on poverty lines defined at a national level and conventionally used in relevant comparisons. Thus, 38.2 per cent of the population in Greece and 54.3 per cent in Portugal have similar low levels of living to those of the 13.3 per cent of the poorest Danish and the 10.5 per cent of the poorest Dutch.

It is therefore evident that even before the crisis, Greeks did not enjoy high standards of living, compared to the other Europeans, unlike claims by the dominant rhetoric. Furthermore, bearing in mind that during that period Greece enjoyed high rates of growth, these findings question the conventional belief of the sort of impact that economic growth has on poverty.

So, high poverty rates were evident in Greece during the pre-crisis period. Because they were hard to ignore, attempts were made to explain them without questioning the mainstream hypotheses of Neoclassical theory and the proposed

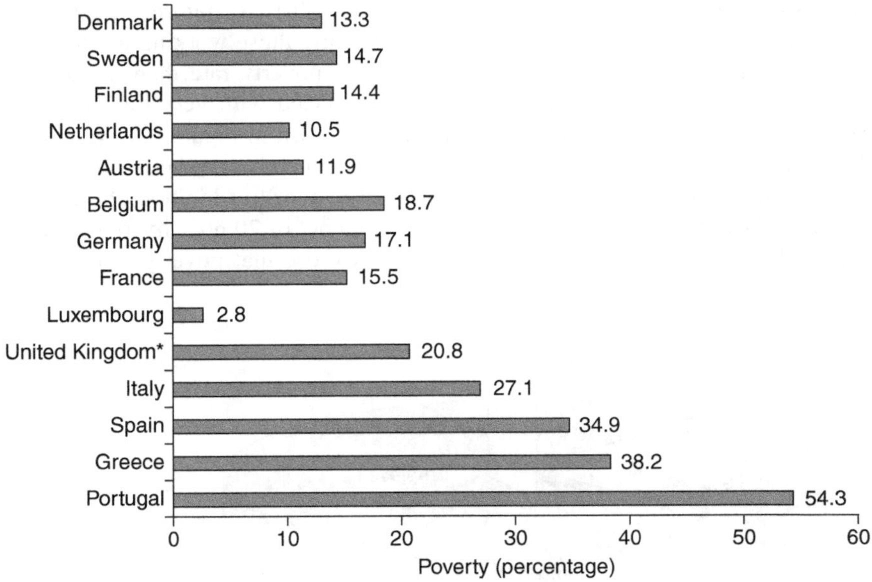

Figure 9.3 Poverty rates in the EU, based on the Danish poverty line and adjusting for differences in purchasing power, 2009 incomes (poverty threshold is set to 60% of the Danish median equivalised disposable income) (source: www.ine-observatory.gr (estimates based on EU-SILC UDB)).

Note
* 2010 incomes.

austerity measures. Since earnings are considered as reflecting people's productivity (or net marginal product) these high poverty rates were attributed to Greeks working fewer hours or less hard than other Europeans. But, how valid is this argument widely reproduced by the media? Eurostat's official data provides an entirely different picture. Greeks work on average more hours per week than the average European. Even before the onset of the economic crisis, the average hours (full-time and part-time) that Greeks worked per week in their main job was the highest among all the EU-27 countries. Since 2008 and until the most recent estimates of 2013, Greeks have been working on average more than 42 hours weekly in the main job.[5] This is significantly higher than the corresponding figures for the total EU-27 and EU-15 which are below the 38 and 37 hours weekly respectively. Compared to the other Europeans, Greeks work more hours and have one of the highest poverty rates.

As earlier discussed, within the mainstream framework lack of paid employment is a crucial factor in determining poverty and inequality. Thus, reducing unemployment is believed to be the most effective remedy to alleviate poverty. The relation between unemployment and poverty is justified by the high poverty risk the unemployed face. No one could expect that unemployment is associated with low incomes and poverty. However, a careful examination of the available data reveals that other occupational categories are also associated with similarly high poverty risks (Papatheodorou and Dafermos (2010)). Before the onset of the economic crisis, farmers in Greece and generally those working in the agricultural sector, appeared to have an even higher poverty rate than the unemployed. Additionally, part-time employees were faced with very high poverty risk. Focusing on the contribution to poverty, as shown in Figure 9.2, we notice that more than 58.4 per cent of those in poverty are members of households with a head employed. Almost 85 per cent of the Greek poor lived in households that are headed by an employed or a retired. Only one out of 20 poor lived in households with a head unemployed. These figures expose that poverty is not only

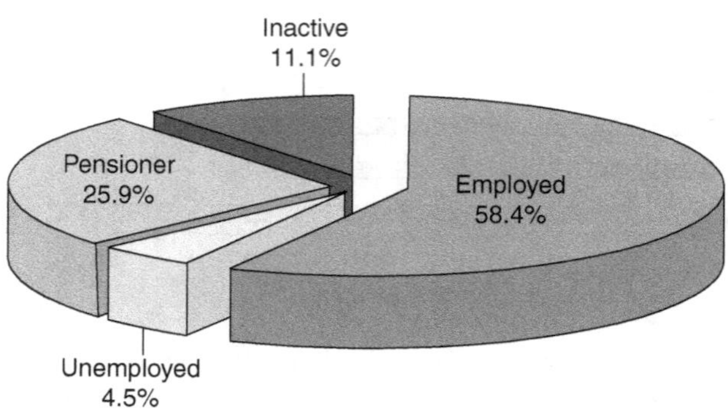

Figure 9.4 Contribution (%) to total poverty by the employment status of the head of household, Greece, 2008 (2007 incomes) (source: Papatheodorou and Dafermos (2010)).

associated with unemployment. A comparative analysis by Dafermos and Papatheodorou (2012) showed that in-work poverty plays a prominent role in shaping overall poverty. Higher flexibility in the labour market is associated with high poverty risk among working people in the EU. The structure of the social protection system appeared to significantly affect in-work poverty, and could explain a large part of cross-country variations. Employing also panel data techniques in exploring the macroeconomic and institutional determinants of inequality and poverty, Dafermos and Papatheodorou (2013) found that the impact of employment is not empirically sound.

Finally, the role of economic growth has been emphasised in the dominant discourse regarding the impact of macroeconomic factors on inequality and poverty. The claim that all population will benefit from the expected economic growth, assisted the implementation of austerity measures. The cuts in public expenditures and the deregulation of the labour market that has mostly affected the low income population, were presented as the main remedies to alleviate economic crisis, and to promote economic growth. It is not within the scope of this chapter to discuss whether these measures would in fact promote economic growth. Other chapters in this volume will cover this large topic. What is of interest to us is the association between economic growth and poverty. As shown in this section, the high rates of growth that Greece experienced during the pre-crisis period did not have a profound impact on reducing poverty. Empirical research in developed countries does not support the strong effect of economic growth on poverty (e.g. Brady (2005), Caminada *et al.* (2012)). Dafermos and Papatheodorou (2013) found that in the EU economic growth does influence inequality and poverty. However, their analysis showed that poverty and inequality are greatly affected by social expenditures. More importantly, their findings suggest that the distributive role of economic growth is largely affected by the social protection system.

Back to the important role of the social protection system: as mentioned before, social spending in Greece was accused of being particularly generous and to contribute to the huge public debt. However, the official data does not support these views. Social expenditures in Greece, as a per cent of GDP have been significantly lower to corresponding figures for total EU-15 and EU-27 for the most of the pre-crisis period.[6] This gap between the Greek and the EU figures has only been narrowed since 2007.

The prominent role of the social protection system in determining poverty risk is portrayed in Figure 9.5. Differences in relative poverty rates between EU countries are greatly attributed to the impact of social transfers. Compared to the other EU-15 countries, the Greek social protection system is particularly feeble in alleviating poverty reflecting its own structural weakness and peculiarities. It is broadly acknowledged as a highly fragmented system, with rudimentary and uncoordinated provisions, deeply polarised, where families play a crucial role in social care (Papatheodorou (2009), Petmesidou (2006)). For income before social transfers, poverty rates in Greece are not among the highest in the EU-15. Even more, for incomes after pensions but before other social transfers in cash, poverty rates in

Greece were among the lowest in the EU-15. It is therefore the weak distributional impact of the other social transfers except pensions that explain the country's high poverty rates. Social transfers in Greece are exhausted in pensions while the role of the other benefits is quite marginal. The latter have by far the weakest distributional impact in reducing poverty among all EU countries.

IV The impact of the economic crisis and of neoliberal remedies

The austerity programmes that were implemented in Greece are presented in other chapters (see Introduction to this volume). Barriers to assessing the impact of economic crisis and of stabilisation policies on poverty and deprivation are imposed by existing time lags between the collection and accessibility of the necessary data and estimates. By the time this chapter was written, the most recent published estimates by Eurostat and the Hellenic Statistical Authority was those of the 2012 EU-SILC survey's that referred to 2011 incomes. As far as the micro-data are concerned, available are those of the 2011 survey that referred to 2010 incomes. Also, the impact of the economic crisis on employment and people's income has become more evident since 2010, when the austerity measures were also introduced, and became more severe the following years. Thus the available data cannot portray the true magnitude of this impact on poverty and deterioration of the level of living.

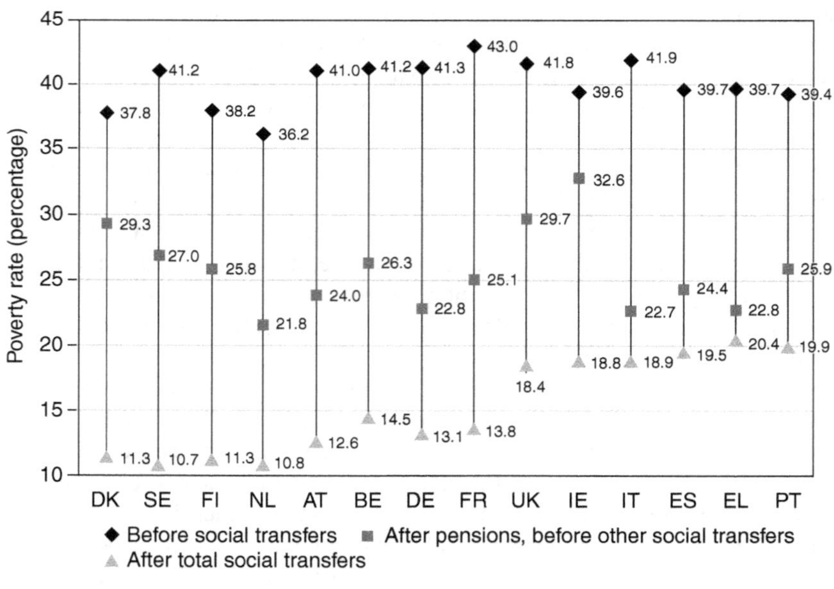

Figure 9.5 Poverty (%) before and after social transfers in cash, EU-15, average values, 1994–2009 (1995–2010 surveys) (source: www.ineobservatory.gr (based on Eurostat's data)).

The economic crisis and the austerity measures that were implemented since 2010 have a devastating effect on poverty and the level of living. According to the broadly used relative poverty definition (60 per cent of average equivalent disposable national income) poverty rates increased from 19.7 per cent in 2008 to 23.1 per cent in 2011. Particularly noticeable is the increase of poverty risk between 2010 and 2011. However, this index is not considered as the most proper one for capturing the deterioration of the level of living. As aforementioned, it is calculated as a percentage of national median income and thus it is affected by changes in the incomes of those in the middle of the distribution. Therefore, this increase in poverty risk took place despite the fact that the poverty threshold reduced dramatically between 2010 and 2011. In only one year the poverty threshold for a single member household reduced from €549 in 2010 to €476 in 2011. At the same period, the risk of poverty or social exclusion increased from 31 to 34.6 per cent. Similarly, the poverty gap has significantly enlarged, from 23.4 per cent in 2008 to 29.9 per cent in 2011. This means that the poor became poorer. In 2011 one out of two poor have an equivalent disposable monthly income lower than €334.

Most revealing for the worsening of the standards of living are the estimates based on a poverty threshold anchored at a fixed moment in time. These are estimates of poverty risk using the same poverty threshold of a particular base year, adjusted for inflation. In Figure 9.6 estimates of poverty risk based on the 60 per cent of the median equivalised disposable income of 2007 (2008 survey) are provided. According to this line, poverty rate increased from 18.9 per cent in 2008 to 35.8 per cent in 2011. In other words, in 2011 more than one-third of the Greek population was living below the poverty line. It is noticeable that in just one year (2010–11) the proportion of the population that was living below

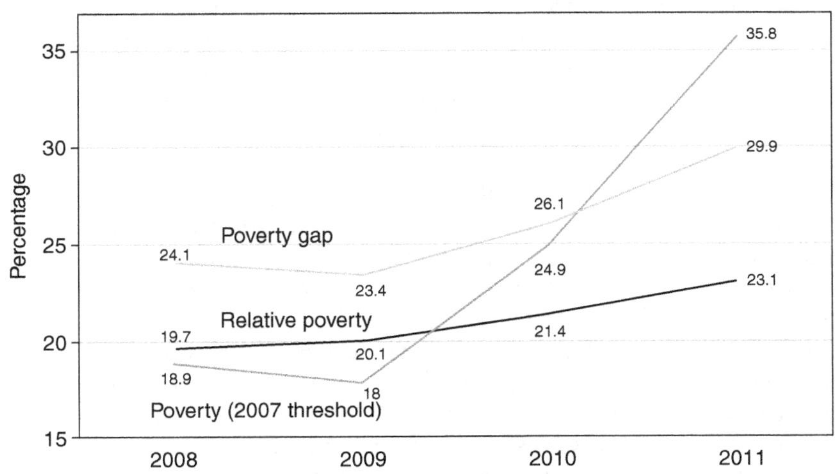

Figure 9.6 Poverty (%) in Greece, 2008–11 (2009–12 surveys) (source: www.ineobservatory.gr (based on Eurostat's data)).

2007's poverty threshold increased by 11 percentage units. This is the year that the austerity policies were introduced, following the three party memorandum agreement signed by the Greek government and the troika (EC, ECB and IMF). Taking into consideration that in 2012 and 2013 the austerity measures had a more devastating effect on people's income, we could safely assume that in subsequent years poverty and deprivation will increase even more dramatically compared to the 2011 figures.

Similarly, in just one year there was a noticeable increase in income inequality as measured by the Gini coefficient and the S80/S20 ratio.[7] This indicates an increase in polarisation as a result of the unequal distribution of the crisis and austerity measures burden. Low and middle income strata were mostly affected, thus disputing governmental claims on this matter. It is indicative that the monthly disposable equivalent income for those in the middle of the distribution was reduced to €793 in 2011 from €915 in 2010.

Dramatic was also the increase in material deprivation as illustrated in Figure 9.7. This measures people's inability to afford a number of items and expenses that are considered necessary for maintaining a certain level of living. People or households are considered materially deprived if they cannot afford three or more of the nine items and expenses presented in Figure 9.7. Those materially deprived in Greece rose to 33.4 per cent of the population in 2012 from 21.8 per cent in 2008. More than half of the population cannot afford a week's holiday. Also two out of five people reported difficulties in facing unexpected financial expenses or are unable to pay mortgages, rent payments, utility bills and so on. Significant was also the increased proportion of those being unable to keep their home adequately warm.

The rapidly increased unemployment rates since 2009 had a devastating effect on poverty and deprivation. Yet, the neoliberal remedies to reduce unemployment not only failed to raise employment but also proved catastrophic on people's income. As noted above, having a job in Greece cannot guarantee the escape from poverty. Even before the crisis the largest part of the poor population was living in households headed by an employed. In just one year in-work poverty risk rose from 11.9 (2010) to 15.1 per cent (2011) reflecting mainly the effect of austerity policies on the labour market. That is, the deregulation of the labour market, the abandonment of collective bargains, the reduction of minimum wages and salaries, and the increase of labour flexibility and particularly of part-time contracts. Also, for a large number of employees (particularly the young) the minimum net monthly wage for full-time employment has been reduced to an amount lower than that of the country's relative poverty line for a single person in 2010.

One would expect that during the crisis the social protection system in Greece would have been reinforced in order to protect people from the increasing risk of poverty and deprivation. But this practice would have also been against the dominant neoliberal perspectives for organising and administrating society. In reality though, austerity and stabilisation measures have undermined welfare rights and have worsen the Greek social protection system which was already rather weak (see Petmesidou (2011, 2013)). For instance, pension incomes

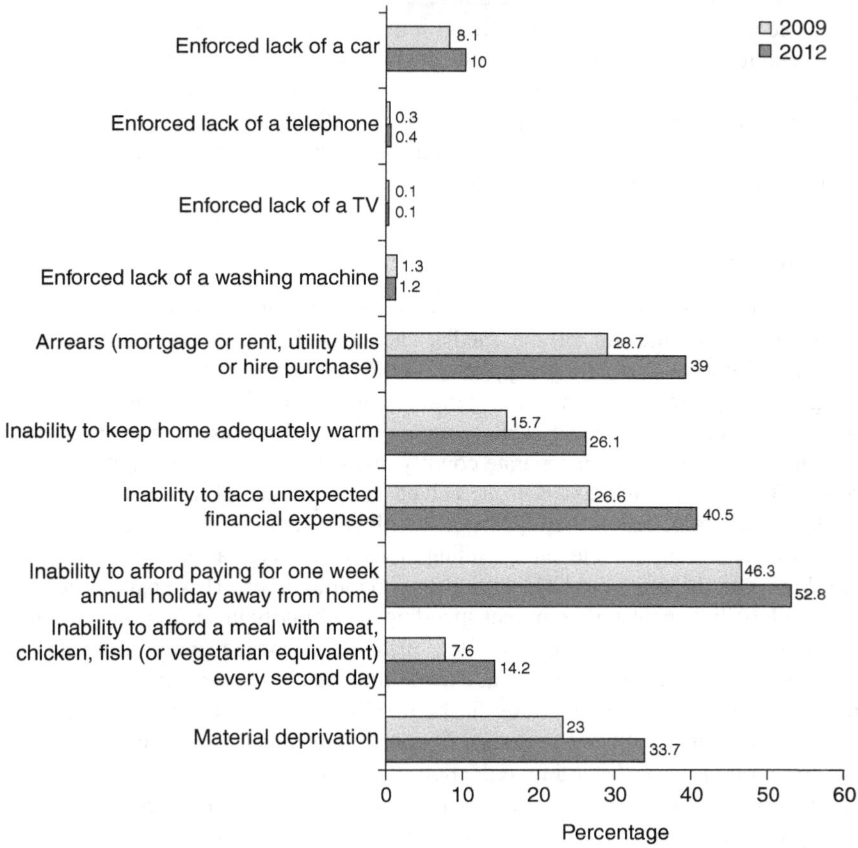

Figure 9.7 Material deprivation (%), Greece, 2008–11 (source: estimates based on Eurostat's data: http://epp.eurostat.ec.europa.eu).

(current and future) and social assistance benefits have been significantly reduced, and large cuts in social services have taken place. The basic pension of €360 per month that has been introduced, funded by general taxation, is well below the country's 2011's poverty line for a single person. Note that this amount is not fixed and could be further reduced. Unemployment benefits are also set at a level well below the country's poverty line. Empirical evidence has shown that the high poverty rates in Greece are mostly attributed to the weak distributional impact of its social protection system (see also Dafermos and Papatheodorou (2012, 2013), Papatheodorou and Dafermos (2010)). The neoliberal remedies have further weakened the distributional role of social protection by transforming the system towards a liberal one, which performs badly in alleviating poverty, and by further cutting on social transfers. These will have a further devastating impact on poverty and deprivation.

The reader is reminded that the above estimates refer to a period before the current economic crisis had a significant impact on people's income. The effect of the economic crisis on poverty and deprivation in Greece will not only be restricted to that of the huge increase of unemployment and the shrinkage of GDP. Poverty will also and most importantly be affected by the neoliberal remedies that promote fiscal discipline, reduction of public spending, particularly on social protection, and labour market deregulation.

V Conclusion

The current global economic crisis has apparent negative effects on poverty and deprivation. With the aid of the media, the crisis has been presented in the dominant discourse as a strong support of neoliberal perspectives rather than as a strong challenge to the mainstream paradigm for organising and administrating economies. Rooted to Neoclassical economics, the crisis has been treated as a problem 'belonging' to each separate country and not as endemic in capitalist economies. The Greek crisis has been perceived as an individual incident for which Greeks are to blame rather than a part of the global economic crisis. Furthermore, social protection and the relevant spending have been treated as the main demonic contributors to the huge public debt and to economic crisis. This position helped cultivate hostility against government spending, particularly in social policy, which was considered part of the problem. One of the main consequences is the strong pressure for further decrease of social expenditures and for transforming the social protection systems in order to better fit the neoliberal paradigm for administrating the economy. The neoliberal remedies imposed under the austerity measures are those promoting fiscal discipline, reduction of public spending and labour market deregulation. In the same vein, the dominant perception on income inequality and poverty is also rooted to the main Neoclassical hypotheses: a society consisting of individuals, whose incomes are mainly gained through their participation in the labour market. Earnings are largely determined by personal characteristics and choices, rather than the macroeconomic factors. The proposed remedies to alleviate poverty are narrowed to those that help people improve their skills and employability (through education and training) and to access the labour market. Also considering unemployment as structural, deregulation of the labour market is proposed as the main remedy to reduce unemployment.

The analysis reveals that these perspectives are not empirically sound. The evidence also documented that the economic crisis and, more importantly, the neoliberal remedies have dramatically increased poverty, deprivation and income dispersion in Greece in just one year. These estimates refer to a period when the current economic crisis and the austerity measures had a less severe impact on people's income. Due to the impact that these neoliberal remedies have on the macroeconomic environment, it is anticipated that they will have an even more devastating effect on people's incomes, and will affect mainly those at the low and middle income strata. These are the populations that have the highest rate of consumption with profound implications to aggregate demand and to growth.

Notes

1 On a theoretical ground, Kuznets' (1955) hypothesis of the inverse-U shaped curve has been questioned by a number of studies (i.e. Bourguignon (1990), Alderson and Nielsen (2002)) but has gained support by others (i.e. Aghion *et al.* (1999), Caselli and Ventura (2000)).

2 Empirical evidence does not provide support to the view that personal attributes could have a determinable impact on people's incomes. Decomposing inequality by population sub-groups in EU countries reveals than none of the broadly used characteristics in these theories could alone explain a large part of the overall income dispersion (see Papatheodorou and Petmesidou (2005), Papatheodorou and Dafermos (2010)).

3 This does not imply superiority of this poverty index against the plethora of alternative ones that have been proposed in the literature (see Alcock (1993), Gordon *et al.* (2000)). On the contrary, it could be argued that it is a rather arbitrary chosen index that lacks any strong theoretical foundation (see Papatheodorou (2008), Papatheodorou and Dafermos (2010)). The particular poverty index was chosen because it is easily estimated with available data and it is broadly used by official statistics and by several studies in the field which helps result comparability.

4 The modified OECD scale assigns a weight of 1.0 to the first member of the household, of 0.5 to each additional adult member and of 0.3 to each child.

5 See http://epp.eurostat.ec.europa.eu.

6 The corresponding figures for social expenditure as a per cent of GD in Greece and EU-15 were 19.9 and 27.4 per cent in 1995 (http://epp.eurostat.ec.europa.eu).

7 The S80/S20 is the total income ratio of the 20 per cent of the population with the highest incomes to the 20 per cent of the population with the lowest incomes.

References

Aghion P., Caroli E. and García-Peñalosa C. (1999), 'Inequality and economic growth: the perspective of the new growth theories', *Journal of Economic Literature* 37(4).

Alcock P. (1993), *Understanding Poverty*, London: Macmillan.

Alderson A. and Nielsen F. (2002), 'Globalization and the great U-turn: income inequality trends in 16 OECD countries', *American Journal of Sociology* 107(5).

Atkinson A.B. (1998), *Poverty in Europe*, Oxford: Blackwell.

Atkinson A.B. and Bourguignon F. (2000), 'Income distribution and economics', in Atkinson A.B. and Bourguignon F. (eds), *Handbook of Income Distribution*, Vol. 1, Amsterdam: Elsevier.

Becker G. (1993), *Human Capital: A Theoretical and Empirical Analysis, with Special Reference to Education*, 3rd edition, Chicago, IL: University of Chicago Press.

Bourguignon F. (1990), 'Growth and inequality in the dual model of development: the role of demand factors', *Review of Economic Studies* 57(2).

Brady D. (2005), 'The welfare state and relative poverty in rich western democracies', *Social Forces* 83(4).

Caminada K., Goudswaard K. and Koster F. (2012), 'Social income transfers and poverty: a cross country analysis of OECD countries', *International Journal of Social Welfare* 21(2).

Caselli F. and Ventura J. (2000), 'A representative consumer theory of distribution', *American Economic Review* 90(4).

Dafermos Y. and Papatheodorou C. (2012), 'Working poor, labour market and social protection in the EU: a comparative perspective', *International Journal of Management Concepts and Philosophy* 6(1/2).

Dafermos Y. and Papatheodorou C. (2013), 'What drives inequality and poverty in the EU? Exploring the impact of macroeconomic and institutional factors', *International Review of Applied Economics* 27(1).

Esping-Andersen G. (1990), *The Three Worlds of Welfare Capitalism*, Oxford: Policy Press.

Ferrera M. (1996), 'The "southern model" of welfare in social Europe', *Journal of European Social Policy* 6(1).

Gordon D., Pantazis C. and Townsend P. (2000), 'Absolute and overall poverty: a European history and proposal for measurement', in Gordon D. and Townsend P. (eds), *Breadline Europe: The Measurement of Poverty*, Bristol: Policy Press.

Kuznets S. (1955), 'Economic growth and income inequality', *American Economic Review* 45(1).

Leibfried S. (1992), 'Towards a European welfare state? On integrating poverty regimes into the European community', in Ferge Z. and Kolberg J.-E. (eds), *Social Policy in a Changing Europe*, Frankfurt am Main: European Centre for Social Welfare Policy and Research.

Levitas R. (1996), 'The concept of social exclusion and the new Durkheimian hegemony', *Critical Social Policy* 16(1).

Levitas R. (2000), 'What is social exclusion?' in Gordon D. and Townsend P. (eds), *Breadline Europe: The Measurement of Poverty*, Bristol: Policy Press.

Mincer J. (1958), 'Investment in human capital and personal income distribution', *Journal of Political Economy* 66(4).

Papatheodorou C. (2004), 'Conceptual and methodological issues in measuring inequality: what is the impact of alternative assumptions and interpretations', in Petmesidou M. and Papatheodorou C. (eds), *Poverty and Social Exclusion*, Athens: Exantas [in Greek].

Patheodorou C. (2008), 'The public debate on poverty in Greece and the legitimization of dominant national and supranational policies', in Agelidis M., Sakkas D. and Gravaris D. (eds), *Social Theory and Political Responsibility*, Athens: Gutenberg [in Greek].

Papatheodorou C. (2009), 'Inequalities and deficiencies in social protection: the welfare system of Greece', in Schubert K., Hegelich S. and Bazant U. (eds), *The Handbook of European Welfare Systems*, London/Oxford: Routledge.

Patheodorou C. and Dafermos Y. (2010), *Structure and Trends in Economic Inequality and Poverty in Greece and EU, 1995–2008*, Observatory of Economic and Social Developments, Labour Institute, Greek General Confederation of Labour, Athens: INE-GSEE [in Greek].

Papatheodorou C. and Petmesidou M. (2004), 'Inequality, poverty and redistribution through social transfers: Greece in comparative perspective', in Petmesidou M. and Papatheodorou C. (eds), *Poverty and Social Exclusion*, Athens: Exantas [in Greek].

Papatheodorou C. and Petmesidou M. (2005), 'Inequality, redistribution and welfare regimes: comparing Greece to other EU countries', in Argitis G. (ed.), *Economic Changes and Social Oppositions in Greece: The Challenges at the Beginning of 21st Century*, Athens: Tipothito, Yorgos-Dardanos [in Greek].

Papatheodorou C., Sakellaropoulos S. and Yeros P. (2012), 'Greece at a crossroad: crisis and radicalization in the Southern European semi-periphery', *MRZine*, 30 May.

Petmesidou M. (2006), 'Tracking social protection: origins, path peculiarity, impasses and prospects', in Petmesidou M. and Mossialos E. (eds), *Social Policy Developments in Greece*, Aldersot: Ashgate.

Petmesidou M. (2011), 'Is the EU-IMF "rescue plan" dealing a blow to the Greek welfare state?' *CROP Poverty Brief 4*, www.crop.org/viewfile.aspx?id=225.

Petmesidou M. (2013), 'Crisis and austerity: A painful watershed for the Greek welfare state', *Politica Insight*, 8 November.

Taubman P. (1978), *Income Distribution and Redistribution*, Reading: Addison-Wesley.

10 A comparative study of aspects of employment and unemployment in Greece before and after the crisis

Alexis Ioannides

I Introduction

Greek capitalism's crisis and the troika EAPs that followed had an unprecedented impact on Greece's labour market. For Marxist Political Economy an over-accumulation crisis (caused by the TRPF) can be overcome only through a drastic devalorisation of capital and the revitalisation of the counteracting to the TRPF forces. The most important of the latter is the increase of the rate of exploitation (i.e. the rate of surplus-value). The rate of surplus-value can be improved by increasing unpaid labour-time and decreasing the value of labour-power. Both these elements are undeclared but essential parts of the Memoranda strategy (i.e. the type of capitalist restructuring organised by the EAPs co-opted by Greek capital and the dominant EU imperialist powers).

The Memoranda strategy argues that a critical aspect of Greece's crisis is its poor competitiveness (see Chapter 1 of this volume). High wage increases are unjustifiably accused of being the culprit for this. Then it is argued that because Greece is part of the EMU it cannot rectify its falling competitiveness through devaluation (as it has no currency of its own) and has to resort to 'internal devaluation'. This latter is a euphemism – or even a contradiction in terms – denoting a drastic decrease of wages. This is also associated with a generalised deregulation of the labour market and a monstrous worsening of labour relations. The most powerful tool for this strategy to succeed is the tremendous rise of unemployment and underemployment. This augments the reserve army of labour that has a 'disciplining' effect on the working class. Because of the fear of unemployment workers are obliged to accept lower wages, increased unpaid work-time and worse working conditions. Thus, despite the official utterances about the problem of very high unemployment, the latter is a conscious element of their strategy.

The implementation of the Memoranda strategy has already dire impact on the working class. Workers' rights, that took decades and many sacrifices to be achieved, have been attacked and eliminated. In the public sector there are for the first time mass redundancies, the increase of work-time and drastic cuts on nominal wages by 20 to 40 per cent. In the private sector we watch the easier allowance of collective dismissals and the drastic diminishing of severance pay for dismissals, the encouragement of flexible working time arrangements and atypical employment, the further reduction of the (already too low) minimum wage, the reduction of unemployment benefit and the abolition of almost any other workers' benefit. Unions are also attacked by undermining collective bargaining and the coverage of collective agreements, by legislating the prevalence of company level collective agreements compared to sectoral or general ones and by conceding the right to sign collective agreements not only to unions but also to any informal group of employees. These have already led to a rapid decrease in nominal wages in the private sector too (INE-GSEE (2013)).

The mainstream mantra argues that these labour market reforms will re-establish equilibrium in the labour market. Wages will be adjusted to the level of marginal productivity and this will finally lead to the reduction if not the vanishing of unemployment. According to orthodox economics these labour market reforms will restore the normal functioning of the labour market, so that workers under their free will and maximising behaviour could choose the hours they would like to work and accept a wage that leads to labour market equilibrium and the reduction of unemployment.

The mainstream mantra is a feeble ideological masquerade of capital's ruthless restructuring strategy. As we intent to show using the data from EUROSTAT's Labour Force Survey (LFS), there is not much free will left to the workers to guide their actions in contemporary Greece. It is the sheer fear of unemployment and rapid deterioration of the workers' living standards together with the weakness of the trade unions that dictate terms. The examination of the conditions regarding work-time, part-time and full-time employment and unpaid overtime disputes the Neoclassical explanation of the labour market function and verifies the Marxist one. Additionally, the real unemployment rate is estimated, using a moderate approach, proving that the conditions for the Greek working class are much worse than they seem to be.

The next section offers an overview of the Greek labour market, focusing on the issue of employment and unemployment. In section III the level of real unemployment is estimated, using the LFS data. The conditions concerning work-time and overtime are analysed in section IV. All estimations are based on our own processing of the available LFS micro-data, available until the year 2011. Finally, the last section concludes.

II An overview of the Greek labour market

The post-2009 rapid GDP decline led to a great reduction of employment by 16.5 per cent from 2009 to 2012. This reduction is continuing in 2013 as well, as EUROSTAT data reveal.[1] Analogous was the decline in the employment rate (for the ages 15–64) while the active population remained practically stable and the activity rate as well. This has created an explosion in the unemployment rate that increased from 9.5 to 24.3 per cent in 2012 and to 27.3 per cent in October 2013.[2] And the situation is even worse. This horrendous figure is in fact underestimating the real unemployment rate in Greece. As we intent to prove below,

Table 10.1 General overview of labour market statistics

	2009	*2011*	*2012*
Total employment	4,508,662	4,090,711	3,763,000
Unemployment	471,107	876,891	1,204,000
Labour force	4,979,769	4,967,602	4,967,000
Unemployment rate	9.5%	17.7%	24.3%
Employment rate (15–64)	61.2%	55.6%	51.3%
Activity rate (15–64)	67.8%	67.7%	67.9%

Source: Own estimations using LFS micro-data and (for year 2012) Eurostat statistic databases.

unemployment rate is at least 4.4 per cent higher for the year 2011 which is the last year for which LFS micro-data are available.

While the labour force shows only a small decline in total, the results are quite different if men and women are examined separately. In this case it can be observed (Table 10.2) an important reduction in male participation and an equally important rise in women's rate. Observing the differences between men and women, the struggle between workers' discouragement and addition to work force is obvious, as it will be observed below.

Table 10.2 Main labour force statistics by sex

Employment status	*2009*	*2011*	*Rate of change (%)*
Employed	4,508,662	4,090,711	–9.3
Male	2,717,790	2,441,485	–10.2
Female	1,790,872	1,649,226	–7.9
Unemployed (%)	471,107 (9.5%)	876,891 (17.7%)	86.1
Male	199,997 (6.9%)	428,896 (14.9%)	114.5
Female	271,110 (13.1%)	447,995 (21.4%)	65.2
Long-term unemployment	192,396 (3.9%)	434,685 (8.6%)	125.9
Male	68,856 (2.4%)	192,971(6.7%)	180.3
Female	123,540 (6.0%)	241,714 (11.5%)	95.7
Labour force (PR)*	4,979,769 (67.8%)	4,967,602 (67.7%)	–0.2
Male (PR)	2,917,787 (79.0%)	2,870,381 (77.7%)	–1.6
Female (PR)	2,061,982 (56.5%)	2,097,221 (57.5%)	1.7
Inactive	4,287,659	4,374,279	2.0
Male	1,602,930	1,691,203	5.5
Female	2,684,729	2,683,076	–0.1
0–14	1,571,176	1,583,204	0.8
Male	809,374	815,858	0.8
Female	761,802	767,346	0.7
Total population	10,838,604	10,925,085	0.8

Source: Own estimations using LFS micro-data.

Note

* Participation rate in the labour force for 15–64 years of age.

Another interesting fact is that the unemployment rate gap that existed between men and women tends to decrease. As can be seen in Table 10.2 male unemployment rate has more than doubled, while women saw only an approximately 60 per cent increase. It must be noticed that this impressive increase is only for the 2009–11 period. The situation is much worse for 2012 and 2013 according to EUROSTAT's press releases. The main reason for this asymmetric effect on men and women is the uneven way the crisis has hit the various branches of the economy (and especially male-dominated sectors like construction) and not some tendency to sexual equality during the crisis.

Especially important is the impact of unemployment on the different age groups. As can be expected, young people are the ones most severely hit, with youth unemployment climbing over 44 per cent for 2011. The interesting fact is that unemployment rates increased analogously for every age group, despite the fact that they were already very high for young people even before the crisis.

III Hidden unemployment and the real unemployment rate

Despite the remarkably high official rate of unemployment in Greece during the last years, the real rate is even higher due both to general factors that are valid for most of the countries and to specific reasons that hold for the Greek economy and the Greek labour market in particular.

The first reason is the well-known discouragement of the workers because of the persistently high unemployment rate and the effect of long-term unemployment. This has been called the 'Discouraged Worker Effect' (Cahuc and Zylberberg (2004): 116–17). As is acknowledged, LFS and the statistical surveys in general that follow the standards of the International Labour Organization (ILO) have as a precondition, among others, the continuous search for a job for a jobless person to be registered as unemployed. This methodology is rightfully criticised for failing to count as unemployed people who, because of the long unemployment spells and high unemployment rates, have been discouraged and stopped actively searching for a job, although they remain available to accept a job and this will probably happen when the economy rises again. The existence of this hidden labour force is pointed out by macroeconomic considerations too, that are common in business cycles models. Although an old debate exists on whether the discouraged workers should be added to the unemployed,[3] our thesis (which will not be argued further at this point) is that they should and so we will try to estimate them.

On the other hand, during a crisis the reverse effect also occurs. Some people not previously working or wanting to work are now entering the labour force because a person in their family lost a job, or suffered income loses (Added Worker Effect, Lundberg (1985)). Most of the relevant literature agrees that the first effect is stronger meaning that discouragement prevails and the rise of unemployment is negatively correlated to the participation in the labour force.

It has been also estimated that a 1 per cent increase in the unemployment rate leads to a reduction of the labour force at a rate of 2 per cent for young men and

Table 10.3 Unemployment by age groups

Age group	*2009*			*2011*		
	Employed	*Unemployed*	*% Unemployed*	*Employed*	*Unemployed*	*% Unemployed*
15–24	257,001	89,271	25.8	176,716	141,132	44.4
25–34	1,187,370	168,526	12.4	988,116	320,073	24.5
35–44	1,331,248	112,532	7.8	1,270,639	216,195	14.5
45–54	1,093,502	73,406	6.3	1,051,886	148,408	12.4
55–64	554,091	26,645	4.6	529,233	49,115	8.5
>65	85,451	727	0.8	74,120	1,968	2.6
Total	4,508,662	471,107	9.5	4,090,711	876,891	17.7

Source: Own estimations using LFS micro-data.

women and less than 0.5 per cent for the older (DeFreitas (1986)). The adoption of this estimation would lead to a major reduction in the labour force in the case of Greece (compared to the one that would exist otherwise) so we will follow a much more moderate approach to obtain an estimation of the labour force reduction due to the crisis.

A first approximate estimation can be given by the examination of the male and female participation in the labour force. As can be seen in Table 10.2 the male participation rate has decreased by 1.3 per cent of the total population between 15 and 64 years of age. This number can be a rough estimation of the difference between the discouraged and the added workers for men. So this 1.3 per cent can be an approximation of the minimum level of the degree that the male labour force has been negatively affected by the crisis. It can be assumed that women's discouragement is at least at the same level, since this is a modest estimation and the long-term unemployment is much higher among women. This means that at least 80,000 people were added to the discouraged workers during these two years. This number is much bigger than the one that is estimated by the LFS, particularly by the variable that measures the number of people that would like to work but are not actively searching for a job. According to this estimation there were 103,687 people in this category in 2009 and raised to only 112,535 in 2011 (our estimations using the LFS micro-data). This is a clear indication that this LFS variable clearly underestimates the discouraged workers. One reason for this is perhaps the probability that a discouraged worker difficultly reveals that he or she has quitted efforts and became inactive.

But even according to this underestimating source, there is 2.3 per cent of the labour force that is not accounted for and this would lead to an extra 2.2 per cent rate of unemployment (see Table 10.5, below), even after adjusting for the increased labour force.

One extra source of hidden unemployment is the underemployment of the labour force. For the employees, underemployment takes the form of working fewer hours than the preferred ones or working as part-timers although they would prefer a full-time job. There is also the case of working in a job which requires inferior qualification, in which case it is the skills of the worker that stay unutilised; but this case, which is very common among the highly educated Greek youth, will not be examined here, since we focus on the quantitative aspects of unemployment.

For the self-employed, underemployment takes also the form of fewer working hours as a result of client scarcity, or it can take the form of performing tasks that have minimum probabilities of being paid, only as a means of increasing the potential customers.

It has to be noticed that the number and the share of self-employed to the total employment in Greece is very high. This fact reflects some basic structural peculiarities of the Greek economy. The self-employed category contains people and jobs with quite diverse characteristics. Many of them can be found in the primary sector where the small ownership doesn't allow for big farms with paid labour. But most of the self-employed are found in sections G and M.[4] Among them are doctors, engineers, architects, accountants or financial advisers, lawyers, small-shop owners without employees, even secondary education professors that work in private schools. They accounted for 31 per cent of the labour force in 2011 which is a rather big share. One reason for their extended existence is the lack of big enterprises in many sectors of the Greek economy, where they could work as employees. This fact makes inevitable for many scientists and other professionals to become self-employed in order to find a job and to secure health care and pension. In the last years an extra phenomenon is also increasing the number of self-employed in Greece. Employers in some sections (mostly in the service sector) tend to press their employees to convert themselves to self-employed and keep on doing the same job as before. In this way they avoid paying insurance taxes, which are now obligation of the worker. This is an additional method for reducing wages in contemporary Greece. This fact led to an increase in self-employment despite the crisis in some sections of economic activity (e.g. in section M that covers professional, scientific and technical activities). Although this practice in not legal it is tolerated by the authorities.

The underemployment can be estimated with LFS's help. In Table 10.7 (below) we can see the number of part-time workers that would like to work full-time but failed to find a full-time job. It is obvious that the majority of part-timers would prefer a full-time job and this number is increasing with the crisis. This statistic can be used to estimate the extent of unemployment among the part-timers. But LFS provides us with another statistic which measures the desired hours of work per person. This allows for a comparison between desired and actual or usual work-time. This variable also allows for the estimation of underemployment not only among the part-timers but among the 'full'-timers as well, since many of them might still prefer to work more hours.[5] The same variable can be used for an estimation of self-employed and family workers underemployment. The results of this comparison can be found in Table 10.4. As it is estimated, the effect of underemployment is equivalent to approximately 140,000 more unemployed workers than the official count accepts.

It has to be noticed here that this statistic seems to seriously underestimate the effect of underemployment for self-employed workers. As it can be seen in Table 10.7 (below) the reduction of the number of employees was almost 9 per cent while the reduction of self-employed was less than 6 per cent. Since the majority of self-employed in Greece are without personnel and do similar jobs with similar compensations to the workers, this difference in reduction rates is rather surprising. The main explanation for this is that many self-employed – even if they don't earn enough money – cannot easily get out of business because they lose not only health care for them and their families but also the right for a pension when they grow old. This is because they belong to separate pension funds and are obliged to pay their contribution to them whether they work or not; otherwise they lose all pension rights. So it is very common to stay officially as self-employed and pay the insurance contribution even though they don't have any clients or have closed their businesses. If we only assume that the reduction in self-employment was analogous to the reduction of the number of

Table 10.4 Underemployment estimation

Year	*Employment relationship*								
	Self-employed			*Employees*			*Family workers*		
	More hours (mean)	*Number of persons*	*Equiv. full-time workers*	*More hours (mean)*	*Number of persons*	*Equiv. full-time workers*	*More hours (mean)*	*Number of persons*	*Equiv. full-time workers*
2009	16.96	35,636	15,110	17.38	150,343	65,324	18.08	8,372	3,784
2011	17.64	75,468	33,281	16.56	237,420	98,292	18.83	17,584	8,278

Source: Own estimations using LFS micro-data.

employees, then we can speak for thousands more self-employed that are practically unemployed because of underemployment and are not accounted for in official measurements. Nevertheless we will, for the present, stay to the number estimated with the help of LFS micro-data; although it seriously underestimates the effect of underemployment among the self-employed, as argued. This estimation is also presented in Table 10.4.

If only the modest estimations of underemployment and hidden labour force are used (which as argued lead to underestimation of underemployment) still there is a significant increase in unemployment rate. As estimated in Table 10.5 for the year 2011, the unemployment rate is rising from the official 17.7 per cent to the 'real' 22.1 per cent; an increase of 4.4 per cent.

Unfortunately the micro-data for the year 2012 are not available yet. But we can project that the hidden unemployment rate of 4.4 per cent must have grown bigger and if this is added to 24.3 per cent for the year 2012 or to 27.3 per cent for October 2013 it leads to the conclusion that total unemployment in Greece has already surpassed one-third of the Greek labour force and this is still an optimistic estimation. This has already resulted in a reduction of real unit labour costs at 13.8 per cent from 2009 to 2013 (AMECO) and this seems to be only the beginning in the process of diminishing the value of labour-power in Greece.

IV The work-time dimension

The second quantitative dimension of labour supply is work-time. According to the Neoclassical approach, work-time is defined by the preferences of workers (supply determined) since enterprises are forced sooner or later to adjust work-time to the will of their employees or suffer profit losses. According to Marxist and other heterodox approaches work-time is determined socially through a complicated process of class struggle. Capital benefits from longer work-time whereas workers benefit from its reduction. Nevertheless, this thesis is valid only within the broader limits of an historical framework of social evolution (high level of abstraction), since only in this historical perspective work-time can be detached from wage and the value of labour-power.

Table 10.5 Real unemployment rate estimation

Year 2011	*Magnitude*	*Rate*
Labour force (LFS)	4,967,602	–
Adjusted labour force	5,107,453	–
Unemployed officially (LFS)	876,891	17.2% (17.7%)
Discouraged (LFS)	112,535	2.2%
Underemployment (LFS)	139,851	2.7%
Estimation of total unemployed	1,129,277	22.1%

Source: Own estimations using LFS micro-data.

On the contrary, within the narrow time limits of the crisis, total compensation of employees is in most of the cases dependent upon their work-time. In periods where the wage rate is falling (especially as in contemporary Greece) it is observed that workers wish to increase their work-time in order to minimise the wage loses they suffer and to try to keep their life standards unaltered (income effect prevails). Workers' volition contrasts with their employers' tendency to temporarily reduce work-time as one of the means to respond to the rapid reduction of consumer demand. This is the reason why the preferred work-time is lower from the usual before the crisis and the opposite during, as the Greek data reveal.[6]

As for the usual work-time of the employees in Greece, it has been reduced from 39.5 hours per week in 2009 to 39 in 2011.[7] This reduction is relatively small considering the magnitude of the crisis; a crisis that has provoked a rapid decrease not only of the weekly working hours but also of the weekly working days for many enterprises in Greece. This, surprisingly small, work-time reduction can be explained only if we consider an opposite effect that is observed in Greece the last years; which is the increasing trend of work-time. This trend is not observed in Greece alone, but in other countries (e.g. US and Britain) as well (Bluestone and Rose (2000), Ioannides and Mavroudeas (2007), Schor (1991)).

This long-term increasing work-time trend moderates the decline in work-time caused by the crisis. In our opinion the crisis will only temporarily lead to less work-time and will finally lead to an increase compared to the situation before the crisis; reinforcing and not weakening the increasing trend that was active for many years before. This is because increasing work-time is a means used by capital to reverse the falling rate of profit through the extraction of absolute surplus-value. The crisis strengthens even more this need of capital. On the other side, this crisis and the high unemployment has weakened the ability of the working class to resist to pressures towards work-time increases. As we have also seen, at the individual level there are many workers who already wish an increase in their work-time (even if part of it is unpaid) in order to compensate for income loses. So when the first wave of the crisis is over and enterprises adjust their capital to a new lower level, the temporary job-sharing policy (which was preferred in the short run for social, productive or legal reasons) will be replaced by fewer jobs with increased work-time. Our estimation is that the pressure from employers for increased work-time has not flinched but is hidden under the work-sharing policy that is used throughout the first severe phase of the crisis.

This conclusion is supported from the examination of the evolution of paid and unpaid overtime. The incidence of unpaid overtime has been emphasised and examined by many authors during the last years (Anger (2008), Bell and Hart (1999), Pannenberg (2005)). One reason is of course its increasing importance, since in many developed countries unpaid surpassed paid overtime. Various explanations were offered for this 'strange' phenomenon. Neoclassicism, almost unreasonably, argues that in fact unpaid overtime is not really unpaid, but paid in different ways such as future promotions, and deferred compensation. Marxist Political Economy, more realistically, argues that unpaid overtime is a clear indication of the pressure put upon the employees to work more time without the corresponding wage increase. The tendency of increasing unpaid overtime is consistent with the explanation of absolute surplus-value extraction and the observed and parallel increase in total work-time.

In Greece unpaid overtime was present the years before the crisis as well. As Ioannides *et al.* (2014) have argued, the incidence of unpaid overtime in Greece is stronger to more vulnerable workers with less union or legal coverage. So there is strong evidence to support that unpaid overtime in Greece is not a voluntary action of workers but the result of their weak position against their employers. Under this explanation it would be expected that unpaid overtime should amplify its relative position compared to paid overtime, although it could be possible for both to decline, since work-time is declining in total due to the acute crisis. The facts for Greece support this explanation. As is shown in Table 10.6, paid overtime decreased during the crisis which is rather expected due to the shrinking demand and the decline on total working hours.

On the other hand, not only the relative magnitude of unpaid compared to paid overtime has increased, but the absolute magnitude of unpaid overtime has increased by almost 20 per cent and this has happened in a period of diminishing working hours in general. This is a clear indication, if not proof, that workers are increasingly under pressure. It is not by their own will that they act, but under the increasing pressure of their employers with the help of the reserve army that is growing in vast numbers, as shown above. This fact is also a clear indication of the explanatory superiority of the Marxist explanation of the process of work-time determination and the function of the labour market as opposed to the Neoclassical mythologies.

V Part-time and temporary work contracts

As shown in Table 10.7, part-time workers increase by 1 per cent from 2009 to 2011. This alone is not that remarkable, since Greece has one of the lowest rates of part-timers in Europe. What is really important is the portion of part-time workers that would prefer a full-time job but could not find one. This part was already high before the crisis (66.4 per cent) but got even higher (74.8 per cent) in two years' time for employees, while there is a similar increase for self-employed. Although a common accusation against the Greek labour market is that it was so rigid that part-time could not blossom, as is obvious it blossomed more than the workers would like to. And there is no excuse like legal rigidities or union contradiction for the employers who fail so totally to adjust to the preferences of their workers. Since it is well known that labour law in Greece favours full-time jobs and trade unions do so as well. So the only explanation is that some employers – for their own interest and contrary to the interest of their workers – employ part-time workers when no one other seems to want this. In our opinion this gives additional support to the Marxist thesis that work-time and in general working conditions are mostly imposed on workers and are not the

Table 10.6 Paid and unpaid overtime

	Paid overtime		*Unpaid overtime*	
	2009	*2011*	*2009*	*2011*
N of employees (% of employed)	117,193 (4.0%)	78,350 (3.0%)	96,776 (3.3%)	94,276 (3.6%)
Hours/week (mean)	7.88	7.93	5.86	6.50
Hours/week on total employees (mean)	0.32	0.24	0.20	0.24

Source: own estimations using LFS micro-data.

Table 10.7 Part-time and temporary employment

Type of employment	*Professional status*											
	2009						*2011*					
	Self-employed		*Employees*		*Family workers*		*Self-employed*		*Employees*		*Family workers*	
	N	*%*	*N*	*%*	*N*	*%*	*N*	*%*	*N*	*%*	*N*	*%*
Full time	1,276,216	94.8	2,738,653	94.5	221,555	84.0	1,196,322	94.2	2,430,895	93.5	186,388	83.9
Part time	70,651	5.2	159,425	5.5	42,161	16.0	73,056	5.8	168,310	6.5	35,740	16.1
Total	1,346,867	100.0	2,898,078	100.0	263,716	100.0	1,269,378	100.0	2,599,204	100.0	222,128	100.0
Could not find full time	16,788	23.8	105,864	66.4	5,634	13.4	25,240	36.8	124,802	74.8	6,461	18.9
Permanent	–	–	2,547,830	87.9	–	–	–	–	2,298,583	88.4	–	–
Temporary	–	–	350,248	12.1	–	–	–	–	300,622	11.6	–	–
Could not find permanent	–	–	246,706	82.2	–	–	–	–	228,681	86.1	–	–

Source: Own estimations using LFS micro-data.

outcome of their free choice and/or their preferences. And, unfortunately for them, this situation is deteriorating dramatically because of the crisis and of high unemployment.

The picture is almost the same for another kind of employment: the temporary one. Although the percentage of temporary employed is a bit smaller in 2011 than in 2009, the reason for this can be found in the layoff of most of the temporary employed personnel that used to work in the public sector; being the first to pay for the downsizing of the public sector in Greece. Ironically, if we consider the preferences of the temporary workers, it is only a 'modest' (*sic*!) 86.1 per cent of them that would prefer to have a permanent job; of course, as permanent as it can be in Greece today.

VI Conclusions

Greek capitalism has entered an era of economic turbulence and decline that is unprecedented in its modern history and throughout the developed world as well. The reasons can be found in the global economic crisis and the position of Greece inside the EU. The failure of Greek capitalism's modern 'Big Idea' of participating in the European imperialist integration is leading to its downgrading within the international division of labour (see Mavroudeas (2013)). The result is the direct intervention of the dominant EU capitalism (i.e. the euro-core economies) even in the core of the production process (i.e. the labour and exploitation process) with the aim of increasing the extraction of surplus-value, both absolute and relative. This goes hand-in-hand with Greek capital's interest but it can also 'overshoot' (i.e. surpass its historical social and technical limits) and endanger the very foundations of Greek capitalism.

This uneven 'partnership' is materialised in the EAPs for Greece. Its labour market restructuring strategy is based on the use of unemployment and the reserve army of labour as the mean to put every worker individually and the working class as a whole in an inferior position against capital. As argued earlier – using a modest approach and methods that in our opinion underestimate unemployment and underemployment but at least cannot be accused of exaggeration – the real unemployment rate is substantially greater than the one officially calculated by European and Greek authorities. For example, for the 2011 official count of 17.7 per cent unemployment an extra 4.4 per cent (at least) must be added in order to attain a more realistic estimate. It is indicated from anecdotal evidence that for 2013 hidden unemployment is even larger: most probably one out of three Greek workers is unemployed.

This situation in the Greek labour market is used by enterprises at both the individual and the collective level to further curtail workers' rights and increase their exploitation. This is far away from the Neoclassical myths of labour contracts under the free will of both sides; even if one accepts that some free will can survive an extremely high unemployment rate. We have used two facts of the contemporary Greek labour market to indicate this contradiction. The first is the increasing trend of unpaid overtime while both paid overtime and working time are decreasing due to the crisis. Unpaid overtime is not voluntary in Greece and its increase during the crisis proves that workers are under pressure from their employers to work more, for no pay at all. The second fact is the failure of employers to adjust to their workers' preferences to work full- instead of part-time, although there is no corresponding market rigidity; quite the contrary.

So, the contemporary Greek drama leads to some strict conclusions. The labour market does not adjust to employees' preferences as Neoclassicism expects. The force of high unemployment is used to minimise not only wages and the value of labour-power but also all other aspects of labour market conditions against the interests of the workers. This is happening both at the central political level and at the decentralised level of every enterprise or economic branch. Workers don't seem to have any possibility of achieving their goals in an individualistic basis, since their preferences are not satisfied, not even in the fields they should be (like part- and full-time work). The only way of improving their position is through collective action and mass movement against capitalist restructuring.

Notes

1 http://ec.europa.eu/economy_finance/ameco/user/serie/ResultSerie.cfm.
2 http://epp.eurostat.ec.europa.eu/cache/ITY_PUBLIC/3-29112013-AP/EN/3-29112013-AP-EN.PDF.
3 For a detailed discussion, old but important, see Lucas and Rapping (1969: 721–54).
4 Section G is covering wholesale and retail trade and repair of motor vehicles and motorcycles and section M professional scientific and technical activities according to NACE Rev. 2 from 2008.
5 In periods of rapid changes in wages and working conditions, the 'desires' of workers reflect – and thus can be used as an estimation for – the previously existing social norms for working time and for the value of labour power, since they tend to adapt in the long run to these socially determined variables.
6 Own estimations using the LFS micro-data.
7 Own estimations using the LFS micro-data.

References

Anger S. (2008), 'Overtime work as a signalling device', *Scottish Journal of Political Economy* 55(2).

Bell D. and Hart R. (1999), 'Unpaid work', *Economica* 66.

Bluestone B. and Rose S. (2000), 'The enigma of working time trends', in Golden L. and Figart D. (eds), *Working Time: International Trends*, London/New York: Routledge.

Cahuc P. and Zylberberg A. (2004), *Labor Economics*, Cambridge, MA: MIT Press.

DeFreitas G. (1986), 'A time series analysis of Hispanic unemployment', *Journal of Human Resources* 21.

INE-GSEE (2013), *Greek Economy and Employment*, Athens: Institute of Labour, GSEE.

Ioannides A. and Mavroudeas S. (2007), 'Overworked Greeks? Working time trends in Greece', *Asian-African Journal of Ecomonics and Econometrics* 7(1–2).

Ioannides A., Oxouzi E. and Mavroudeas S. (2014), 'All work and no ... pay? Unpaid overtime in Greece: determining factors and theoretical explanations', *Industrial Relations Journal* 45(1).

Lucas R. and Rapping L. (1969), 'Real wages, employment and inflation', *Journal of Political Economy* 77.

Lundberg S. (1985), 'The added worker effect', *Journal of Labor Economics* 3.

Mavroudeas S. (2013), 'Development and crisis: the turbulent course of Greek capitalism', *International Critical Thought* 3(3).

Pannenberg M. (2005), 'Long term effects of unpaid overtime: evidence from West Germany', *Scottish Journal of Political Economy* 52(2).

Schor J. (1991), *The Overworked American: The Unexpected Decline of Leisure*, New York: Basic Books.

11 Recession and atypical employment

A focus on contemporary Greek metropolitan regions

Stelios Gialis

I Introduction

Greece has been an EU member since 1981. Since then, a series of economic and institutional restructurings including several labour market reforms, have been enacted in the country. The majority of them were either directed or monitored by EU official authorities, which, in most cases, endorsed these restructurings and praised the prospects of the Greek economy (EC (2009), Clauwaert and Schömann (2012)). All of a sudden, in early 2009, it was realised that Greece should have never entered the Eurozone as its economy was suffering from 'huge public spending and debts', 'widespread tax evasion' and 'counterproductive patterns'. The country's labour markets were found to be a lot more 'rigid' than those of Northern EU member states, mainly due to a lower incidence of part-time labour and due to strict dismissal regulations (OECD (2012)). Based upon such a discourse, and the official requests of successive Greek governments for EU bailout packages in order to deal with the 'spectre of default', one of the most tragic periods in the country's modern history began. The result was the imposition of a painful devalorisation[1] – which has been presented as largely inevitable – to subordinate classes and social groups so that the Greek economy could attempt to overcome overaccumulation and the tendency of the rate of profit to fall (Michael-Matsas (2010), Armingeon and Baccaro (2012), Karamessini (2012)).

This chapter focuses on the regional dimension of the Greek crisis. It argues that the Greek regions' problem was not that they were insufficiently incorporated into the EU and the global capitalist economy but, rather, that they were too well incorporated while at the same time being constrained by certain peculiarities and traditional patterns. This also applies to employment norms and practices in the country which have been aligned to EU regulations for over three decades despite the existence of divergent trends and practices such as the high dispersion of self-employment (Leontidou (1993), Gialis and Herod (2013)).[2]

To substantiate this argument, the chapter explores the reproduction of atypical forms of employment, both at the national level, and, importantly, in the two crisis-hit metropolitan regions which make up for more than 60 per cent of the Greek population, employment and production namely Attica-Athens and

Central Macedonia-Thessaloniki; the former hosts the capital city of Athens and the latter the second major Greek urban area of Thessaloniki. It does so by bringing to the fore official data on part-time, temporary, self-employed and family work; while also relating these data to changes in production and unemployment between 2008 and 2012. The chapter evaluates these data, by taking into account several key informants interviewed and other secondary sources,[3] and finds that, despite the existence of common national trends, the response of the different local labour markets to crisis and devalorisation is non-uniform and is necessarily place-specific (Smith (1986), Harvey (2007)). Different patterns in the response of local labour markets to casualisation of employment are linked to the regions' socio-economic profiles and are highlighted. Following an alternative Marxist explanation, the findings are also discussed within the context of the historical background of Greek capitalism and recent restructurings of its labour markets. Finally, the chapter reflects on whether or not the contradictory reproduction of atypical employment, combined with informal employment and the huge unemployment, signifies the revival of an expanded industrial reserve army for combatting falling profit rates.

A deeper understanding of such factors, we would suggest, may contribute to a strengthening of the prospects for resistance in places and spaces where painful capital devalorisation is diminishing workers' rights and dismantling social and employment protections (Bergene *et al.* (2010), Herod (2012)).

The structure of the chapter is as follows. In the next section a brief theoretical framework that contextualises flexibilisation and atypical employment within capitalist structures is presented. Next, the potential interrelationship between uneven socio-spatial development and various forms of employment, such as the atypical ones, is outlined. A brief historical background on the atypical employment phenomenon in the pre-crisis era provides a context for discussing the post-2008 devalorisation and restructuring of the two major Greek regional labour markets, and relating these effects to diversified trends in atypical forms. The final section concludes by offering some wider policy implications of the study.

II Flexibility, employment arrangements and the capitalist production

Wage labour, and the (either implicit or institutionalised) employment arrangements that are associated with it, is a historical product of the evolution of the capitalist mode of production. There are many implications for the labourers arising from the fact that competition has to be reproduced on a continuous and expanding scale, because individual capitalists must search for increasing rates of profit by expanding the surplus-value they absorb relative to the socially averaged rate of exploitation (Harvey (2007)). One of the most important implications has to do with the need for firms to flexibly use their labourers, at least as far as fluctuations in demand and the organisation of production is concerned. Thus, despite its contemporary use in describing 'post-modernity' and the recent changes in the field of production and reproduction, flexibility has always been a historical pursuit of the capital (Buzar (2008)). Two fundamental ways this is achieved is either through expanding working-day limits, which labourers seek to keep on a normal basis, or through expanding the relative surplus-value derived from workers. The latter is usually achieved through technological modernisation of the production and/or by cheapening the basket of wage-goods the labourers buy to live, and thus reduces the value of their labour-power (Harvey (2010)).

The struggle of labourers to increase wages and to work under stable and humane employment arrangements has an impact on the surplus-value and the exchange-value of products brought to market. The value of labour-power is then socially determined and diversified according to cultural, historical and geographical factors, as well as according to power relations between opposing classes (and the same applies for the employment arrangements, either typical or atypical). Employment patterns and practices are unevenly developed as the development of the capitalist and the working classes takes on a variety of intermediate forms and proceeds unevenly by sector and by region. The geographical part of this unevenness is commonly neglected in many studies, and its importance will be discussed later (Peet (1975), Bergene *et al.* (2010)).

During the period that Marx's *Capital* was written employment patterns and arrangements were a lot different from existing ones and no typical pattern in the sense it is usually conceived nowadays (i.e. regulated, long-term employment for five days and a total of 40 hours per week) existed. Similarly, 'atypical' and 'irregular' employment were a long way from the contemporary norms. Having said this, Marx directly connected the capitalist accumulation and the production of wealth and profits, to the expansion of the 'reserve army of labour'. In the latter, he included as much the unemployed as those who were 'partially employed' (Peet (1975), Clark (1980)). To be specific, he grouped the relative surplus population into three groups: the *floating*, the *latent* and the *stagnant*. The former of the three comprised the unemployed who had lost their jobs either due to technological modernisation or due to employers' will to replace them with cheaper/younger employees. The latent group, found mostly in the primary sector's activities, at that time, included all the 'underemployed' in activities which had been marginalised by advanced capitalist production and turned into traditional sectors. Finally, the stagnant relative surplus population consisted of those, natives or immigrants employed under 'extremely irregular employment'.

Nowadays, stagnant-like groups can be found among 'very atypical' employees and informal labourers. These labourers are usually subjected to part-time, seasonal and temporary employment norms that are deprived of important security aspects, and underpaid in comparison to the average wages of the 'typical' workers. Compared to the former two groups, the stagnant group has a relatively higher weight in the overall composition of the reserve army, and acts as a 'pool' of living labour – a porous buffer zone between the employed and the unemployed segments of the working class. In any case, defining the industrial reserve army is not reducible to empirically observing and measuring the groups that it comprises; rather it has to do with defining how the reserve army is derived from capitalist expansion (i.e. how and where it increases in line with increases in the organic composition of capital) (Clark (1980), Dorre (2010)).

To contextualise the discussion among the 'advanced' countries and the twentieth century, the introduction of massive production and related Taylorist working practices signified a turn towards a relatively long period of development during which the reserve army of labour lost much of its potential in acting as a disciplining force *within* these capitalist countries (although large numbers of cheap living labour could be recruited from other parts of the globe). This was, among other things, an organisational and technological change that corresponded to the productive needs and profitability rates of the so-called 'Fordist period of expansion' (Harvey (2007)). Since then, typical employment became the norm, while, at the same time, a new dichotomy between typical and atypical workers came to the forefront, marginalising informal employment (Kalleberg (2003)).

The analytical and empirical validity of such trends is highly contested, especially for the countries of the semi-periphery, as there are many sectors, regions and employment groups where typical employment was the exception rather than the norm. This is also verified for certain periods of Greek capitalism as discussed later. Despite such exceptions, well-regulated work arrangements became an everyday reality, at least for the majority of (mostly) male breadwinners involved in industrial and public sector activities, for several decades between the mid-1930s and the early 1970s. The flexibility that employers could exert upon their workers, especially typical ones, had been highly regulated during this era; while unemployment remained modest for many years and across many spatial entities (Clark (1980), Hudson (2013)).

Since the 1973 crisis and the recession that followed, so-called 'flexible accumulation strategies' eventually came to the fore, and a new period of relative surplus extraction with its associated working practices was established. The 'flexibilisation' agenda, pushing for re-/deregulation of the labour markets was gradually introduced, aiming for employment norms and regulations to come in line with the new imperatives of accumulation. The politics and guidelines that are associated with flexibilisation should be seen within the context of evolving class relations and contemporary politics. In other words, they aim to redefine temporality, which is as essential for the survival of capitalism as the search for increasing rates of profit (Herod (2012)). This is also an essential goal of the 'flexicurity' agenda[4] and other policies applied in the EU and beyond, on the back of a period of labour movement retreat and de-unionisation (Buzar (2008)).

Notably, flexibilisation has multiple goals and meanings. It is related to the expansion of working-day limits in some sectors and regions and, through this, the absolute surplus-value derived from labourers therein. The maximum working hours per day, while subject to specific physical and social limitations, can be very flexible. Recent EU-triggered working time arrangements that expand the working day up to 12 hours or so, by compensating overtime work with equivalent days off provided during periods of reduced production, contribute to this argument. Another goal is related to how enhanced competition among employers can often take super-exploitative forms that endanger the reproduction of the labour force – the source of capital itself. This is why nation states, and transnational authorities, which tend to play a decisive role in the formation of the employment agenda, act in favour of collective capitalist interests and institutionalise new forms of employment with relevant regulations. These regulations facilitate the use of 'more flexible' and 'very atypical' employment relations while simultaneously setting limits on the rate of exploitation that individual capitalists can exert upon their workers (Harvey (2006), Mitchell (2011)).

Overall, flexibilisation is related to re-deregulation during eras of escalating global antagonisms where accumulation needs to be continued and capitalist production needs to be efficiently reorganised. It is also a way for redefining power geometries within and between the labour markets in favour of capital interests. For countries and regions suffering severe crises of overaccumulation and also subjected to imperialist exploitation, flexibilisation may be coupled with the revival of the arithmetic size and disciplining role of the industrial reserve army and jeopardised local labour markets (Dorre (2010)).

New spatial formations and flexibilisation: devalorisation is necessarily region specific

Wage-capital relations do not unfold on a uni-dimensional space; rather they evolve within and across space and, thus, hold inherent spatial dimensions. The dispersion of different types of employment relations and flexible practices is tightly interconnected with the geographical reformations of (uneven) capitalist development. This is also the case of the industrial reserve army, which has its own geography following the spatial configurations of uneven regional development (Clark (1980), Massey (1996), Harvey (2010)).

These spatial configurations, which are socially produced, are active moments within the temporal dynamic of the accumulation process. Spatial integration, conceptualised by Marxist theorists as the, more or less, coherent linkage of different locations and spaces through commodity exchange, is essential in order for the accumulation process to be completed and reproduced on an expanding scale. Within this spatially integrated framework capital circulates either in the form of commodities, money or as labour process (Harvey (2007), Herod (2012)).

Contemporary labour market reforms and EU employment policies should, then, be theorised within this context. Their aim is to foster a common set of 'less rigid' labour markets with certain and less protective security provisions than those of the previous era. In other words, EU policies are seeking to homogenise local labour markets in terms of labour and employment regulations by overcoming the barriers posed by previous (especially national) legislation provisions. This in an inherently contradictory attempt since uneven geographical development unavoidably reproduces different local labour realities which free labourers from their local constraints (Buzar (2008), Mitchell (2011)).

'Freeing' labour from rigid employment provisions and geographical immobility (akin to typical employment), is in sharp contrast to the necessity of capital to immobilise workers in certain regions and keep them, as well as a sufficient reserve army, 'in place'. Policies that promote atypical employment officially seek a proper equilibrium between these two poles, but stability and balance between two such opposites is a mere exception to the overall contradictory dynamic of uneven geographical expansion (Massey (1996)).

Things get more complicated when a crisis occurs. Recession and the associated devalorisation trends, destabilise coherent spatial linkages between different localities and regions, and at the same time act as the catalyst for the emergence of new spatial fixes that are in line with the general needs of accumulation. Political and institutional measures imposed on the regions from outside, and from internal rivalries over who pays the burden, are decisive. The imperative to lower wages reflects the need to adapt the regional mode of labour and social reproduction to aggregated and abstract modes of labour on a global scale; the latter is currently determined by the overwhelming role of low-wage competitors such as China or India in worldwide commodity production and by the subcontracting activities of multinationals. Consequently, regions become more vulnerable to imposed devalorisation. Their ability to counteract and oppose such devalorisation and, at the same time, 'export' their internal problems (e.g. inflation, unemployment, debt, stagnation in production) is diversified according to their political and economic power, and temporal alliances. Imperialist politics are of importance for this process (Harvey (2010), Mavroudeas and Papadatos (2012)).

Overall, a general trade-off between overaccumulation in one region and devalorisation in another is always present and mediated through various socio-political and historical peculiarities. Under the guiding and often repressive role of supra-regional powers such as the EU, people in one region can be seen to be 'exploiting' others in another region (not necessarily of the same country), while both are being subordinated to the will of capital (Peet (1975), Hudson (2013)). And this uneven distribution of the burden of devalorisation, depicted in the next section through the case of two Greek regions, is what helps capital accumulation to proceed.

III Flexible employment in Greece and the crisis

During the second semester of 2007, the US housing and mortgage market started to reel under the pressure of the financial inability of loan recipients. A seemingly US-based instability soon proved to be a severe wave of recession, for many, comparable to the one witnessed between the two World Wars of the last century. The recession spread across the EU and other global regions. Mainstream scholars and economists immediately associated the crisis with the increasing 'public indebtedness' of certain states and economies. As analysed in previous chapters of the collective volume at hand, these perceptions gave emphasis to policy-driven mistakes and structural deficiencies associated with such 'wrong choices' (Matsaganis (2011), Pitelis (2012)). Other post-Keynesian and radical explanations associated the crisis with extreme 'financialisation'; while revealing the role of the 'golden boys' of the financial sector and 'toxic' products, such as synthetic CDOs (Karamessini (2012)). Marxist scholars and economists have directly linked the crisis to falling profit rates and overaccumulation; while revealing the consequent devaluation that is coercively, though unevenly, imposed upon different states due to hierarchical imperialist relations existing among them (Harvey (2006), Mavroudeas and Papadatos (2012)).

In early 2009 the effects of the crisis were prevalent in the EU, and more intensely in the Eurozone. As soon as these effects emerged, the so-called PIIGS of the EU South and the periphery (i.e. Portugal, Ireland, Italy, Greece and Spain) were targeted and blamed. An already existent division line between these countries and the Northern, industrious and highly competitive economies, came to the fore. In particular, Greece was portrayed as the 'black sheep' of the Eurozone due its high public debt and deficit; at the same time, fears about the collapse of the Eurozone due to a Greek default were widely magnified by the mass media. A true understanding of the peculiarities of the Greek political economy and an analytical discussion into the causes of its post-2008 crisis, is presented in previous chapters of this collective volume (see also Hadjimichalis (2011), Selçuk and Yılmaz (2011), Eichengreen *et al.* (2013)). As far as this chapter is concerned, a brief background on the political economy of flexible and atypical forms in the Greek socio-economic formation is described below.

A brief note on the background of Greek capitalism and atypical employment

Atypical patterns and 'informality' have been highly dispersed in this relatively developed country of the Southern European semi-periphery during its entire modern period and, specifically, between the 1950s and the late 1970s. Typical employment and high levels of security have never been the norm as *Keynesian*-type social contract policies were weakly penetrated (Karamessini (2008), Hadjimichalis (2011)). In addition, advanced scientific organisation of production in the form of rational production norms, efficient use of available resources and machinery, and an advanced technical division of labour were also only weakly implemented; in parallel the majority of those employed either in the private or in the public sector was subjected to paternalistic policies and anti-unionist practices. As an outcome, the capitalist imperative for efficiently organising the production process was often reduced to practices increasing the output extracted from workers through authoritarianism, extensive use of atypical and informal work, and prohibitive, if not repressive, actions against the workers' agency (Leontidou (1990)).

Taking for granted the unequal postwar division of labour and power across the European capitalist countries, the most important industrial firms that developed were in labour-intensive sectors. Capital-intensive goods were mainly bought from the markets of the advanced North, continuously boosting the trade balance deficit (Leontidou (1993); Karamessini (2008)).

Indeed, accumulation rates had been quite important during many phases and gross output increased significantly (e.g. during the 1960s or the 1990s), while the spatial fixes necessary for the reproduction of capital became both quite viable and 'profitable' (Gialis (2011)). Eventually, Greece became a member of the major institutions and organisations that act in favour of transnational capitalist integration (e.g. OECD, WTO, NATO, EU) and followed many of their directives and suggestions (Pitelis (2012)).

Family has always had extended socio-economic functions in this pattern, and served as the epicentre of various, often informal, modes of living and working (Leontidou ((1933)). This was, in part, an implicit reaction against quite poor state welfare and protection policies. Other ambivalent aspects of what has been called a 'Southern welfare regime' (Karamessini (2008)) were insufficient industrial relations, the lack of planning and housing policies and the various and mixed land uses within cities and regions. Mobilisations of civil disobedience were often coupled with unionism and organised strikes despite the fact that most unions were subordinated to state paternalism and employers' repression until the late 1970s (Leontidou (1990, 1993).

The absence of social support, along with the continuous reproduction of small businesses, frequent labour redundancies in the low-skilled sectors and the seasonal nature of many activities, were amongst the basic factors driving intense mobility in the labour market and atypical or informal forms (Leontidou (1993), Gialis (2011)). Due to the fact that advanced labour markets favouring the complete proletarianisation of the economically active were not promoted, the dependence on formal wage labour remained low. In parallel, the share of wages over the total value added remained stagnant or decreased constantly (especially until 1974). Following tendencies that surfaced during the inter-war era, a new wave of internal migration causing a great urbanisation trend in Athens, Thessaloniki and other urban centres came to the fore. This trend led to the further promotion of micro self-employment practices. Small industrial units and microestablishments became a dynamic pillar of an integrated socio-spatial system rather than being just a marginal phenomenon (Leontidou (1993), Matsaganis (2011), Pitelis (2012)).

After the 1973 crisis and the fall of the seven-year dictatorship in 1974, formal salaried employment in densely urbanised regions increased significantly, while, at the same time, important flexibilisation trends emerged. The typical working patterns mainly concerned an expanding core of workers in the public sector and large industrial and service firms, sufficient enough to create a relatively wealthy and expanded petty-bourgeoisie for the first time in Greece's modern history. However, self-employment continued to increase and the vast majority of firms remained small, often involving members of the owner's family or employees in informal practices. All these changes took place during a new era where global re-/deregulation policies surfaced and labour movements were reeling under de-unionisation and advanced capitalist imperatives (Harvey (2006)).

Vertical disintegration, tertiarisation and the first pro-austerity policies of the mid-1980s and early 1990s were coupled with extensive privatisation and legislative interventions that sought to enhance stagnating profit rates while introducing new flexible labour regulations (Hadjimichalis (2011), Gialis and Herod (2013)). A series of 'traditional' atypical (e.g. seasonal employment, overtime) or even informal forms (e.g. undeclared work) are now being reproduced, often part and parcel of modern adaptation strategies, while 'new' forms more akin to Northern EU patterns (i.e. part-time work, temporary agencies) are being constantly institutionalised and expanding. In the early 1990s, Greece's turn to a migrant-receiving destination, for the first time since its post-war period, gave new impetus to informal and undeclared work across the localities of the country. Cheap migratory labour deepened the already existent segmentation in local labour markets and was heavily utilised both by small to middle size as well as by more advanced segments of Greek capital (Gialis (2012)). In any case, it helped Greek capitalism maintain an important dynamism in an era of developmental stagnancy across the EU (Mavroudeas and Papadatos (2012)).

Overall, Greece had followed a divergent pattern of development compared to Northern European countries, which in turn changed its character from a traditional society of under-development and marginality to a semi-peripheral capitalist country (Leontidou (1990), Hadjimichalis (2011)). Both in the post-war as well as in the post-dictatorship period, flexibility and informality, and the combination of capitalist with traditional practices and modes of production, were a vital component of a hierarchically structured though divergent capitalist formation that was well integrated into global capitalist structures. This also made the expansion in arithmetical size and, more importantly, the disciplining role of the industrial reserve army across many sectors and localities, *relatively weak*. The members of latent and stagnant groups managed and continue to just manage to make a living supported by various familial and informal networks, while at the same time being flexible and not demanding. The prospects for attaining influence in core and privileged groups of employees were supposedly frequent, and division lines between the typical and the flexible 'other' were not as strong as they are nowadays (Gialis (2012), Karamessini (2012)). Social consensus was achieved, but in a rather peculiar way.

The post-2008 period

In the post-crisis period, all quantitative and qualitative indicators reveal the highly intensive devalorisation and ongoing disintegration of the Greek economy. It is indicative that, according to Eurostat's data between 2008 and 2012, the Greek nominal GDP reduced by more than 20 per cent. The GDP further decreased in 2013 by about 4 per cent, while governmental optimism for small marginally positive increments by the end of 2014 is already (early 2014) being disputed. Such negative rates are comparable only to those of countries experiencing military invasion or witnessing fundamental socio-political transformation as in the case of the state-socialist countries in post-1990s Europe. It is not surprising then that the structural reforms imposed by the government and the troika (i.e. the committee formed by the EU, the ECB and the IMF to monitor the Greek economy) were unsuccessful in almost all of their major ambitions. For example, it is commonly acknowledged that the increasing public debt, expected to return after 2020 to its pre-2008 level (i.e. below 120 per cent of the GDP), is currently being derailed. The spectre of default is still haunting the Greek economy, while the devalorisation that is impoverishing the working and middle classes is fast becoming unsustainable.

An absolute drop in all employment and security figures has propelled Greece in less than a four-year period to top of the national unemployment ranking across EU-15. In 2012, the unemployment rate was 24.8 per cent and the number of officially unemployed individuals is 1.25 million; an increase of +218.5 per cent compared to 2008. Employment decreases in all major sectors of the economy (see Tables 11.1 and 11.2). During 2012, 40 people were losing their jobs every hour. Unemployment among young people has hit the dramatic rate of 56.6 per cent with almost half not being entitled to or receiving any form of unemployment allowance. As an outcome, it is the first time in the post-war period that the employed (some 3.7 million individuals) is significantly smaller than the economically non-active (4.6 million).

Ironically, these profound changes, despite talk of the 'rigidity' of Greek employment patterns, are turning Greece's labour markets into the most flexible in EU-15. Labour forms such as part-time employment, which were uncommon to the Greek productive patterns, are now highly increasing. In parallel, other embedded atypical forms such as self-employment and temporary employment are either stagnant, or decreasing at lower rates than the decline in total employment. Indeed, when we look at changes in employment forms, which may in part or in total belong to the industrial reserve army, during the period 2008–12, the share of part-timers over total employment increased from to 5.6 to 7.7 per cent, and the share of the self-employed with no personnel also increased from 21.3 to 24.7 per cent. The share of temporaries marginally reduced to 11.6 per cent (from 12.1 per cent in 2008) due to waves of mass dismissals and the share of family helpers also modestly lowered to 5.0 per cent (from 5.9 per cent in 2008) due to the failures of thousands of family-run businesses and micro-enterprises (as shown in Table 11.2). Thus, according to even the most moderate accounts, more than one out of every three employed persons are now working under flexible arrangements (by the end of 2012), and a significant proportion of them is now subordinated to 'very atypical' employment forms.[5] This argument is substantiated by many direct and indirect reports as well as by the key informants interviewed; according to the Labour Inspectorates Organisation (LIO), more than 60 per cent of newly hired persons are on an atypical basis, while contracts that have been changed from full-time to part-time employment increased by +126 per cent. (Labour Inspectorates Organisation (2012)).

Severe outward migration and upcoming trends in undeclared employment and informal activities have also been recorded. In early 2013, labour inspectors from the LIO were astonished to learn that the share of undeclared labourers among a representative sample of firms inspected exceeded 38 per cent (it was 25 per cent in 2010). Thus, patterns such as tax evasion, tax fraud and

Table 11.1 Total and change in employment and Gross Value Added (GVA) by sector: a comparison of two Greek metropolitan regions and national figures (2008–10, 2008–12) with Eurozone figures (2008–12)

Metropolitan area	*NUTS-2 region and code*	*Employment (in thousands, population 15 years and over)*								*GVA at basic prices (in millions of euro)*							
		Primary		*Industrial**		*Secondary*		*Tertiary*		*Primary*		*Industrial**		*Secondary*		*Tertiary*	
		Total, 2012	*Change (%), 2008–12*	*Total, 2012*	*Change (%), 2008–12*	*Total, 2012*	*Change (%), 2008–12*	*Total, 2012*	*Change (%), 2008–12*	*Total, 2010 (2012)*	*Change (%), 2008–10 (2008–12)*	*Total, 2010 (2012)*	*Change (%), 2008–10 (2008–12)*	*Total, 2010 (2012)*	*Change (%), 2008–10 (2008–12)*	*Total, 2010 (2012)*	*Change (%), 2008–10 (2008–12)*
Athens	Attica (EL30)	14.1	–7.8	164.3	–34.6	228.7	–40.3	1,161.5	–12.1	386	+7.3	7,466	+3.9	11,842	–16.7	81,480	–1.0
Thessaloniki	Cen. Macedonia (EL12)	83.1	–8.7	73.0	–41.5	98.8	–47.6	432.9	–10.7	1,236	–7.4	3,495	+8.1	5,172	–15. 5	20,031	–4.5
Greece		490.0	–5.2	420.8	–32.3	627.0	–38.3	2,646.0	–12.6	6,300 (5,751)	–1.5 (–10.0)	26,371 (24,404)	+3.8 (–3.9)	33,143 (28,020)	–15.7 (–28.7)	155,780 (136,750)	–2.2 (–14.2)
Euro–area		4,805.2	–6.7	24,573.0	–9.2	34,440.0	–11.8	100,357.0	+0.8	(143,679)	(+1.4)	(1,640,579)	(–0.2)	(2,131,120)	(–3.4)	(6,231,700)	(+4.7)

Source: Eurostat and HELSTAT, author's compilation.

Note

* Secondary except construction.

Table 11.2 Total and change in employment, unemployment and atypical employment forms: a comparison of two Greek metropolitan regions and national figures with Eurozone figures (2008–12)

Metropolitan area	*NUTS-2 region and code*	*Employment*		*Unemployment*		*Part-time*		*Self-employed*[*]		*Family helpers*		*Temporary*[**]		*Permanent*[***]		*Total atypical*[****]	
		Total in thousands, 2012	*Change (%), 2008–12*	*(%), 2012*	*Change (%), 2008–12*	*(%), 2012*	*Change (%), 2008–12*	*(%), 2012*	*Change (%), 2008–12*	*(%), 2012*	*Change (%), 2008–12*	*(%), 2012*	*Change (%), 2008–12*	*(%), 2012*	*Change (%), 2008–12*	*(%), 2012*	*Change (%), 2008–12*
Athens	Attica (EL30)	1,404.4	−18.4	25.3	+301.7	7.6	+54.0	15.2	−6.8	2.5	−44.2	6.5	−38.0	72.4	−16.7	22.0	−20.2
Thessaloniki	Cen. Macedonia (EL12)	614.8	−19.6	26.0	+211.4	6.8	−20.0	26.4	−4.1	4.7	−40.4	10.3	−34.5	54.3	−19.5	37.3	−16.9
Greece		3,763.0	−17.5	24.2	+218.5	7.7	+13.8	24.7	−3.1	5.0	−30.6	10.0	−29.8	56.9	−17.9	36.0	−13.6
Euro-area		140,584.0	−2.7	11.3	+52.7	21.4	+8.1	10.1	+2.0	1.1	−26.4	15.2	−8.5	71.2	−1.4	23.8	−5.2

Source: Eurostat and HELSTAT, author's compilation.

Notes
Employment figures refer to the population aged 15 years and over; * self-employed on own basis over total employment; ** over total employees; *** over total employment; **** temporary and self-employed and family helpers over total employment.

social/health care contribution avoidance, frequently stigmatised by EU bureaucrats and Greek elites as signs of backwardness and popular misbehaviour, are now exacerbated by policies that nominally seek to restore competitiveness (Kondilis *et al.* (2013)).

Despite the numerous protests and general strikes that tried to resist austerity (Gialis and Herod (2013)), devalorisation strongly affected the wages and the price of labour-power. Indicatively, the labour share over GDP has fallen from 55.8 per cent to less than 48 per cent since 2008 (ten times larger than the average fall in the Eurozone); while the labour cost index for secondary sector activities is currently 16 per cent lower than it used to be.

The data in Table 11.1 show clearly that the recession that all productive sectors in Greece are facing is severe. This is especially so for the secondary sector and more intensely documented for industrial activities that lie at the core of advanced capitalism despite their reduced relative contribution. Despite some comparability issues,[6] a closer look at the data reveals some interesting discrepancies, strongly apparent both among sectors as well as between the employment and output of each sector. First, the fall in the secondary output is mostly related to the collapse in construction activities. Industrial GVA is only slightly decreasing.

Second, the diminishment of employment in the industrial, secondary and tertiary sector is much more important than reductions in the productive capacity of these sectors. In other words, an intensification of work is observed, especially of the industrial work which is, in turn, a signal of advanced productivity and enhanced surplus-value extraction from those still employed in the sector.[7]

As expected, the diversified devalorisation and fall of employment is positively connected to a dramatic, proportional increase of unemployment as can be seen in Figures 11.1a to 11.1c. Table 11.2 depicts how this generic trend is differently attributed to the distinct employment forms, especially atypical ones.

Interestingly, the aggregated share of those atypically employed, is higher than it used to be in 2008, at least on a national level; verifying one aspect of the increasing flexibility in post-crisis labour markets. This is so despite the divergent contribution of the atypical forms under study (for example self-employment is marginally affected at the national level and in Thessaloniki in 2012 while temporary and family work on these spatial scales is significantly reduced). Additionally, the incidence of part-time employment (i.e. usually an engagement of four hours per day and less than 300 euros monthly salary in Greece nowadays) is increasing, especially in Athens.

The data on hand substantiate the argument that devalorisation is geographically sensitive and, thus, region-specific. Central Macedonia, which encompasses the urban area of Thessaloniki, has a higher rate of total atypical employment and is hardly hit as compared to Attiki and the capital city of Athens found therein. Reductions in output and employment are more intense in the former region, which was suffering from higher unemployment shares and which had a reduced productive

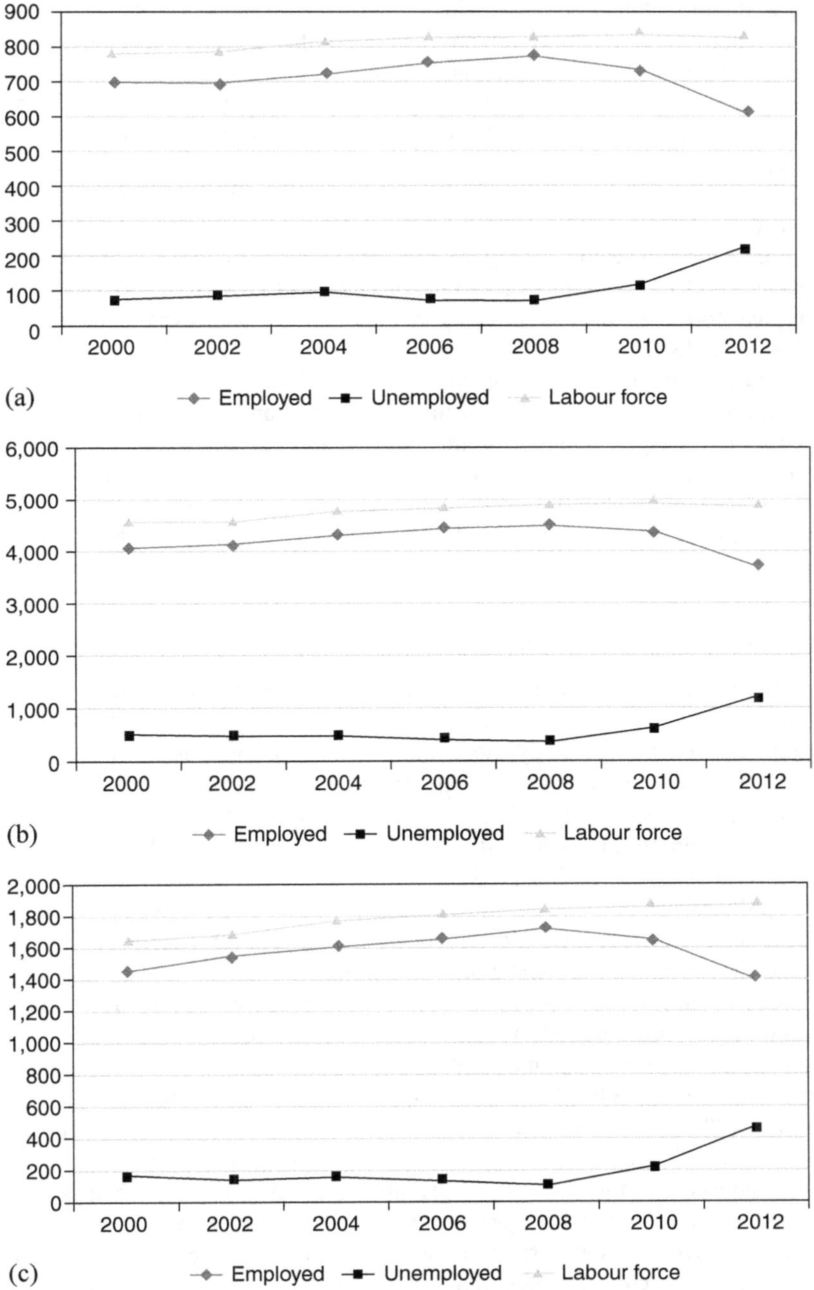

Figures 11.1a–11.1c Absolute change in the labour force, employment and unemployment for (a) Greece, (b) Attica-Athens and (c) Central Macedonia-Thessaloniki respectively, 2000–12.

capacity in the pre-2008 period also. This is partly due to the fact that, during the past two decades or so, hundreds of plants fled out of the region towards the neighbouring Balkans, in search for cheaper labourers.

Other reasons exist, such as the less expanded and poorly diversified tertiary sector of the region, and specifically the public sector (where a great part of Greek permanent employees can be found) compared to a far more developed one in Athens. On the other hand, Attica-Athens which was more affluent and less crisis prone before 2008, having a booming labour force (see Figure 11.1b), an expanded financial sector and big investments in infrastructure developments, has now reached the unemployment rate of Thessaloniki; while thousands of poor atypical forms, mainly underpaid part-time employment, expand across its urban space (Gialis (2011)).[8]

A thorough comparison of the above trends and figures in the context of the wider Eurozone is out of the scope of the chapter on hand but Tables 11.1 and 11.2 depict that, despite common trends such as falling output and increasing unemployment, the Greek crisis is a far cry from that impacting the Eurozone at large. At the same time, part-time work may be relatively undeveloped but atypical forms such as self-employment and family work are much more dispersed in Greece.

IV Discussion and conclusions

An absolute and intense decline in employment combined with a dramatic fall in output, especially in the secondary sector, has been recorded for the Greek metropolitan regions under study. Secondary data reveal that the fall is accompanied by an equally important drop in the average and minimum wages. This is one of the most important devalorisations in the history of modern capitalism and 'externally' imposed upon well integrated into global capitalism regional labour markets of the EU periphery, through international directives and national austerity policies. Irrespective of which segments of Greek capital will finally survive the crisis, the prospects for enhanced profits through decreased labour costs have nevertheless been substantially enhanced.

The way devalorisation proceeds proves the dependence of collective agreements and employment protection provisions (e.g. dismissal rates) and wage-bargaining mechanisms upon (inter)national and sectorial economic necessities and political choices, rather than reliance upon local demand–supply balances (Matsaganis (2011), Armingeon and Baccaro (2012)). To give but an example, thousands of employees across various knowledge-intensive sectors in Athens and Thessaloniki are now less paid, despite there being no important documented reduction in output for these sectors, and their labour pools remaining the same. Moreover, the data presented deconstruct the pro-capitalist narratives about the rigid character of Greek and the Southern-EU labour structures. The high incidence of self-employment, increments in part-time work and the thousands of dismissals, applying equally to permanent as well as to atypical employees, substantiates this argument.

By focusing on the different mechanisms that lead to the observed reproduction of atypical employment in the study areas, interesting patterns are revealed. As the recession unfolds and demand for products or services of most firms falls, the pressure put on employees to accept reduced wages and more flexible types of contracts, is escalating. The contracts can be either explicit (i.e. following official employment regulations) or implicit (i.e. holding one or several informal aspects). According to the record produced by key-informants and secondary sources, the responses are varied but can be roughly categorised into the following groups; (i) firms that dismiss their permanent employees and/or do not renew the contracts of their atypical employees, (ii) firms that reduce the working hours and/or salaries of their permanent or atypical employees; (iii) firms that turn the employment status of their permanent employees from a typical to an atypical one and also (iv) firms that outsource part of their activities while simultaneously reducing the number of employees. Last but not least, (v) there are thousands of firms that implement informal practices upon their existent workers (i.e. not compensating overtime work, forcing employees to resign and be rehired with a new/precarious contract, those engaging in undeclared work and/or illegal immigrants, etc.), and do not adhere to contractual obligations. Reduction in wages goes hand in hand with proliferation of 'very atypical' employment such as part-time work in Attica and self-employment in Central Macedonia; employers do not only seek cheaper employees but due to the ongoing instability they also need to be able to flexibly recruit them.

Many of these different practices can be simultaneously found across many enterprises, proving the symbiotic relation between the typical, atypical and informal patterns in the Greek framework (Hudson (2013)); while some of them are currently exacerbated due to post-crisis flexible legal provisions that re-regulate (if not jeopardise) labour markets in favour of capital interests. The intensity according to which different combinations of the above practices are implemented across various spatial and sectorial settings, needs to be explored with specific case studies.

In any case, these trends may point to the increasing significance of an industrial reserve army in Greek regions, especially in the deprived ones like Central Macedonia (Dorre (2010)). Its floating part comprises all those who lost their jobs due to costs reductions. Many of them are currently recruited as informal workers. Its latent part is either directly or indirectly pictured in the reproduction of self-employment with no personnel. Indeed, many among these micro-entrepreneurs are underemployed due to the fact that their activities (e.g. small manufacturers or shops) have been marginalised by devalorisation and cut-throat competition. Finally, the stagnant part of the industrial reserve army comprises all of the poor and underpaid atypical forms discussed earlier. What is more important than defining the potential groups of workers that belong to the reserve army or its size (which can be more than half of the economically active population of the study regions), is to reveal how this powerful segmenting mechanism is acting in favour of collective capitalist interests. It does so by dividing workers while making those who still have a typical job more frightened and dispensable than in the pre-crisis period (Pratschke and Morlicchio (2012), Gialis and Herod (2013)).

In parallel to the primary contradiction between labour and capital, various other contradictions are reproduced within the same labour market: those between different segments of employees, different employment forms, different security and welfare provisions, different firms and sectors, let alone the divisions between different nationalities and ethnic groups, etc. The picture becomes even more uneven and mixed when spatial competition and antithesis between different regions and localities is introduced. This is a necessary outcome of the deepening division of labour under the capitalist mode of production and the expansion of flexible practices.

The way that flexibilisation is implemented follows the antinomies of capitalist accumulation, especially in an era when devalorisation accelerates. Labour processes across the EU are re-theorised in order to adapt to the average rate of profit worldwide (Mavroudeas and Papadatos (2012)). The outcomes of such a re-theorisation are necessarily uneven within EU regions due to unequal internal power relations and productive structures. Flexible employment arrangements are as specific to particular localities and time periods, at least as much as devalorisation is sensitive to place and time.

Marx's analysis on the reserve army of labour seems to be rediscovered in the case of Greece. Within just a few years, conditions that seemed to belong to the early capitalist period are being re-established; yet, history repeats itself, first as tragedy, second as farce.

Acknowledgements

This research is conducted in the frame of the author's post-doctoral activity under the title 'The Southern EU flexicurity project' which is jointly funded by the Greek Ministry of Education, General Secretariat of Research and Technology and the EU. Many thanks to Don Mitchell who generously provided me with the electronic copy of N. Smith's unpublished paper, and to Mike Taylor for reading, commenting and improving the manuscript.

Notes

1 Devalorisation is a precise expression of the dialectic between the change of form and the quantitative loss of the value of capital. Here, it is understood as *periodic devalorisation*, i.e. the absolute destruction and loss of value that affects the general capital of a sector or a region. Periodic devalorisation takes place at moments of crisis and it is necessary violent and sudden, while it affects all forms of capital (i.e. money, commodities and productive). For a thorough elaboration on the concepts of devalorisation, depreciation and devaluation, see Smith (1986).

2 Greece's responsiveness to 'Going for Growth' recommendations (OECD (2012)) and EU directives increased the most between 2009 and 2012, as unpopular reforms were implemented in employment protection and labour market regulations (e.g. dismantling of collective agreements, reduction in minimum wage, increments in the maximum permitted dismissals).

3 The interviews and data collection are part of the author's post-doctoral research on 'flexicurity' in the Southern EU regions. The key informants interviewed were trade unionists, atypical employees in both industrial and service activities, labour inspectors and members of the executive boards of regional authorities and the employers' associations. Interviews were conducted between July and October 2013 in both the regions under study.

4 Flexicurity, a neologism derived from the words flexibility and security, is probably the most important pillar of the EU's employment agenda. It is defined as a policy strategy that seeks to enhance the flexibility of labour markets, flexible or atypical employment relations in particular, while promoting some forms of employment and social security for certain groups of employees (EC (2008)).

5 Only three out of the four atypical forms, either fully dependent (i.e. temporary workers) or quasi-dependent (i.e. self-employed with no personnel and family workers) are included in this account. Part-time work is excluded due to the fact that labour force statistics do not provide data on the number of part-time wage-dependent employees while do not distinguish between different forms of part-time work (e.g. temporary part-timers or part-time business owners).

6 Unfortunately, data for GVA in 2012 are only available on a national level. The most recent GVA for the study regions are those of 2010 (see Table 11.1).

7 The divergent contribution of permanent, atypical and informal workers, engaged under different working-time patterns, into this phenomenon cannot be derived from official statistics.

8 For example, in 2011, 67.4 per cent among the part-time employed in Attica-Athens were seeking a full-time job, according to Eurostat. This skyrocketing share (it was 37.9 per cent in 2009) signifies unwanted low-paid jobs, and it is one of the highest in the EU.

References

Armingeon K. and Baccaro L. (2012), 'Political economy of the sovereign debt crisis: the limits of internal devaluation', *Industrial Law Journal* 41(3).

Bergene A.C., Endresen S.B. and Knutsen B.M. (2010), *Missing Links in Labour Geography*, Aldershot: Ashgate.

Buzar S. (2008), 'Towards a critical geography of flexibility: facets of adaptability in society and space', *Geography Compass* 2(4).

Clark G. (1980), 'Capitalism and regional inequality', *Annals of the Association of American Geographers* 70(2).

Clauwaert S. and Schömann I. (2012), 'The crisis and national labour law reforms: a mapping exercise', European Trade Union Institute, Working Paper, 2012.04.

Dorre K. (2010), 'Social classes in the process of capitalist 'landnahme': on the relevance of secondary exploitation', *Socialist Studies* 6(2).

EC (2008), 'Mission for flexicurity', European Commision, EMPL/D/XPM/DD D(2008) 2899, Brussels.

EC (2009), 'Implementation of the Lisbon strategy structural reforms: annual assessments', COM-2009 34/2, Brussels.

Eichengreen B., Jung N., Moch S. and Mody A. (2013), 'The Eurozone crisis: phoenix miracle or lost decade?' *Journal of Macroeconomics* (dx.doi.org/10.1016/j.jmacro.2013.08.005).

Gialis S. (2011), 'Restructuring strategies, firms' size and atypical employment in the local productive system of Thessaloniki, Greece', *Industrial Relations Journal* 42(5).

Gialis S. (2012), 'Integration a few kilometres away from the motherland: Albanians' internal migration, settlement and voluntary return in Epirus and the Ionian Islands in Greece', *Migration Letters* 9(2).

Gialis S. and Herod A. (2013), 'Resisting austerity: the case of Greece's powerworkers and steelworkers', *Human Geography: A New Radical Journal* 6(2).

Hadjimichalis C. (2011), 'Uneven geographical development and socio-spatial justice and solidarity: European regions after the 2009 financial crisis', *European Urban and Regional Studies* 18(3).

Harvey D. (2006), 'Neo-liberalism as creative destruction', *Geografiska Annaler: Human Geography* 88(2).

Harvey D. (2007), *Limits to Capital*, London: Verso.

Harvey D. (2010), *A Companion to Marx's Capital*, London: Verso.

Herod A. (2012), 'Workers as geographical actors', *Labor History* 53(3).

Hudson R. (2013), 'Thinking through the relationships between legal and illegal activities and economies: spaces, flows and pathways', *Journal of Economic Geography* (doi: 10.1093/jeg/lbt017).

Kalleberg A. (2003), 'Flexible firms and labour market segmentation: effects of workplace restructuring on jobs and workers', *Work and Occupations* 30(2).

Karamessini M. (2008), 'Still a distinctive southern European employment model?' *Industrial Relations Journal* 39(6).

Karamessini M. (2012), 'Sovereign debt crisis: an opportunity to complete the neoliberal project and dismantle the Greek employment model', in Lehndorff S. (ed.), *A Triumph of Failed Ideas: European Models of Capitalism in the Crisis*, Brussels: ETUI.

Kondilis E., Giannakopoulos S., Gavana M., Ierodiakonou I., Waitzkin H. and Benos A. (2013), 'Economic crisis, restrictive policies, and the population's health and health care: the Greek case', *American Journal of Public Health* 103(6).

Labour Inspectorates Organisation (2012), 'Annual Report of the Greek Labor Inspectorates Organization', Ministry of Employment and Social Protection, www.ypakp.gr [in Greek].

Leontidou L. (1990), *The Mediterranean City in Transition: Social Change and Urban Development*, Cambridge: Cambridge University Press.

Leontidou L. (1993), 'Informal strategies of unemployment relief in Greek cities: the relevance of family, locality and housing', *European Planning Studies* 1(1).

Massey D. (1996), *Spatial Divisions of Labour: Social Structures and the Geography of Production*, London: Macmillan.

Matsaganis M. (2011), 'The welfare state and the crisis: the case of Greece', *Journal of European Social Policy* 21(5).

Mavroudeas S. and Papadatos D. (2012), 'Financial regulation in the light of the current global economic crisis', *International Critical Thought* 2(4).

Michael-Matsas S. (2010), 'Greece and the world capitalist crisis', *Critique* 38(3).

Mitchell D. (2011), 'Labor's geography: capital, violence, guest workers and the post-World War II landscape', *Antipode* 43(2).

OECD (2012), 'Structural reforms in times of crisis', *Going for Growth: Economic Policy Reforms*, Paris: OECD.

Peet R. (1975), 'Inequality and poverty: a Marxist-geographic theory', *Annals of the Association of American Geographers* 65(4).

Pitelis C.N. (2012), 'On PIIGs, GAFFs, and BRICs: an insider–outsider's perspective on structural and institutional foundations of the Greek crisis', *Contributions to Political Economy* 31(1).

Pratschke J. and Morlicchio E. (2012), 'Social polarisation, the labour market and economic restructuring in Europe: an urban perspective', *Urban Studies* 49(9).

Selçuk B. and Yılmaz N. (2011), 'The effects of global crisis into Euro region: a case study of Greek crisis', *European Journal of Economic and Political Studies* 4(2).

Smith N. (1986), 'The concepts of devaluation, valorization and depreciation in Marx: toward a clarification', Unpublished paper.

Index

For Product Safety Concerns and Information please contact our EU
representative GPSR@taylorandfrancis.com
Taylor & Francis Verlag GmbH, Kaufingerstraße 24, 80331 München, Germany

www.ingramcontent.com/pod-product-compliance
Lightning Source LLC
LaVergne TN
LVHW011123300926
849160LV00008B/488

* 9 7 8 1 1 3 8 2 2 6 8 5 2 *